New Progressiv

To every member of my family,
from youngest to oldest,
present or absent, with love.

New Progressivism

Peter Silcock

| UK | Falmer Press, 11 New Fetter Lane, London, EC4P 4EE |
| USA | Falmer Press, Taylor & Francis Inc., 325 Chestnut Street, 8th Floor, Philadelphia, PA 19106 |

© Peter Silcock 1999

All rights reserved. No part of this publication may be reproduced, stored in a retrieval system, or transmitted in any form or by any means, electronic, mechanical, photocopying, recording or otherwise, without permission in writing from the publisher.

First published in 1999

A catalogue record for this book is available from the British Library

ISBN 0 7507 0969 3 cased
ISBN 0 7507 0968 5 paper

Library of Congress Cataloging-in-Publication Data are available on request

Jacket design by Caroline Archer

Typeset in 10/12 pt Times by
Graphicraft Limited, Hong Kong

Printed in Great Britain by Biddles Ltd., Guildford and King's Lynn on paper which has a specified pH value on final paper manufacture of not less than 7.5 and is therefore 'acid free'.

Every effort has been made to contact copyright holders for their permission to reprint material in this book. The publishers would be grateful to hear from any copyright holder who is not here acknowledged and will undertake to rectify any errors or omissions in future editions of this book.

Contents

Acknowledgments		vii
Foreword		ix
1	Introduction	1
2	The Value of Educational Ideologies	11
3	Progressivism, Traditionalism and Pragmatism	23
4	Progressivism and National Curricula	39
5	New Progressivism: Principles to Be Reviewed	53
6	Developmentalism	59
7	Curricular Values: The Relationships between Learners and their Knowledge	77
8	Informal Teaching Methods	101
9	Choice	121
10	Modern Progressivism	135
References		149
Index		163

Acknowledgments

Thanks are due to my wife for her constant support and forbearance during long periods of time while the book was being written. A debt of gratitude is owed to Colin Richards, whose unstinting efforts and encouragement kept my project alive when it could easily have collapsed. I am also grateful to Dr David Scott for his ready agreement to let me use material taken from a paper already published in the *Curriculum Journal* in one of the book's early chapters. Finally, I thank all those headteachers who welcomed me into their schools, and the class teachers who welcomed me into their classrooms at various times during the past ten years to talk to me about their hopes and fears. Their wise words taught me much about child-centredness. I hope this book gives something back to them and to the values we share.

Foreword

This is an important book. It articulates a very important viewpoint and represents a very significant contribution to educational theorizing. At a time of increasing bureaucratic influence on schools and classrooms it reinforces the importance of teachers' beliefs and how they affect practice. It challenges us to reconceptualize teaching and learning *à la fin de siècle* with a key role for both learners and teachers in what Peter Silcock characterizes as the essence of the educational process, the 'co-construction of minds'.

There has been much discussion about education since the Education Act of 1988 and, more recently, since the election of a New Labour government with its education-dominated mantra. Many views have been expressed; many interest groups have had their say; many parties to the educational enterprise have attempted to make their voices heard. During this time there have been many references to progressivism, almost all of them critical. Progressivism and 'trendy progressive teachers' have been scapegoated for the alleged deficiencies in primary education, for the alleged problems of the education system generally and even for contributing significantly to the declining fortunes of the nation state. The voice of progressivism has been muted, almost silent, in this furore about declining standards and quality.

This book gives progressivism a new voice, one based, not on simplistic polarizations and caricatures of opposing views, but on reasoned, though complex, argument referenced in particular to recent thinking and research in developmental psychology. It systematically reviews and reinterprets progressivism's main principles — developmentalism, humanism, democracy and pragmatism. It identifies progressivism's key values and beliefs and explores their relevance to contemporary theory, policy and practice. It provides its own critique of old-style progressivism and takes seriously the considered criticism of its critics. The book itself not only justifies progressivism's principles, values and beliefs but embodies them.

The *neo-progressivism* it articulates provides a theoretically resilient response to critics. It provides theoretical support for those 'primary school teachers whose beliefs have survived the past decades and are unabashed in advertising their ideas about the "whole child", integrated topic-based teaching and informal approaches'. It reasserts the learner's role in the educative process without diminishing the role of teachers in that process or in the wider debate about primary education's purposes and direction.

It is a profoundly optimistic book which, in my judgment, does justice to the complexities of primary education and to the idealism of so many primary school

Foreword

teachers. It could, like progressivism itself, be 'an engine of real power' in influencing primary theory, policy and practice. As a reasoned, updated and reformulated articulation of a major tradition in English primary education a publication of this kind is long overdue.

Colin Richards
Professor, St Martin's College;
Honorary Professor of Education,
University of Warwick
November 1998

Chapter 1

Introduction

The need for a revised progressivist ideology

As a set of values, beliefs and professional ideals, held mainly by primary school teachers (i.e. as an educational ideology), progressivism has been in decline for around three decades, since its high point of influence, in England, immediately following the publication of the Plowden Report (Central Advisory Council, 1967). Unrelenting attacks upon it from politicians and from others during this period prepared the ground for a series of political 'root-and-branch' changes to the educational system which have not only transformed the schoolteacher's job but have pushed ideological issues well outside the public spotlight. Such issues no longer merit much attention. Debates about whether progressivist or traditionalist curricula provide effective solutions to the problems of teaching appear to have 'run out of steam'. In particular, when progressivism itself is discussed, its favoured methodologies, once believed innovative, are as often as not used as foils for newer approaches. Compared with more 'enlightened' methods applied elsewhere (such as in countries of the western Pacific: Reynolds, 1996; Reynolds and Farrell, 1996), these have been condemned for preventing teachers from reaching the standards of excellence a modern society demands.

Progressivism has few friends these days, and many detractors. From time to time, a member of some pressure group or other proposes it is time to move 'beyond progressivism' towards better ways of adjusting school pupils to technological change, the hurly-burly of postmodern life, an unjust society or whatever. Since 1989, value-positions established by reformers in England have been traditionalist not progressivist — the English/Welsh National Curriculum, for example, is a structured framework imposed on schools through a highly textured system of controls. It seeks to standardize curricula, not encourage the diversity of practices 'child-centred' teachers have always preferred. A 'skilled traditionalist' model of good practice is embodied in the current OFSTED (Office for Standards in Education) framework for school inspection (Lee and Fitz, 1997), while the chief inspector for schools (Christopher Woodhead) regularly lectures teachers to return to formal methods and give up on child-centredness which he believes does not work (OFSTED, 1996).

It is tempting to turn one's back on this beleagured ideology! Surely it has outlived its usefulness and should give way to ideas better fitted for the times? Yet — somewhat surprisingly perhaps — a number of primary school teachers are reluctant to give up their child-centred beliefs. Research in classrooms up and

New Progressivism

down the country (Francis and Grindle, 1998; Pollard et al., 1994; Silcock, 1995; Silcock and Wyness, 1997; Vulliamy and Webb, 1993) finds that these survive, albeit shakily, in the thinking and attitudes of teachers. At the same time, the educational scene soon, again, becomes fluid and uncertain. Renewed doubts about the future of the 'broad and balanced' primary school curriculum, in the light of government drives towards a 'neo-elementary' concentration upon basic skills (see Richards, 1998), promises to revitalize debates about competing models, while the collapse of 'Pacific Rim' economies during 1998 suggests that their educational philosophies may not be as appropriate for this country as we once thought.

Uncertainties about the best way forward for primary schools must encourage us to study alternatives. But they are not, in themselves, good reasons for revisiting older positions, which might still be thought too remote from present circumstances to warrant time being spent on them. Nor should we pretend that progressivism is likely to be the first 'port of call' for anyone wanting to point us in a different direction. If policy makers are to take a fresh interest in what may still be the dominant primary school ideology, its supporters have yet to respond fully to their many criticisms. However, there are grounds for believing that such a response would be worthwhile. Although the educational world has changed since the Plowden Report was published, not all changes are antagonistic to the progressivist movement. There are more solid research-based theories now, on which child-centred teachers can depend. And the fact that a number of primary school teachers resolutely keep to their child-centred beliefs is evidence that these do, still, sustain them within their jobs. It is a fair question, then, to ask, as this book asks: exactly how far can a progressivist primary school ideology be adapted to modern, twenty-first century expectations?

To an extent, the answer to such a question must depend on how any revision is accomplished. Educational debates are engaged with at different levels of argument, and it is often hard to jump between these. Politicians, academics, researchers, administrators, industrialists, publishers, technologists, all invest directly or indirectly in the business of getting children educated, and it is never straightforward deciding whose brief has most merit when arguing about a type of school curriculum or the virtues of a teaching strategy. Sensibly, we may conclude that what happens in school classrooms is multi-determined. There is no single argument which will persuade us to prefer one approach to another. Child-centredness will earn its credentials as a third millennium ideology when it is shown as viable within the many practical, socio-political and academic contexts where it is likely to be tested.

In a somewhat masochistic sense, a plethora of criticisms mounted against the ideology is helpful to someone writing about the subject. An obligation to revise progressivist claims rather than merely defend them arises partly because so many damaging reproaches have been made. Not that the most perceptive critiques have always been the most influential. What seems to have worked, historically, is how well critics' ideas were wedded to the political mood of the times. Nevertheless, some criticisms are effective just because the circumstances in which these criticisms were made are still with us. The economic conditions which have turned politicians — especially — against child-centred primary school practices, for instance, regularly recur. This fact has produced an ongoing climate of sometimes covert, sometimes open hostility to these practices which presents a difficulty to anyone trying to reassess the ideology: within this climate, arguments become debased by prejudice, and it is not easy to pin down any truth they might have. As a preliminary, it is worth looking at the historical context within which a downturn in progressivist fortunes has occurred in order to detect what *are* the recurrent problems it has faced and why it has faced them.

Recent historical background

In 1992, during that phase of educational reform when the pace of change was breathtaking, a review paper on primary school curricular organization was sponsored by the Conservative government (Alexander et al., 1992) to attempt a broad and wide-ranging overview, rather as the Plowden Report achieved in 1967. Lady Plowden herself (1991) welcomed the initiative, having recommended a ten-year review cycle: it had been 25 years since her own report was published. The paper drew on ideas from a substantial British research tradition established since around the 1960s. Professor Alexander, one of the so-called 'three wise men' who authored the document, had acquired prominence, during his time at Leeds University, through questioning ideologically inspired educational orthodoxies (1992). During his research, he had found progressivist dogma used to excuse much mediocre teaching: this led him to realize how ideologies can hinder rather than help teachers deal with the variety of problems facing them in classrooms. He continues, still, to argue for a restructuring of primary education to suit diverse concerns, stressing a balancing of expressive aims such as personal welfare and social justice with vocationally linked training needs (Alexander, 1998).

The report's (1992) dossier of criticisms backed by its body of evidence reflected badly on the child-centred cause. Alexander himself subsequently denied that it was meant as a clarion call for a return to more traditionalist thinking, complaining that — like progressivist beliefs — his report was the victim of politicians looking for scapegoats for the country's economic ills (1994, p. 28). He reminded us that it was written as a discussion paper not a policy document. Yet its most substantial recommendations promoted the idea of more specialist teaching in primary schools, i.e. focusing on subject-based knowledge, rather than on the thematic, topic-based work commonly found in primary schools and associated with child-centred teaching. It did not solidify as government policy, and it is questionable whether it has had much long-term influence. But at the time, its credibility lay not so much in the quality of its arguments as in the way these culminated a long line of criticism of standard primary school practices. Whatever validity it had rested, really, on what had gone before rather than on any novel conclusions. The report was a review document, not a call to the government to change course.

We can date the starting point for the line of criticism for which the Alexander et al. paper was the culmination fairly precisely — simply because its focus was those progressivist methodologies originally recommended by the 1967 Plowden

Committee. Shortly after publication of the 1967 report, a group of philosophers and social scientists (Peters, 1969) protested at its reliance on developmental psychology as a main reference and queried, among other things, its inadequate emphasis upon subject-based learning. Nine years on, public opposition to what were becoming known as 'Plowden' methods, grew stronger when Neville Bennett's Lancaster research (Bennett, 1976) purportedly found that progressivist teaching was less effective than the traditional when pupil progress was assessed using standardized tests and observational measures. Bennett confessed to having been a progressivist, and his book became a high-profile text. As such, it exploded an educational bombshell among teachers and others barely used to the new child-centred orthodoxy. In fact, it wasn't alone in its criticisms, but was simply the latest in a series of largely damning publications (see Francis and Grindle, 1998, for a brief discussion of these; also Galton, 1989a; Sugrue, 1997). Equally damaging to progressivism — though for very different reasons — was the 'William Tyndale' affair (Ellis et al., 1976). In a North London primary school, a group of teachers giving their pupils considerable freedom of action and curricular choice defended their practices using a mix of progressivist and politically charged arguments. Their actions were denounced by parents, politicians and newspapers, leading to a court case which became a *cause célèbre* (Ellis et al., 1976). Teachers were suspended, then the school closed, eventually reopening with a changed staff.

It is hardly coincidental that the year of the Bennett research and the 'William Tyndale affair' was the year the Labour Prime Minister of the day, James Callaghan, decided to make a major speech on education, which he eventually delivered at Ruskin College, Oxford (1976: Batteson, 1997; Chitty, 1989). To help him prepare, DES civil servants compiled a 63-page confidential memorandum, sometimes called 'The Yellow Book' (Chitty, 1989), analysing the worries about primary and secondary schools which were beginning to surface in articles and the popular press. The Yellow Book noted that the 'new' progressivist approach in primary schools 'could have positive results, but . . . could also be applied uncritically, with a consequent undermining of standards of performance in the three Rs' (cited Chitty, 1989, p. 75). The Yellow Book's judgments were fairly even-handed about primary school achievements. But, given that political fears of economic failure were growing daily (because Callaghan's tottering government might be linked to it), there was some need to look for villains. Could not one cause of a poor trade performance be shoddy workmanship? And could not shoddy workmanship arise from poorly taught formal skills? Civil servants advised that 'the time is almost certainly ripe for a corrective shift of emphasis' (paras 12–13: Chitty, 1989, p. 75).

Added to what he would know about public opinion, this sort of advice persuaded Callaghan that it was time for a wider debate about the purposes of schools. In the speech he actually made (Batteson, 1997; Chitty, 1989 and 1996), he hinted at a future centralizing of control over education policy, questioning the right of the educational establishment to tend its own 'garden' of professional secrets. In terms of policy commitments, he was circumspect, pointing out that schools had social, economic and industrial responsibilities as well as catering for individual welfare, but denying that he wished to return teachers to pre-Plowden days or was condoning

Introduction

the opinions of the political right wing, as had been expressed in the, then, notorious 'Black Papers' (Cox and Dyson, 1960, 1971). His attitude did not at all resemble the 'back to basics' philosophy the 'Black Paper' writers wanted and which were eventually adopted by the Conservative administrations which followed his. But he would have been aware of the public backlash against what was being castigated by the press as 'permissiveness', in education as well as in society at large (see Lawton, 1992, p. 9). Callaghan's Ruskin speech, launching what he called a 'great debate' about schools, gave us the first warnings of a political campaign which would in time wholly capture educational and curricular policy making within the public sphere. It led, if indirectly, to the demonizing of progressive education and the wholesale curricular reforms of the late 1980s and 1990s.

The ending in 1997 of a long era of Conservative government has, in some ways, changed little. Under a Labour administration, we still have a National Curriculum, an OFSTED inspectorate and a punishing teacher accountability system. A 'new' Labour government, rejecting an earlier socialism it believes too 'ideological' ('old Labour'), continues to implement reforms it judges as sensible in their own terms. Maclure (1998) wonders whether the Labour Party might not complete Margaret Thatcher's educational revolution for her, and pleads for a 'change of style'. What he would like is the Labour Party to try to swing the teaching profession behind government policy rather than leaving it alienated by a tightly centralized control. This seems unlikely to happen. Allegedly, HMCI (Her Majesty's Chief Inspector) Christopher Woodhead, an advocate of formal teaching methods and enemy of teacher unions, was one of the first political appointments the new Prime Minister, Tony Blair, made. David Blunkett, present secretary of state for education, openly allied himself when he was opposition spokesman with the views of Professor David Reynolds (Rosenthal, 1996), whose comparative studies (1996; with Farrell, 1996) direct him towards 'whole-class' modes of teaching.

However, whereas a Conservative prime minister like John Major, and Conservative secretaries of state, liked, also, to advocate didacticism in schools (Clarke, 1991; Major, 1991) the present prime minister and a number of other influential Labour politicans have begun to promote a 'third way' in education as in other areas, refusing to make overtly ideological pronouncements. This 'third way' option is meant to bypass ideologies at the level of policy, and, on the ground, so to speak, break down barriers between 'teachers and pupils . . . staff and the parents . . . school and the local community' (Kellner, 1998, p. 15). Margaret Hodge, chairperson of the Commons education and employment select committee, tells us what the 'third way' is:

> Pragmatism has replaced ideology. It is what works that counts. Who provides it and how it is provided is less important. (1998, p. 15)

Pragmatism is the natural beneficiary of public and political impatience with educational ideologies. It is a supposed alternative to ideological decision making. As such, it exerts an awesome power over modern political and academic life (Mounce, 1997). 'Goodness of fit' is a very end-of-century slogan, drawing us towards a utilitarian and materialistic disregard for longer lasting considerations. Popular versions of pragmatism, such as the Hodge dictum that 'it is what works that counts' do generate educational policies. And when pragmatism is couched within more sophisticated theories, it gives us excellent examples of the difficulties we have finding reliable criteria to use to justify what and how teachers should teach. Pragmatic criteria masquerade as alternatives to the justifications for actions we should really employ. They are a replacement for theory, during a period when we are suffering a crisis of faith within educational studies. As Sixsmith and Simco (1997) have it:

> There is currently a 'theoretical vacuum', a lack of widely accepted validated theory to underpin . . . current orthodoxy. (p. 4)

To restore some confidence in still developing progressivist theories, it will be important to test out how pragmatic ideas have or have not successfully usurped those we once used as foundations for educational policy.

At the same time, the theories themselves need scrutiny, since a telling problem for the academic side of progressivism has been its reliance on developmental psychology. The Plowden Report's message that activity-based teaching (seemingly sanctioned by psychologists) was synonymous with good primary practice was, itself, new. It represented a revision of the child-centred ideology which had relied on older philosophical ideas, usually traced back to Rousseau (1911/1762: see Darling, 1994; Grimsley,1973) and associated with Dewey's work in America (1900, 1902, 1916, 1976/1899). Plowden progressivism was an updated version, thought to be more reliable than the older kinds. The writings of Piaget (with Inhelder, 1969; Sutherland, 1992) and Bruner (1972) were around mid-century becoming immensely popular in England and America, and were disseminated as an underpinning of primary school teaching. Although this theoretical backing was believed needed to rescue progressivism from what had become a rather 'precious' view of children, its very exclusivity turned out to be an Achilles heel. A number of British academics became converted from 'Piagetian' doctrines placing children's voluntariness at the centre of their own learning to views about the part adults and other children play in intellectual development — reinforcing pragmatic tendencies begun elsewhere. Today, while some teachers cling to their 'Plowdenesque' child-centredness, the discrediting of Piaget's ideas has theoretically armed those preferring the socio-historical approach of the Russian, Lev Vygotsky (1962, 1978).

As is often true when sudden changes of direction happen, advances in our knowledge lead, temporarily, to an over-hasty discarding of insights. Some (though not all) judgments made by the Genevan school of child development are being reappraised by psychologists and reinterpreted in educationally relevant ways. And just as progressivist principles coincided so closely with the Piagetian that to abandon one set meant our abandoning the other, by that same token, a putative Piagetian revival must return us to some study of progressivism, if only to see what this recovered knowledge implies for the ideology. Following such a course need not return us lock and stock to the position of thirty years ago! There are other developments within the world of education to help moderate our conclusions. Yet, some attention to psychological issues will prove promising in that we can now take two complementary perspectives on children (the Piagetian and the Vygotskian), and, in combination, recognize how they point to more practicable ways of resolving standard problems than the singular Piagetian perspective provided.

Summarizing this brief historical discussion: it is educative to see how tightly bound together political, academic and practical ideas can become. For around 30 years, progressivism has suffered from an increasing lack of public trust in its theories, in the empirical justification for its theories and in classroom practices based on them. Reasons for this lack of trust can be blamed on adverse publicity about 'over-permissive' classrooms, a long tradition of hostile research and a 'paradigm' shift in our developmental explanations. Politicians are not wholly cut off from such things. They have noticed public misgivings and have exploited these when trying to excuse a less than perfect industrial and trade performance. We are returned to earlier conclusions: a revised progressivism has to take note of many different criticisms and debates but especially the ones grounded in curricular practices, academic theories and the socio-political world of policy making. It is these which will help shape an argument.

Structuring the argument

A brief, historical discussion clarifies priorities and helps us begin ordering these. Updating progressivist theory is, it seems, only justified if two further questions are answered. Firstly, there is a question as to whether ideological influence *is* a proper way to judge what is or is not sound educational practice. It could be that teachers' dependence on personal values will fade as research evidence mounts and the technologies based on them reveal sure principles of practice, supporting the wisdom of politicians enforcing a central control over school curricula. Secondly, if it can be shown that ideologies have a serious part to play in educational thinking, we have still to demonstrate that progressivist beliefs have sufficient latent virtue to merit re-examination. Even though child-centred approaches may not be shown to have been, factually, flawed, technological advances or consensual decisions may have condemned them to becoming side-issues. To deal, satisfactorily, with these questions, the book's first section looks at the value of ideologies in educational decision making *per se,* and, also, at what, overall, can be gained from reinserting progressivist language into educational discourse.

Following on from that, the book's second half works through a systematic revision of progressivist principles — not, fundamentally, to change them, but in order to calculate their relevance to modern classroom conditions. Invariably, a gradual unwinding of arguments presages a hopefully conscientious look at what is practicable for teachers to achieve, and how far political policies can facilitate channels of communication between the two worlds of classrooms and academia. Politicians have to serve a number of masters: at times they must bend to the practical dilemmas of teachers, maybe imposing demands on the back of stringent financial constraints; at other times, they try to implement what they have come to accept as sound theoretical advice about managing effective schools. What matters as much as arguments about theoretical correctness are arguments about utility and economy, recognizing that there should be no built-in conflict between these.

The balance between the book's different sections is dictated by the type of questions asked, and each chapter will present its own perspective upon such questions. Given the recurrent risk of ideology phobia submerging any attempts to breathe new life into child-centred teaching, Chapters 2 and 3 try to justify educational ideologies as worthwhile ways of dealing with practical matters, and include an initial exposition of the main value-oriented stances which teachers normally take. While exposing the difficulties of building school curricula either on an older traditionalist model or on the shifting sands of pragmatic decision making, progressivism's long association with the humanistic movement is introduced in anticipation of lengthier treatment. In many ways, it is progressivism's humanitarian ideals which have sustained it in countries right across the world (Rohrs and Lenhart, 1995). These will be recurring themes within the book's central discussions.

The fourth chapter summarizing research findings into the way the progressivist movement has fared internationally and in England, especially among child-centred teachers, estimates how any newly revised movement is likely to be received by British practitioners. There would be little sense in recommending classroom policies for teachers whose professional tastes already bias them in other directions. And teachers' own reasons for holding to their personal value systems should give clues as to their lasting viability and practical worth. What's more, although child-centred beliefs are discoverable in research interviews with teachers, this does not mean they aren't, themselves, evolving under the pressure of constant change. A modern progressivism must come to terms with naturally evolving forms if the movement as a whole is not to fragment completely. This chapter ends the book's preliminaries, apart from a summary statement (Chapter 5) of the principles thought to be most in need of review.

Chapter 6 recovers progressivism's developmental rationale. It assesses modern developmental child psychology and analyses how this impinges on educational practices. A main difference between educational and religious or political ideologies is that we can test out the former with research evidence about human thinking and intellectual problem solving. Lady Plowden touched on this matter when, in 1991, she looked ahead, optimistically, to the 'three wise men's' report. While conceding that much social upheaval since 1967 meant that educational organizations had to change also, she is reported as saying:

> The economic needs of the country have changed, but I cannot believe that the nature of children and the way that they learn best has changed fundamentally in the past 25 years ... (C)hildren will continue to need to be understood as individuals ... (1991, p. 17)

She was implying that if we kept to what we knew about children's learning, there ought to be some continuity of judgment between her own report and that which was, soon, to follow. One might say that she had a point (though events proved her personal optimism misplaced). Schools exist to improve their pupils' minds. The best factual knowledge we have explaining how that process happens has to be taken account of somewhere within a teacher's professional behaviour: the problem is, to be sure that we have the correct factual knowledge.

Chapters 7, 8 and 9 clarify how we can apply revised values and beliefs to issues of school curricular organization and primary school teaching methodology. Throughout these chapters, criticisms of the effects of teachers' child-centred attitudes on their practices will be reviewed either to accept a modification of principle or to show that no such modification is needed. Finally, Chapter 10 summarizes what has gone before in terms of the main arguments for and against progressivist teaching. It lifts main points from the preceding text, naming writers and publications in such a manner as to ease the work of anyone wishing either to agree or dispute conclusions. The roots of an educational ideology stretch down to many depths and layers of argument — not just within the educational literature. Ascertaining where these are is a useful concluding task.

Chapter 2

The Value of Educational Ideologies

What are educational ideologies?

In education, as in politics, the terms 'ideology' and 'ideological' are now more often than not used as pejoratives: to label an action ideological is to condemn it as probably biased and doctrinaire. This is unfortunate. If human thought and action are regulated by our developing values and beliefs, to condemn that form of self-regulation we call the ideological out of hand is to cut us off from the origins of our own behaviour. It may be that professional teachers, like doctors, politicians, priests and social workers, need easily accessed belief systems to guide them through the difficult social encounters which compose their jobs.

How true this is has to depend on what we believe educational ideologies are — whether they are 'easily accessed', for instance, or whether they are so deeply embedded in our psyches they can only work in ways we will never fully understand. Sociologists who study the functions and operations of ideologies (Apple, 1990; Billig et al., 1988; Larrain, 1979; Thompson, 1984) find the term hard to define because it is so conceptually versatile. It can be used descriptively to identify the values and beliefs of a social or professional group; or it can be used evaluatively to suggest the 'false consciousness' a group of people might develop as a result, perhaps, of prolonged oppression (a Marxist interpretation: see Swinglewood, 1991). When examining the communal basis of school life, Kainan and Shkolnik (1994) turn to the more affectively neutral idea of a 'belief system', since this lets them examine group decision making without having to worry about 'irrelevant associations' (p. 3). But, as they discuss it, the determining effects of belief systems on school policy are virtually identical to ideological determinacy.

As is often the case within educational study, reaching an agreement about definitions is not so important as discovering how a term is used, and, accordingly, what is assumed by those who use it. What would be lost if the term 'ideology' were not in our educational vocabularies? What would we stop saying if we discarded words like 'progressive' or 'traditional'? Taking this approach, a brief analysis of usage criteria contained in the sorts of debates which progressivists undertake should reveal what is distinctive about ideological belief systems, as these apply to schools. These criteria pick out, from such a consideration, the purpose or function of educational ideologies, their form and content, and their range of application to circumstance. Because much already written about the subject (e.g. by Lawton, 1989, 1992, 1996; Morrison and Ridley, 1989; Scrimshaw, 1983; Taylor and

New Progressivism

Richards, 1985) involves such criteria, analysis is meant to clarify matters relating to school classrooms, not break new ground.

The function of educational ideologies

If teaching were like carpentry or accountancy, where the problems posed by a job of work were to be met purely in technical ways or through following well documented procedures, there would be no obvious role for professional values and beliefs. But only the most commonplace educational questions let us resort solely to technicalities or factually based theory. And even then, a hidden background of assumptions always threatens the practical implications of our answers. The value-laden nature of professional work is part of the way we recognize it as professional. Unavoidable questions for priests and politicians (e.g. how, if God exists, we should heed His/ Her wishes, or whether a redistribution of wealth is the right way to improve society) constantly tug them back to their basic belief systems. Educational questions of the same fundamental kind surface rapidly during discussions on the purposes of education, which, in turn, foster debates about curricular design and method and those accountability networks attendant on our first decisions. What we find is that we have to square up to these issues before we can deal with most others. And we confront the various value-claims which groups of people make when answering associated questions, not by way of the values themselves but, usually, by discussing the beliefs rising from them.

It is simple enough to illustrate how this process works by identifying what may be the most ideologically resonant issues in education, which are also, not coincidentally, among the most central. They are captured by three questions:

1. What is education for (why do we oblige children to attend school)?
2. How should pupils be taught, in the light of what we understand about theories of learning and cognitive development?
3. Who should control schools and school curricula (how should we limit the spheres of influence of politicians, parents, teachers, curricular specialists et al.)?

The point about these questions is that in order to answer them we have to think through many different issues, a number of which are concerned with professional beliefs organized around values. This will be seen when we study each in turn.

The first question tends not to provoke the heated disagreements it once did. These days, we are likely to say that schools have many purposes, including the personal, the utilitarian, the social and vocational. Alexander (1998), for example, finds no natural conflict between the utilitarian and economic imperatives of education and the personal and vocational functions of schools. But he reminds us of the two types of purpose because he detects an imbalance towards the former in the minds of those members of government committees currently organizing the English/Welsh National Curriculum. He is acknowledging that what most occupies curricula designers is not so much having to concede the absolute legitimacy of competing claims but having to settle priorities between them.

It is seldom possible for teachers or headteachers to give to a type of teaching programme all the time they find that it, ideally, requires, so they find themselves choosing between options. To reckon that in general all options are equally worthy is unhelpful (even when true), because in the face of a forced choice, there has to be some means of making a decision. Not only that: we may suspect that in trying to serve all aims equally we achieve none especially well. A teacher convinced that pupils learn best when pursuing their own aspirations and experiences may take pains over the planning of interest-based tasks that someone trying to prepare students for a vocationally related exam would not take. The two teachers need not be in any conflict about the value of both types of aim. But as soon as we agree the legitimacy of both we are brought face to face with dilemmas of priorities, calling into question the major directions we believe that our educational policies should take.

This is why Richard Peters (1966) divided those educational processes he believed intrinsically valuable from the training and instruction programmes which were important, but were not to be called 'educational'. It wasn't because the latter do not matter. He knew that they did. But within an educational system where all resources are finite (especially teacher time), value-issues arise not because everyone hotly disagrees about aims ('pious statements of the obvious' as Peters called them), but because we have to get our priorities right. It is precisely the function of beliefs arising from our value-systems (as Kelly, 1994, shows) to lead us through the labyrinthine procedures of deciding about priorities.

The second question is different from the other two, in that it has two halves. It is two questions, umbilically tied — though how how we pass from answering the one to answering the other is not always clear. Once we have chosen our best theories of learning, the matter of deciding the forms of teaching which respect them still has to be moderated by a study of resource possibilities and a closer look at what is actually to be assessed within a school curriculum, even though teachers cannot ignore what we know about learning and intellectual development when deciding a teaching strategy. The factor which currently might seem to a teacher most binding on his or her actions could be that of keeping to the legally established framework of the National Curriculum. 'Early years' teachers convinced that it is not directly in children's interests (for example) to struggle through a 'literacy hour' in some predetermined manner might think twice about refusing to conform to an enforced ruling. But the 'dumbing down' of their beliefs doesn't terminally paralyse them, in that, as soon as they feel less inhibited in their actions, they will look to other sources of knowledge — possibly found in college-taught developmental theory — in combination with their own experiences, to shape their pedagogy in ways they themselves appreciate.

The third question is not, usually, a teacher's to answer. It is the business of politicians to govern and in order to govern the domain of education they are wont to set up bureaucratic hierarchies. Teachers cannot prevent politicians taking charge of the organization of school curricula. Yet it is perfectly proper for them to query whether political authority is the right backing for such decisions, and try, as soon

New Progressivism

as they are able, to reinsert their own voice within what they might feel is their legitimate sphere of authority. Further, it is just as correct for a teacher to continue a re-examination of the rights of pupils to make curricular choices, as this intercedes into her professional life, given that the educational system exists to promote pupils' welfare. A teacher's ideological commitments will unavoidably come into play within areas concerning accountability just as they do when puzzling over questions about methodology. A number of child-centred practitioners presently regard their hands as tied by legislation (Pollard et al., 1994; Silcock and Wyness, 1997), as far as issues of pupil involvement in curricular matters are concerned. But the issues have only been put on the back burner of professional thinking until the day bonds of restriction are eased. A number would undoubtedly wish to give some degree of control back to pupils, just as a number of even the youngest pupils themselves see that idea as an attractive option (Pollard et al., 1994; Trigg and Pollard, 1998).

How questions such as the three listed above are answered very much influences what teachers do in classrooms, day by day, throughout their careers (it is not of course suggested that these are the only questions which influence actions). Since teachers have to answer such questions, consciously or tacitly, and since the questions cannot be answered in a wholly factual manner, teachers resort to their own beliefs for guidance. One might still think that there is a difference between a loosely organized set of beliefs and an ideology, but what will be shown is that the sorts of questions professional people have to deal with are associated with yet more fundamental questions about the nature of human beings and the role of societies in human affairs. Answering them consistently implies a structured set of values and beliefs on which we can draw. The term 'ideology' is the one we normally use to identify such hierarchically structured, psychological systems (Billig et al., 1988; Taylor and Richards, 1985; Thompson, 1984). As said, similar forms of cognitive guidance help other professionals manage their affairs. Priests must have some opinion on how to please the particular deities they worship, just as politicians must come to some decisions about what counts as fair recompense for manual labour *vis-à-vis* managerial skill. Few questions which intervene in deciding our most critical decisions are answered factually. That is why we have values, belief systems and structured cognitive and affective organizations of these.

The content of educational ideologies

Ideologies are belief systems gathered around values (Taylor and Richards, 1985; Thompson, 1984). And although, technically, it would be possible to answer questions such as those listed above without developing an ideology, once we are sure of our long-term educational priorities we will find that these priorities impress themselves on thoughts about curricular design and accountability. Beliefs about one set of questions become interrelated with beliefs about another. The first judgment teachers have to make concerns aims which will spring, most purely, from their publicly known value systems. Modern presumptions about 'life-long learning' or 'continuing education' (Alexander, 1998; Jarvis, 1995; Wain, 1985) are that schools exist not only to teach useful skills and known concepts but to enrich our lives in a more profound manner, helping us to appreciate as continuing sources of pleasure many aspects of the physical and social environment. So what at bottom teachers believe makes for an educated person affects almost everything they do: relatively trivial decisions about which chores they will polish off in a busy day will reflect, somewhere, their short-term priorities born from overarching ideals.

Recognizing that ideologies are structured belief systems does not mean that they cannot be tested out through argument. Questions which do have factual answers will bear weightily upon decisions taken, and there are many of these asked by educationists if only because of their socio-psychological nature. This is why it should be quite impossible to exclude a study of the social sciences from teacher education if anyone were to think about doing so. It also explains why ideological debates in education are often worth pursuing through to a conclusion: sooner or later, we will find that matters of fact do intrude, and might sway us one way or another. Many of our beliefs (though not all) falter before those research outcomes we can trust. The point of this is to stress that defining ideologies as value-related belief systems does not relegate ideological debate to a never-ending swopping of anecdotes or expressions of faith. We can, and must, not only know what beliefs we hold, educationally speaking, but why we hold them. Empirical evidence may well play the decisive role in settling the fate of our beliefs. Of course, it needn't. This will depend on the beliefs in question and how fundamental they are. Educational ideologies cling less tenaciously to facts than to values — the area where moral and philosophical questions rule (i.e. concerning the kinds of creatures we not only believe that we are but believe that we should be). As soon as we enter an educational debate (as with political or religious argument), we find the two sorts of elements, the factual and the ethical, mix together. The special way in which these interrelate is what composes an educational ideology.

Applying educational ideologies

Although ideologies have wide application, they affect our lives in well-demarcated ways. A teacher's professional ideologies will overlap at the level of values with his or her political, religious or academic belief-systems, but they may not overlap at the level of precise belief and will seldom overlap in terms of actions taken. This is because the ideological beliefs which govern actions refer to discrete sets of questions, which, in themselves, set the parameters of the study, pursuit or job concerned. Seeing that ideologies have precise limits of application (thus 'political', 'religious', 'educational' ideologies) also helps separate the notion of an ideology from the broader idea of a culture or way of life (Billig et al., 1988; Thompson, 1984; Waters, 1994). Our cultures embrace all activities in our lives; our ideologies give us an overview of only one part. One benefit from asserting a specificity of application is that it clarifies the common error of confusing political with educational ideologies. The 'William Tyndale' affair (Ellis et al., 1976) was a case in point, where 'progressivism' and left-wing politics probably fused together in the public mind. It is quite usual for people with 'left-wing' political motivations to be progressivists and share common values; but questions about the purposes of education do have educational answers. How they are answered reveals our ideologies, and these have to be answered separately from questions about inherent injustices within our class system. Although holding one type of belief might prejudice us towards another, teachers with identical political ideologies might be at loggerheads over how they believe school curricula should be organized.

This should not conceal how the same values can be parents to very different beliefs. A religious sentiment and a humanitarian ethic may span many areas of activity. But not only do beliefs arising from common values differentiate as soon as they are applied to groups of questions, they obey distinct sets of rules. Teachers who are religious, or are politically committed, obey different decision making criteria when they pursue each activity. It is true that one type of ideology can subsume another: schools have always seemed promising places to start restructuring society. Yet the motivations to improve pupil learning in a school environment are subtly distinct from motivations to 'improve' society in general. And when distinctions are not made (again, the 'William Tyndale' affair gives us an example), we risk abusing one set of professional duties in obedience to another. We can, sometimes, by the same actions serve the educational interests of learners and other interests too, but sooner or later conflicts between the two sets of interests arise. At such moments, different justifications must come into play so that proper conclusions can be reached.

The contested nature of educational ideologies

Ideological belief systems evolve in order to deal with problematic circumstances. This is why we can so quickly get bogged down with religious, political, academic and educational questions. They preoccupy our discussions, whether we are professionally engaged or not. Proof of this lies in the blood spilled (literally and metaphorically) over disputes about the proper way to respect a deity, the fairest strategies for distributing wealth and power in a society, the most valid techniques for testing out academic truths and the most effective ways of teaching children to read. If we could avoid the questions we argue about ideologically, we probably would do so. Because we can't, we find ourselves not only obliged to defend our belief systems against criticism, but often seek to join with others in mounting such a defence. Ideologies are shared value-oriented belief systems, as definitions stipulate. They are: '[Systems] of beliefs and values, held in common by members of a social group, each of which draws on the system of meanings in explaining the world or part of it' (Taylor and Richards, 1985, p. 32).

This final defining feature only extends the other three, being linked to the realization that we commit ourselves to positions on certain issues because those issues are pivotal in our affairs. It reminds us why so much emotion can be expended trying to resolve an ideological problem and why many people try to avoid the discussions altogether. It also brings us face to face with the possibly unpalatable truth that anyone seriously involved in educational debate who wishes to make consistent judgments must really develop an ideology. Only through these 'systems of interacting symbols' can we make 'otherwise incomprehensible social situations' meaningful (Geertz, 1964). Billig et al. (1988) write:

> Thus ideologies in everyday life should not be equated with the concealment, or prevention, of thought . . . [I]n a real sense, ideologies shape what people actually do think about, and permit the possibility of thought. (p. 27)

It is as professionally important for teachers to become ideologically committed as it is for priests, sociologists and ministers of state, if they are to make decisions which will consistently support a (morally and practically coherent) value position. And to neglect ideological commitment is hazardous for any professional group, especially one such as that composing the teaching profession which does not have goverance over its own activities, for it may ultimately find its professional ideals have been submerged in the ambitions of others.

Problems with educational ideologies

Notwithstanding their utility, accusations of bias against ideologies are not quickly dismissed. It is never simple to sort out matters of fact from matters of value when trying to find out why one teaching aim or method is preferable to another, and who should rightly decide such matters. To persistently champion a cause leaves the person concerned open to accusations of one-sided inflexibility. As introduced, in some sociological texts, ideologies are thought to distort our thinking by nature. Napoloeon, apparently, blamed French ideological hang-ups for his Russian defeat (cited in Larrain, 1979, p. 215). Larrain (1979; also Swinglewood, 1991) suggests that the designation of ideologies as forms of mental distortion may be owed to attempts by Marx and Durkheim (who both made extensive use of the concept) to establish the scientific base of sociology. These seminal thinkers felt they had to segregate beliefs about society based on scientific analysis from those dominated by indoctrination and prejudice. Lawton (1992) pins the basis of such educational usage on Mannheim.

Yet value-based belief systems can work neutrally, or beneficially, if those who hold them are honestly committed for defensible reasons. This second mode of application — now widely acknowledged in educational sociology (Apple, 1990; Billig et al., 1988; Morrison and Ridley, 1989; Thompson, 1984) — is the one normally used by those proposing ideological determinants for school curricula (Apple, 1990; Billig et al., 1988; Davies, 1969; Richards, 1988; Scrimshaw, 1983; Taylor and Richards, 1985). Unfortunately, someone wishing to discredit an argument without taking full stock of its meaning can skip evasively from one concept to the other. What those who appreciate value-committed debate have vigilantly to monitor are the objective grounds for their own beliefs. Unyielding dogmas and empty rhetoric do fasten onto ideologies in ways we can overlook. They do so because no one can, realistically, think through complex arguments in order to justify every decision made. We use handy phrases and pithy epigrams as short-hand for deeper principle. These ideological short-forms become slogans when they cease to reveal any vestiges of the case they represent and metamorphose into an inflexible source of meanings in their own right. Critics are right to insist on teachers avoiding the crude polarities of view which are not intrinsic to ideologies but which, often enough, are their lasting by-products.

It is helpful, here, to compare two *ways* in which people hold their ideologies. They can maintain an ideology covertly, being unwilling or unable to profess it openly, so protecting it from criticism, but also making it impossible to update through reflection and review. It is ideologies held in this way which tend to degenerate into dogma and rhetoric. The mediocre progressivist teaching which Robin Alexander found in Leeds (1992) and had earlier worried Sir Alec Clegg visiting other parts of the West Riding (cited Alexander et al., 1992, pp. 9–10) was reckoned by Alexander to be caused by teachers' unwillingness properly to think through a course of action in its own terms. They tended to adopt overly simple solutions to classroom problems and justify these by sloganizing. Sharp and Green (1975) found teachers in London similarly confused about the meaning and effects of their own ideological beliefs. Mediocre practice can arise from beliefs which are, simply, poorly understood. But it is probable that any attitude which becomes wholly dependent on dogma will in time lead to ill-judged practices because these will be unexamined and will not be adapted to social circumstances which do, invariably, alter. Ideologies should be professed honestly, and opened up to the scrutiny of others. Only through such overt assessments can child-centred teachers gain the 'essential skill' Lawton (1996) proposes. They must be able to 'distinguish between educationally valid aspects of progressivism or child-centred education and those which have been rightly dismissed as mere trendiness' (p. 53).

Overcoming this first problem with educational ideologies (their tendency to distort) is achieved by the same means we use to counter bias in any argument. We must regularly think them through. This is a requirement, both for those with ideological commitments and for critics — for anyone can sidestep legitimate complaints in order to conserve an entrenched point of view or avoid difficulties. It is arduous to have to work through every belief behind a proposed action or policy, and no one can do this for every decision they take. But we can, from time to time, re-examine our belief systems, realize what exactly are the values which justify them and check out their relevance to concrete situations.

The second difficulty is more intransigent. Just as the concept of an ideology is, itself, hard to circumscribe, so any one ideology, because of the intricate relationships existing between values, beliefs and actions, not to mention an immensely wide potential sphere of application, will be hard to pin down. Both friends and critics point to this difficulty with progressivism (Bennett, 1976; Billig et al., 1988; Cremin, 1961; Francis and Grindle, 1998; Rohrs, 1995; Sharpe, 1997). And unless we can at least cite criteria which cleanly divide one ideology from another, we cannot defend nor attack either successfully. For example, on observational grounds, alone, some have decided that progressivism has never taken hold at all in primary schools — that it has long been a myth (Galton, 1989a; Richards, 1985; Simon, 1981a; Mackenzie, 1997). Teachers who claim to have 'child-centred' philosophies have seemed to behave no differently from those who have made no such claim. On the other hand, when it is the child-oriented ethos of schools which is hailed as the essence of their progressivism, we can believe, as Holmes (1995) does, that the ideology triumphed during the middle period of the twentieth century and remains dominant, at least in primary schools. If we care only for base principles, we will probably take for granted Sullivan's (1996) contention that once-radical progressivist ideas are now 'accepted practice [having] shaped contemporary and public education systems around the world' (p. 349). Obviously, there is an issue here of what is or is not symptomatic of ideological influence, and how tenuously the association between beliefs and modes of teaching can be before they are still considered legitimate examples of such influence. This is so integral to an ideological study it is discussed separately (Chapter 3).

By the same token, because ideologies are value-charged belief systems, not neatly packaged prescriptions for behaviour, it is very possible to overlook their effects on classrooms. Research shows that the links between teachers' values, beliefs and practices are often indirect (Fang, 1996; Lee and Croll, 1995; Sugrue, 1997). There is a sense in which teacher intentions — born of their beliefs — must decide what they do: we simply may not see how the determination works. What we have to decide is whether the real risks of bias, indoctrination, vagueness of definition and of application, attendant on ideological commitment outweigh their virtues — notwithstanding the contention that it is hard to see how anyone who takes educational questions seriously can avoid having an ideologically framed belief system. It might be that in the context of many other sorts of influence, the ideological is the one teachers have to fight against and minimize.

The value of educational ideologies

The two types of benefit gifted to teachers and other educationists by their ideological commitments are implicit in the earlier discussions, but it is useful to make these explicit, taking into account the problems listed. These two benefits relate to the structural nature of ideologies (their interrelating of values and beliefs) and to their material content. Ideological commitment as a process sustaining teachers in their day-to-day jobs is different from the content of the beliefs and values themselves. With regard to the latter, the strength of educational belief systems is that they respond to research recommendations more obviously than do — for instance — belief systems maintained by politicians and those who minister to people's spiritual needs. Each of these issues is dealt with as a way of summarizing preceding argument.

New Progressivism

Coherence and consistency of interpretation

Firstly, educational ideologies have been defined as *coherent* belief systems, structured hierarchically — that is, there will be core values to which will cling central and subsidiary beliefs about specifications for classroom action. Because values affect many areas of our lives, they bring together diverse ideas taken from lived experience as justificatory arguments. As professional people, teachers have to frame what they do within coherent rationales, connecting one set of decisions (say about objectives) with another set (say concerning methods and assessment). These rationales are devised from a mix of professional judgments, factual knowledge, and an assessment of prevailing circumstances which are likely to be different from situation to situation and time to time. It is never easy in teaching to standardize practices because of the unpredictability of classroom events, and for this reason a teacher's decisions rarely rest on certain knowledge. Even those criteria stipulated by OFSTED to grade teaching performance (1995a) must be interpreted using beliefs of some sort, as studies of Inspection Reports (Northam, 1996) and the expressed opinions of inspectors (Silcock and Wyness, 1998) show. The evidence on which an inspection report is based is not 'objective' in any scientific sense, but results from judgments guided by the inspectors' expectations, which, in turn, arise out of beliefs moulded by experience.

This stays true during periods when teachers cannot use their own value-judgments to decide practices but must follow guidelines set by others — usually curricular and subject specialists working on government-sponsored committees. The implementation of the English/Welsh National Curriculum in 1989 ignored disagreements between educationists about curricular organization and delivery. But increasing standardization based on a contrived consensus does not eliminate disagreements which relate to real value disputes, it merely represses them, making inevitable the tensions and protests which follow from its enforcement. What, feasibly, happens is that teachers interpret their standardized tasks according to their own agendas: some will stress one part of their work, some another. They have no choice but to do this, since the tasks themselves (i.e. the subject orders built into the National Curriculum) are expressed in generalities which require professional judgment to implement. It is teachers' ideological leanings (just as with school inspectors) which gives them the wherewithall to respond to curricular demands. It will certainly be harder for progressivist teachers to respond positively to 'traditionalist' curricula than it will be for those already in tune with the reforms. But without any value-based belief system at all, we cannot imagine a teacher putting together coherent schemes of work to realize programmes of study.

The first advantage for teachers of having ideologies, then, is that these bring experiences together in a manner which can be tapped into when they plan and implement curricula. Teachers' ideological belief systems are, on this argument, near the core of their professional identities, because it is the rationales behind them which give answers to questions which, otherwise, would not be answered. To standardize any practices, we need to reach some consensus about justifications, and it will be remembered that the answers to central educational questions depend not on factual evidence alone but on the working out of a teacher's own values. What teachers believe is the proper way to formulate aims is likely to influence much else that they believe about themselves, their pupils and their job. This is the essence of Vic Kelly's (1994) critique of the English/Welsh National Curriculum, that although education is inescapably concerned with value-decisions, there is no public consensus on values, so (he surmises) we should not tolerate a standard curriculum.

Justifying practices

Educational ideologies consist of value-orientations, giving rise to beliefs about schools and children, some of which are empirically testable. Naturally enough, many teachers enter the teaching profession because of their interest in children and they continue to nurture that interest as they learn further about the best ways of relating to and communicating with younger minds. Piaget's great popularity among 'child-centred' teachers was (and to an extent still is) owed to his elaboration of principles which the teachers already knew intuitively. The merit of this coincidence (not an accidental one, if we accept that there is a strong vocational base to teaching) between a personal interest and a body of research-based knowledge is that teachers, being professional people, will be cued for these core studies. One expects that the personal beliefs of many who come into teaching (the same would apply to those joining themselves to politics and religion, or scholars working in subjects such as psychology or history) primes them to study some sorts of knowledge rather than others. A strong predisposition may of course be owed to other sorts of interest — such as a belief in the injustices of racism or a religious conviction. The point would still hold good: that such a predisposition should encourage teachers to explore a relevant literature, to think creatively about what they read, in ways which will then aid their practices.

If it is said that teachers ought, ideally, to engage in reflective, theoretical study regardless of their ideological leanings, this is true. But, as a rule for all teachers to follow, the proposal avoids two realities. The first is that teachers are usually preoccupied with practical tasks which leave limited time for academic work. The second is that 'Education Studies' consists of a large multidisciplinary corpus of books and papers that can easily inhibit someone whose curiosity is anyway diverted by more mundane problems. It may be that teachers will never read theoretical texts on a regular basis, yet there is a chance that they will read those commenting on a fundamental belief. By nature, teachers' commitment to a view (for example) about the nature of childhood makes it difficult for them to marginalize important books dealing with this subject. So a function of educational ideologies is to provide an *entrée* to a maze of books and papers which might otherwise seem daunting, and bring together bodies of knowledge in support of issues concerning values. This mutually nourishing relationship allows research-based theory to impact on more nebulous views, so that proper professional debate can, from time to time, reach balanced conclusions. Recent changes in our understanding of child

New Progressivism

development (see Chapter 6) illustrate the effectiveness of this interaction between values and research, in that these changes are given as a reason for educationists switching their own ideological allegiance.

Being a 'progressivist' means to have a professional identity combining selected value-orientations with a number of interrelated beliefs — some of which can be tested through research and argument. Teachers have to avoid being bewitched by dogma. But if they are systematically to review their ideas and take proper account of criticisms, they are best equipped to do so if they have a reliable perspective to work from. This does not mean they can never change ideological allegiances. Just as Conservative and Labour politicians, Protestants and Catholics, occasionally switch sides, so do progressivists and traditionalists, for rational reasons (one hopes). Since we should choose our ideologies because we know and accept their arguments (they shouldn't choose us — i.e. swamp any saner views we might have with unexamined doctrines) teachers must, also, look outside their ideologies from time to time and assess alternatives. It is one thing to justify ideological decision making, it is quite another to promote one ideology over another. The scrutiny of any beliefs must refer somewhere to others meant, equally, to give theoretical credence to teachers' work.

Chapter 3

Progressivism, Traditionalism and Pragmatism

How many educational ideologies are there?

Writers propose different numbers and types of educational ideologies (see, for example, Davies, 1969; Lawton, 1973, 1989; Morrison and Ridley, 1989; Scrimshaw, 1983; Skilbeck, 1976), depending on whether they think these are best divided into broad categories, or should be further subdivided to accommodate any subtler differences which can be divined in what practitioners do and say. To an extent, how many educational ideologies are needed to do justice to the potentially enormous divergences of belief within the teaching profession has to be decided arbitrarily, according to our purposes.

The approach favoured here relies on a tripartite analysis made by Richards (1988), splitting off the two main educational ideologies from each other, while judging how far both have been succeeded by a more neutral, even-handed pragmatism. This approach is chosen because when teachers discuss their beliefs, these are most easily grouped under the two familiar headings of progressivism and traditionalism: classroom researchers (such as Alexander, 1992; Francis and Grindle, 1998; Pollard et al., 1994; Silcock and Wyness, 1997) resort to terms such as 'child-centred', 'formal' and 'informal' because teachers also use them. Finer discriminations might show that different teachers actually mean different things by the terms they use, but such discriminations are hard to make with confidence. Even discerning the broad progressive–traditional divide is problematic, as Neville Bennett found in his 1976 research comparing formal and informal teaching styles. Having reached conclusions quite damaging to the progressivist cause, he was forced by critics to re-analyse his data and modify his original conclusions (Aitken, Bennett and Hesketh, 1981). His problem was one of categorization.

To find that 'formal/informal', 'teacher-centred/child-centred' dualisms still have currency among teachers does not make them practically useful or theoretically correct. Morrison and Ridley (1989; also Lawton, 1992; Meighan, 1981; Scrimshaw, 1981) group traditionalist and progressivist ideologies apart from those oriented to social change: teachers might believe that schooling should be a stage towards either improving or altering society. And such a belief stops them from having to opt for one of the two other types of ideology. However, as Morrison and Ridley say (1989, p. 45), it is the nature of society-centred ideologies that they are applied outside the educative process itself. In other words, teachers who might (for example)

23

New Progressivism

believe that their work is geared to society's improvement, ultimately have still to make classroom decisions which will not in general flow from their social commitments. When they make these decisions, their options are, still, vulnerable to traditionalist/progressivist labelling (more than they are to the socio-political). This does not mean that there are not issues to debate concerning the relationships between schooling and social improvement. These will be dealt with in terms of the weaknesses concerning a lack of social orientation writers detect in progressivist beliefs.

Returning to the two main ideologies: Alexander (1994), Pring (1989a) and Sharpe (1997) are among those who warn us against the 'false dichotomies' which polarize curricular process against knowledge content, formal against informal teaching methods, topic-based against subject-based work and so on. Such adversarial posturing, they say, leads to inflexible judgments. Pragmatists, postmodernists and poststructuralists, too, condemn the two dominant ideologies as historical anachronisms, suited to less enlightened times (Littledyke, 1998; Mackenzie, 1997; Sugrue, 1997; Walkerdine, 1994). 'Grand narratives' no longer have the conceptual power to penetrate to the complex truths of a postmodern world.

These two types of accusation make substantially the same attack though from slightly different vantage points. At bottom, they assume the commonsensical notion that teachers should not be restricted for ideological reasons to any one set of practical techniques or another, but should have access to all. Where they mislead us is in their merging of justifiable choices, made at the level of values, with the false polarizations people use as forms of conceptual shorthand to help them effect rapid decisions. There is nothing 'false' about contrasting sets of educational aims against others in order to justify them — we cannot discuss values except as categories contrasted with each other. And the traditional/progressive division (at the level of values) encapsulates in educational terms other divisions which exist in philosophy, sociology, politics and similar academic spheres where human affairs are analysed (see Billig et al., 1988).

Where we can agree with critics is that false polarities (where made) are unhelpful. But this polarizing is not confined to educational ideologies, and it is not essential to them. As explained, ideologies are value-based belief systems linked to mixes of classroom practices: they divide at the level of values and general policy but overlap and indeed interact (i.e. via debate, research comparisons, etc.) at the level of practice, enriching each other over periods of time. The history of each of the two major movements in education is one of their being redefined in reaction to each other. There are almost certainly fewer differences to be marked between the actual behaviours of teachers of different ideological persuasion today than there were 30 years ago, although the value positions themselves have not gone away. What confuses us is that in order to connect values to practices we will use the same language for both. Practices (because they are what we can see and judge) soon become synonymous with the difference at issue, and values (because they are abstract and hidden) are forgotten.

Thus we become bemused by the dichotomies we are forced to invent in order to make sense of what we see. We believe that traditional teaching strategies are *confined* to didactic teaching methods, to knowledge prescriptions or autocratic authority, and progressivism is *synonymous* with small-group or individualistic teaching, with integrated and curricular-based topics. That these associations exist is correct: but what makes a teaching strategy traditionalist or child-centred is the value which provokes it, not the features of the strategy itself. So child-centred teachers who use whole-class teaching are no less child-centred for doing so, providing they can appropriately explain the reasons for what they do.

Criticisms from postmodernists are of a different sort, in that a number (not all) actually do question all dichotomies, even at a level of values. The contemporary world is diverse and unstable (Aviram, 1993; Littledyke, 1998; Mackenzie, 1997; Prain, 1997; Schon, 1983; Sugrue, 1997): universalisms, all-embracing ideas, dualisms, explanatory principles rely on a confidence in absolutes we no longer have. Instead of working from principle, we should 'deconstruct' our habitual perspectives to the conclusions actually suited to circumstance (Prain, 1997). Similar strictures are applied by those pragmatists who wish to look to circumstance for guidance on educational matters. Indeed, the chief difficulty we have accepting the postmodern version of classroom life is that if we abandon our usual ways of talking about educational issues and try to adopt a less partisan stance, either we find we have lost our very reason for tackling the issues at all (the underlying value considerations) or are left with no hard and fast criteria for our judgments. In short, we have only pragmatics.

It is a tiresome fact that, in education as in society generally, *plus ça change* more often than not means *plus la même chose*. Although disputes between educationists today are dissimilar to those of 30 years ago, there continue to be limitations set on ways of looking at the teaching and learning process because we haven't, actually, got straight our basic beliefs about ourselves, which continually take us back to those issues locked into the grand 'meta-narratives' which postmodernists abhor. The fact is that in arguing for and against the major educational changes of recent times we do discover older assumptions. It might seem tedious to continue returning to them, but it would be folly to pretend either that they had vanished from the scene or that through some terminological sleight of hand they can be shown impotent or unreal. The hypothesis broached by pragmatists that the differences are real but they need not be binding on us — that is, we can be eclectic in our attitude to classroom policies — is rather more pernicious in its effects because so many educational policies seem to assume it. Considerations of the way pragmatism and eclecticism intercede into educational policy making will be returned to below and in a later chapter (8), acknowledging that they are as often as not seen as our main avenues of escape from the established ideologies.

Defining educational ideologies

Trying to separate progressivism from traditionalism completely would be a mammoth enterprise. There are a bewildering variety of progressivist movements (see Brehony, 1992; Cremin, 1961; Rohrs, 1995), including newly invented models (Sugrue, 1997). The variety of movements does not in itself prohibit defining mainstream characteristics. As Rohrs (1995) finds, there is 'an astonishing degree of unanimity' (p. 23) in progressivist approaches worldwide, probably because the idea of individualism which is at their heart is applied effectively in modern classrooms in a limited number of ways. So we are able to interpret that handful of principles, recognized by friends and critics alike as illustrating the notion of individualism in education, into a modern idiom where it can be defended (successfully or not) against attacks. What does hinder anyone trying to revise an ideology are the many kinds of analysis we have to take into account when isolating its essentials. There is nothing to gain from reducing a complex belief system to practicalities: this 'bullet-point' method sometimes adopted so as to itemize characteristics leads straight into false dichotomizing. Lists of traditionalist/progressivist beliefs abound, but we have no way of disputing their accuracy outside of a rationale which will explain why they exist. And any rationale has, itself, to turn appropriately on an association of empirical and conceptual precepts which contemporary classroom situations call into being.

This routing of argument from principle to illustrations of practice need not be straightforward, but a *preliminary* conceptual definition has to be established providing a base from which to advance. As a first foray into defining centuries old ideologies, the one which follows is not submitted as superior to all others but is a particular kind of definition put together for a purpose. Its starting point is the modern tradition of progressivist writings focussing on the Plowden Report, which was, itself, a reconceiving of earlier forms begun two and half centuries ago with Rousseau (Darling, 1994; Grimsley, 1973). And what is claimed for it are three sorts of validity. It has a validity of origin — it is a development of the Plowden-type progressivism (itself continuous with older recommendations such as those framed by the Hadow Committee: Board of Education, 1931). It has an internal, structural validity — its justifications will be shown to be internally consistent and potentially resistant to piecemeal criticism. And it has a validity of application. It is to be shown as applying to modern primary school practices in a way making sense of issues arising, for example, from the implementing of standard curricula.

Keeping in mind that a fuller conceptualizing is part of this book's overall purpose and will therefore be fairly slowly achieved, we can see both present and past educational disputes as involving two competing concepts or models of what it means to be an educated person. These are in turn derived from a disagreement between theorists about the sorts of creatures human beings are (Billig et al., 1988; Prain, 1997). Educational ideologies were argued to come into existence because some central questions have to be answered by reference both to values and to factually known evidence (see Chaper 2). And the question which holds sway over others — because answering it dovetails into answers to most other questions — is that of what education is actually for: what do we believe its function is in a society such as ours?

One model explanation sees schools as preoccupied with transmitting a valued ('traditionally tried and tested') knowledge. The fact that the National Curriculum came into being implies that its architects were convinced that we can sufficiently well identify the knowledge, skills and qualities desirable for all who live in modern societies. As Anthony O'Hear puts it (1987), it is *what* we know that empowers us: we have only to decide the form our knowledge should take in order to set our main educational aims. Educationists, teachers, are guardians of our cultural inheritance. Lawlor (1990), O'Hear (1987, 1988), O'Keefe (1990), Scruton (1987) and other members of the so-called 'New Right' take what Brundrett (1997) calls the 'Leavisite' position of supposing, like T. S. Eliot (1948), that our finest intuitions and values are harvested from that 'high culture' produced for us by past thinkers. Any digression from subject-oriented teaching is for some to lose sight of the major objective.

In contrast, another group doubts whether we can ever agree about what everyone should learn, and therefore what teachers in all our schools should teach. Members of this group suppose that each generation (or subculture) of people must discover its own preferences (see especially Kelly, 1980, 1986, 1989, 1994; also Pring, 1997; Rogers, 1983; Silcock, 1993, 1994a). It isn't that we have no inkling at all of what is valuable, but that, given that we have a world-culture to plunder which is in no sense static in its development, reliable barometers are hard to come by. Kelly (1994) chastises those philosophers and sociologists who have thought they could set up criteria for 'selecting' among culturally given concepts and skills by indicating that pluralist values are set to become the norm, not an inconvenient and transient fact of British life. The issue, for this second group, is one of deciding how to give learners 'ownership' over curricula in ways which stop them embracing ideas which will not serve their interests, and which preserve as intact as possible at least the core of those knowledge traditions which give ongoing validity to what we know.

A fruitful way of typifying this division between what Lawton (1973) labels the 'classical' (traditionalist) and 'romantic' (progressivist) ideals of an educated person is to recognize it as a version of the 'positivist/humanist' conflict found in philosophy and the social sciences. Those who aspire to explanations of human behaviour with scientific credibility (positivists) disagree with those who suspect that the whole effort is flawed because human beings are quite unlike material objects (humanists). The positivist approach to education, with its firm foothold in scientific psychology (see Littledyke, 1998; Schön, 1983) takes for granted the belief that we will one day know enough about ourselves to be able to mould our own minds and actions according to trustworthy rules of procedure. Humanists propose the reverse, thinking that human beings are autonomous by nature, creative of rules but not to be bound by them (Blackham, 1976; Popper, 1979, 1994; Rogers, 1983; Sartre, 1948). Progressivism is the best-known humanistic ideology, where teachers seek to adapt what they do to the unique differences they find in all human beings. Traditionalists are those who decide we know enough about people already to fix the rules by which all can be educated. It will be seen at once that separating these two ideologies helps us fix the beliefs of some of the people who are either responsible for the recent English/Welsh educational reforms or have commented critically on them.

New Progressivism

The two concepts of education generate different schedules of aims, formulations of curricular content, methodological and accountability systems. They bestow value on some types of curricula at the expense of others. An immediate objection to them might be that (again) they 'falsely dichotomize' in that they each represent half truths: it is to some extent true that there is no consensus about educational aims and to some extent true that there is. Also, no one would wish to prevent learners having *some* say in their own education. But we must remember the earlier conclusion that in situations of limited time and resource, where we really do wish to, say, democratize schools, achieve social justice and not stigmatize minority views, fulfil pupils' legitimate rights (etc.), we have to prioritize. And prioritizing means making decisions which while not alienating others do stand some chance of realizing those aims being prioritized. Just as importantly, as soon as we accept that no single kind of primary school curriculum can serve the needs of all pupils, we find that there are grounds for believing it which go beyond that of citing an ideal. There are arguments which will make us seriously question the sort of 'transmission' hypothesis which *any kind* of traditionalism (even a watered-down version) implies. In short, a revision of progressivism turns up arguments which solidify rather than dilute its values. These will occupy ensuing pages.

Three ideologies

Traditionalism

People who seek to implement a common curriculum for everyone are, as Dewey thought (see MacDonald, 1972), traditionalists. It follows that preferred teaching methods for this group are the ones most suited to transmitting, in some straightforward fashion, the content which has been prioritized (again as Dewey judged — see MacDonald, 1972). The name we give to teaching methods purveying content with little modification or adaptation is 'formal'. Formality of method is associated with traditionalism because to believe we know what others should learn must also entail the belief that others can, in actuality, learn these things, without too much dilution or simplification. To take a formal stance to methodology is to take a traditionalist stance, but the crux of the ideology lies not with the formality as such, as with its purpose — i.e. to teach in a way respecting a subject's structure and the established details of any explanations and arguments associated with it. It is not at all an out-of-the-way idea that traditionalist teachers will, from time to time, need to compromise their formalisms to keep faith with their aims — depending on classroom circumstances. So 'traditionalism' and 'formal methods', while being closely associated, are not perfectly joined.

Extending the above argument, those with authority in education will be those whose expertise qualifies them to make decisions about what we all should know and do, and are by that token qualified to decide how to turn policies derived from the principle into practice. These people include teachers, headteachers, inspectors, and, in modern times, those subject specialists who sit on educational committees and directly or indirectly advise secretaries of state. These are the people who qualify as protectors of our culture, who have the insights which qualify them to detect what the rest of us most require to learn in schools and colleges. Such a situation is not unproblematic. For although there will never be a shortage of people who believe they can prescribe knowledge for others, there will always be just as many who will disagree with them. However, we mustn't mistake practicality for principle. While debates about knowledge continue, we might get closer and closer towards consensus. Until one is achieved, we might accept an approximation to what educational authorities decree as, for now, our best shot at devising an agreed syllabus.

On the above first analysis, and remembering the three categories of questions ideologies seek to answer, traditionalist ideology is summarized as being tied to prescriptions of curricular content, recommending formality of organization and method, and putting teachers and teacher advisers in authority, making them largely accountable for the effectiveness of schools. The extent to which teachers are really 'in charge' in a traditionalist system is a moot question, for in the context of a politically centralized organization teachers may have little decision making power. The point is not that authority is vested in teachers as a professional group, as that it is vested in the knowledge which teachers have by virtue of their roles and which binds them as much as it binds the responsibilities of learners. This fact explains the attraction to politicians of traditionalist beliefs. If we optimistically think that we know what should be taught and that the concepts we identify can be 'transmitted', where we find that they are not being so transmitted we have to ascribe the fault as lying somewhere within the teaching process itself.

The traditionalist idea that teachers are responsible for the success or failure of schools justifies the firm control over education which contemporary politicians have come to prefer, and the managerial hierarchies derived from this control. It deems OFSTED is a sensible way of ensuring that the system is working, and it leads to increasing standardizations of practice. What traditionalist ideology throws out of court is any suggestion that differences between pupils, themselves, can (or should) determine educational outcomes. If we know what an educated person 'looks like', it is a teacher's job to select whatever form of pedagogy is deemed appropriate to bring a pupil to that desired state.

Progressivism

Progressivism modifies traditionalist ideas. It is not so much a novel approach to education as a set of perspectives on standard questions issuing from allegiance to a very different ideal. Progressivism begins with the failure of traditionalism to show incontrovertibly that its older approach produces recognizably educated citizens. Yes, we do have cultural richness in western societies. But what also characterizes these societies are degrees of disaffection with educational values among learners, significant numbers of uneducated citizens (on any criterion) and escapist, mass lifestyles. However, Rousseau's (1911/1762) view of education as an antidote

New Progressivism

to social ills has been replaced in modern thinking by conceptions of the child/society relationship which is meant to integrate not separate the two. Modern progressivists will usually agree with Vic Kelly (1994) that though there is no consensus about what we should teach, and that the reliance placed by a number of people upon didacticism is correspondingly misplaced, we might agree about the attitudes learners should develop to school subjects. Accordingly, 'processes' or principles of procedure are taken to signal the quality of classroom tasks. It might not matter so much whether children study the Vikings or the Romans in History, but it certainly matters whether they enjoy and understand what they learn, wish to pursue it further and can apply it to their own lives. So progressivist curricula put 'process' criteria (sometimes called procedural principles: Ruddock and Hopkins, 1985; Stenhouse, 1975, 1983), of the kind Kelly (Blenkin and Kelly, 1981) and Alan Blyth (1984) have described, in place of precisely stated aims.

Different types of progressivism to an extent spring from different theories about what processes make for quality learning. Bruner (1972), whose ideas stimulated much progressivist thinking mid-century, is an educator and psychologist who believes that human beings grow intellectually through employing socially transmitted mental technologies: we learn from school and family environments how to solve problems through actions (enactive thinking), through structured imagery (iconic thinking) and through linguistic explorations (symbolic thinking). From his curricular experiments, Bruner (1972) deduces that it is the procedures which educators adopt to ensure that learners 'discover' ideas for themselves which matters (what he calls 'heuristics'), not their reaching of correct solutions. He is not suggesting that pupils literally have to mimic the evolution of human ideas by discovering afresh all our established achievements, but that as a classroom strategy it is essential that learners come to their understandings in their own ways.

Accepting that some types of learning are superior to others, and that, as Dewey (1900, 1902; see also MacDonald, 1972) and Blyth (1984) suggest, it is learners' personal experiences which provide the main arena for their learning, constrains teachers to use classroom strategies and modes of organization geared to pupils' developing personalities. Methods adapted to diagnoses of learners' developmental 'needs', rather than fitted to pre-decided rules associated with content, are called 'informal'. As with formality, although teachers take an informal stance because of its intimate relationship with their aims, it does not follow that informality is itself an end to be pursued. Chances are that in any progressivist teacher's day, the maintaining of 'quality' learning situations (as these are defined) will require moments of didacticism or judicious interventions using formal instruction. What ties informality to progressivism is its focus upon diversity of learner requirement: teachers who are at a premium watching for the individual problems which learners have in order to deal with these will not already have bound themselves to a tight scheduling of lessons following subject structure (see Chapter 8).

To make learners' relationships with their own learning *the* pivotal issue, deciding teachers' methods and modes of organization, is to embody 'child-centredness' in school curricula. Decisions about the degree and kind of involvement pupils should have will also be child-centred, since they impinge on that relationship, though the decisions themselves may vary from time to time and place to place. And because relationships between learners and knowledge change through time, 'developmentalism' (especially as found in the work of child psychologists) becomes an ideologically fertile area of study. So 'child-centredness' is a synonym for progressivism because both concepts point to education as having the same end point. Darling (1994) defines the progressivist view of education as being that it 'should be designed to reflect the nature of the child' (p. 3).

Still, if we are strict about it, we find that progressivism and child-centredness are not completely identical. We might just suppose that process aims can be achieved through a strict programme of didactic teaching, which would make that form of 'progressivism' not at all child-centred. Although this conception can (and will) be rejected for practical purposes on the grounds that child-centred sorts of classroom organization are crucial to achieving progressivist aims, it will always be possible for someone with a different vested interest to reinstate it as a possibility. Just as traditionalists have difficulty demonstrating what everyone in our diverse society should know, the weakness of progressivism lies in our scanty knowledge of what actually makes the difference between learning situations which succeed in 'empowering' the minds of learners and those which do not. Fortunately, we do make some progress in such matters, as will be seen. Better judgments can be made now about these things than we could make just a few years ago.

The three well-springs of modern progressivism, then, are (in contrast to traditionalism): that its curricula are designed through considerations of process rather than through specifications of content; it recommends informal teaching methods; and it is child-centred in its involvement of pupils in curricular management and decision making. So for a child-centred teacher, pupils' personal welfare and developmental progress are at the heart of the whole business. This criterion speaks not only for teachers' aims and methodology but also for their accountability. If learners' own attitudes and experiences become determinants of curricula in any real sense, teachers', legal and moral responsibilities for their own professional outputs may seem to that degree diminished. Such an inference from progressivist lore explains politicians' disquiet about the ideology. The moment we admit that pupils need not learn for reasons connected with their own psychologies or social circumstances we open the door for teachers to argue that they cannot always be held accountable for either educational success or failure. If they cannot be so held accountable, political control (through, for example, OFSTED) of the educational system becomes equally dubious. But this is to jump to conclusions about what does or does not decide accountability. It is one thing to say that teachers cannot be absolutely accountable for pupil learning (which will be argued), it is quite another to suggest that they should not be held accountable at all.

Because they support very different models of educational practice, premises founded in the two major ideologies invade all aspects of teaching (Meighan, 1981, and Morrison and Ridley, 1989 list many of these). But, to repeat an earlier caution, this does not mean that supporters of either deny the other's recommendations universally or at all times. How we see ourselves as human beings underlies many of our values, and makes sure that we will consistently sit in one ideological camp and not another. Yet people never wholly conform to type, and as circumstances change, so the viability of any given point of view can change. If the National Curriculum had proven to be a spell-binding success, greeted with overwhelming enthusiasm by a majority of teachers, we would question the sense of trying to argue for the curricular diversity which progressivism fosters. The fact that neither of the above conditions has (yet) been realized gives some encouragement to our exploring, once again, what help progressivist beliefs might offer to hard-pressed teachers working, often, in less than perfect circumstances.

Pragmatism

There is a third option. We can surmise that circumstance will always decide our aims, methods and modes of curricular organization, and that we do not need any other rule to advise us. Sometimes it is right for teachers to adopt a traditional approach, sometimes to be child-centred. The philosophy behind this even-handed position is called pragmatism. It is in prevailing circumstances that we will usually find some reason for choosing between options. As a rule of thumb, teachers are encouraged to ask which strategy best 'fits' the purpose or intention they have in mind. 'Fitness for purpose' has become a slogan able to stand in place of ideological belief (Alexander et al., 1992).

Our attitude towards pragmatism as a coherent set of beliefs able to frame our thinking depends, partly, on what we take the beliefs to be. We are all pragmatic from time to time in our work, but this is different from thinking that the approach offers solutions to all major problems. In a revealing account of the way it has come to dominate much of our thinking throughout this century, Mounce (1997) separates the pragmatism of Peirce, James and Dewey from the later sorts found — for example — in the influential writings of Richard Rorty. Mounce illustrates how the rule of searching within the practicalities of human experience for ways of resolving difficulties, seen in the earlier type of pragmatism, respected values concerned with universals of human life and identity which later pragmatists have abandoned. Peirce, William James and Dewey had no doubt that practical experience had, somewhere, to be judged by criteria external to it; they simply forced our attention on actual events as the only reliable sources of knowledge we have of these things.

Modern philosophical pragmatists are (again, as Mounce tells us) the opposite of those who, like Peirce and Dewey, looked to lived experience as *sources* for our knowledge not as *criteria* by which to judge it. They share with postmodernists and poststructuralists a disdain for those 'absolutes' of conduct by which we might judge our day-to-day experiences. For these, we have to select guidelines for our interpretations of events from whatever are 'on offer' within the particular intellectual and cultural contexts we prefer. Safstrom (1996) thus defines pragmatism as 'a holistic movement of thought which denies the existence of permanent, ahistorical criteria of truth and knowledge and whose aim is to clarify meaning' (p. 58). He goes on to explain how the 'pragmatist holds that we attain knowledge when we understand socially based verifications of belief . . . we do not find knowledge, we create knowledge in our interaction with the world' (p. 58). What this tells us is that whether or not an educational practice is a good one or not can only be judged by studying the particular contexts within which the practice itself occurs.

As Safstrom explains (1996), postmodern and poststructuralist thinkers have a foothold in the sort of pragmatism under discussion. Their antipathy towards 'metatheories' leads them, too, to anchor decision making in whatever localized circumstances politicians, academics and professionals face, denying a-priori principles. Postmodernism (and its poststructuralist forerunner: see Cole and Hill, 1995) comprises a rather more explicit abandoning of universalistic precepts than does pragmatism (the latter developing within twentieth-century philosophy). So Walkerdine (1994) characterizes developmental theories supporting progressivist beliefs as stories selected by the ideologically partisan: their so-called 'objective' truths are, on poststructuralist analysis, unsupportable. There are no universal criteria (such as empirical tests for truth) outside contexts which we can use to judge what is happening within contexts. Progressivism as much validates Piagetian developmentalism as Piaget gives tacit credence to child-centred teaching: this circularity of validation is escaped just by our stepping outside the circle. There are no external ways to justify either. Ergo: we abandon both.

The problem the postmodern view creates for anyone whose profession depends on practical decision making is severe. If we reduce disputes about relative values to differences of viewpoint, even questioning our knowledge of these viewpoints (Prain, 1997), without acknowledging any truths transcending classroom and school contexts, we are left floundering when confronted with decisions with implications which reverberate outside immediate circumstance, and risk giving credence to oppressive social and political policies simply because they seem to 'fit' the postures of the times. This is exactly Cole and Hill's critique (Cole et al., 1997). Through a number of papers (e.g. 1995, 1996; Cole et al., 1997), they point out that to dismiss educational 'dualisms' as invalid dismisses not only ideological positions but also class-based dualisms, thus pulling away the carpet from under the feet of anyone who is trying to right social injustices. As they say, postmodernists who find flaws in base-principle, as a matter of principle, are on a journey to nowhere (Cole et al., 1997, p. 193).

Similarly, in a stinging critique of a contemporary postmodern historical analysis, Gabella (1996) hits at the problem for those academics who eschew objective truths. It isn't so much that, in a historical treatise for example, we can be sure that an account has objective (i.e. historical) accuracy: but in order to give any role at all to historical research, we have to assume that there *is* something called a true account to set against the distortions and false conceptions of events to which we might otherwise revert for guidance. If there is no objective historical truth, there can be no history. The postmodern predicament implies '. . . nothingness . . . no story, no narrative, no interpretation and no explanation' (Gabella, 1996, p. 727). Once we accept that truths are narratives and beliefs about them have no credence outside the perspectives we take, we quickly lose sight of the mission of any educational system to steer learners away from ideas with poor justification and argument towards those we can verify by reference to 'metanarratives' and empirical observation. When all is 'pluralistic, relativistic and dynamic' (Aviram, 1993, p. 426), education along with any other organized effort to clear away ignorance and uncertainty dissolves into a fog of inconsequential meanderings through tales of misguided human achievements.

We might also be led into self-contradiction, as there will be moments in any consistent argument when it is imperative to look outside a context for criteria to judge accurately what is happening within it. This is Ciaran Sugrue's (1997) dilemma, when he takes it on himself to 'reinvent' child-centredness. He starts from scratch, watching teachers at work without prior assumptions in order to classify what they do within newly wrought categories. He does this because through his postmodern lens he finds the two 'power blocks' of progressivism and traditionalism so locked into battle with each other that 'the minds and hearts of teachers and children have been pawns in a kind of educational super league' (p. 2). He nearly falls into circularity because he has to use child-centred concepts to describe his teachers' actions (otherwise he cannot make any ideological claims), while at the same time proposing that he has no presumptions about them. So he draws on the British/Irish progressivist tradition in order to reconceive it, tacitly admitting the meaningfulness of the concepts he uses. He eventually situates himself, comfortably enough, within the 'parent ideology' he has felt himself compelled to 'review, revise and revitalise' (p. 7).

Sugrue is not alone in wanting to throw off the ties of those rhetorical devices which can appear to strangle educational thinking. Robin Alexander, whose writings provide us with a consistently pragmatic approach to the organization and management of school curricula (e.g. 1992, 1993, 1995), warns teachers against the 'bizarrely polarised debate' (1992, p. 194) to which ideological struggles easily give rise. Largely, he is telling us to avoid the mindless dogma which can cripple properly balanced discussion, and his reproaches are fair in separating the gold from the dross in our belief systems. However, in so far as he wants us to look to circumstances for educational guidance rather than searching within our professional beliefs (and this is what he does appear to want us to do, regularly enough), it is hard to see where we should look, since it is the point of these to guide our decision making in consistent and principled ways. To look elsewhere inevitably ends with our interpreting what we find in terms of other people's ideologies. Becoming the means to someone else's end is the likely fate for any pragmatists who work within the public arena.

To put this more succinctly, the quandary for educational pragmatists is that the circumstances which affect teachers' lives are diverse, and seldom 'given' to experiences in a pure or transparent form. We usually have to decide which are most relevant to our aims and then interpret the demands they make on us: appeals to circumstance never resolve value-disagreements. At present, many primary school teachers believe that they are teaching more formally than they were before 1989, and there is research evidence that their perceptions are correct (Cox, 1996; Francis and Grindle, 1998; Galton, 1998a; Silcock, 1995; Webb, 1993). When asked, many explain that what most decides this altered approach is their legal obligation to teach the whole of the National Curriculum (Silcock, 1995; Silcock and Wyness, 1997). Their reasoning makes sense. An advantage of formal over informal teaching is its efficiency: we can cover more ground more quickly through instruction than by taking time to adapt to learner requirements. However, progressivist teachers are not satisfied by efficiency or economy of means, important though these constraints are. They will prioritize other circumstances than those of curriculum coverage. They are likely to ask whether we shouldn't really want learners to understand and enjoy their learning and apply it to their own lives, rather than concentrate on covering every last inch of curricular ground. In short, progressivists and traditionalists will regularly disagree about what circumstances most apply in the resolving of any practical dilemma and how circumstantial demands should be evaluated.

All teachers are pragmatists in that they will give due regard to what is practically sensible and can be resourced. That is, they will decide on the most efficient and economic ways to achieve their ends. But once we step outside the practical arena, we discover that the 'fitness for purpose' rule is limited in how far it can help us. Shortages of money, time, energy will always severely constrain what teachers do, but there are few circumstances in teaching where these are the only, or even the dominant, considerations. As Badley puts it (1993), 'goodness of fit' doesn't even give us one necessary condition for good teaching, for it assumes that the more resonant decisions, concerned with matters of value, have already been sorted. We must separate the day-to-day pragmatism of all teachers from *ideological* pragmatism — the idea that *all* curricular questions can be answered by pointing to circumstance (i.e. practical, political, social or whatever). Full-blooded pragmatism, and postmodernism which it resembles, are meant to unchain us from ideological commitment. They are false gods. They allow us to hide our own commitments from ourselves, but do not resolve anything beyond superficially justifying that rather self-satisfying concealment.

Mixing ideologies

Because we rarely answer ideological questions with finality, school curricula are usually judicious mixtures of progressive and traditional elements. This doesn't mean that ideological disputes are so resolved, since we have still to justify one mixture over another. The helpful difference to make here is that between a compromise and a consciously eclectic (pick-and-mix) approach to classroom decision making. We all compromise our views, following proper debate and an airing of opinions, but to be eclectic or to suggest 'hybridization' as a standard way forward rather than an unfortunate consequence of compromise is to return us to the pragmatist's dilemma of someone then being honour-bound to state what criteria they are applying from circumstance to circumstance. And there are no criteria outside those already locked into the traditions themselves.

Mackenzie (1997) declares that the language of the old adversarial politics carried too much unnecessary baggage to work for us any longer. Like Alexander, he believes we can take from all traditions in fashioning the best classroom practice, putting in place as an organizing process a 'perspectivist' discourse. Such a discourse is based on the 'social-constructivist' idea that we have to take adult and child perspectives together (in a relationship) to decide curricula. It is an interesting suggestion, meant to separate Vygotskian inspired approaches to methodology from the older progressivist (Piaget inspired) ideas, and so pluck us out of the dualist trap. Littledyke (1998), very similarly, takes his 'postmodern', social-constructivist philosophy to be superior to progressive developmentalism. Yet, as it happens, both progressivist and traditionalist beliefs subsume views about the respective roles of teachers and learners: and what we find when we examine 'social constructivism' more closely is that its separation from a more progressivist 'constructivism' represents a 'false dichotomy' (Chapter 6). There is no 'third way' between educational ideologies because there is no mid-way course to travel between two possibilities: learners either construct their own unique meanings from socially mediated options or they do not (and *that* is the division we must mark).

When school curricula are decided, there will always be forces tugging in opposing directions. We cannot mix ideologies, for this means supporting two competing educational ideals along with their connected value systems. The apparent mixing of ideologies is always the modification of one from the perspective of another. So a 'child-centred' primary school staff might tolerate traditionalist opinions by setting strict parameters for children's choice of topics for study, while a traditionalist group of teachers might modify its wish to achieve curriculum coverage by arranging a limited menu of optional subjects for students to choose from. It is perfectly rational to hold that, whereas we do not know altogether what subjects to prioritize, we can decide on a framework of possibilities; or, we may not be absolutely sure that specially tailored forms of teaching style will achieve 'quality' learning, but we hedge our bets and try to work along with learners' interests as far as we can rather than mechanically imposing a written curriculum upon them. We all compromise our values and beliefs. But it would be fatal to dislodge them completely from our minds. For what is there to put in their place?

This returns us to the conclusion that ideologies need not polarize our opinions but there remain real dichotomies at the level of values which we ignore at our peril. No one can harbour contrasting ideals at the same time (there remain differences of aim and therefore curricular stress in the above examples), while the practicalities of resource which limit what teachers achieve, force some degree of choice upon them. The same is true for politicians who might clear-sightedly perceive that there are diverging policies they can explore while trying to please as many people as possible. Their quandary represents a common experience, one suspects.

For example, at the time of writing, the problem of 'delivering' the English/Welsh National Curriculum as it stands has once again become acute. It has been obvious for some time that ten primary school subjects, plus cross-curricular themes and RE, cannot properly be managed in a normal school timetable alongside a heavy commitment to basic skills teaching (see Campbell, 1993a and b, for discussion); the Dearing Report which was meant to alleviate the problem is not universally regarded as having worked (Silcock, 1995; Silcock and Wyness, 1997).

Competing policies of 'slimming' the National Curriculum down, or 'relaxing' its prescriptiveness to allow teachers more leeway in interpreting it, are ideologically conceived. To trim it further is to leave it as a set of prescriptions (traditionalism); indeed, choosing such an option risks discarding altogether the 'broad and balanced' pretensions of the existing subject orders in deference to that most traditional, elementary school diet of basic skills. Alternatively, to allow teachers to select their own routes 'through' the National Curriculum, i.e. to relax legal requirements, is to bow to their professional diagnoses of learner need and attitude (progressivism). Whether we go for one policy or another will depend on whether we value prescribed contents and skills over learners' relationships with these, or vice versa (whether we are traditionalists or progressivists). The realization that we normally compromise between these positions in teaching merely recognizes the strength of argument which bolsters each one. Few people would ever concede one wholly to the other.

Chapter 4

Progressivism and National Curricula

Behind teachers' day-to-day decisions (as behind those of doctors, academics, priests, social workers, politicians, lawyers) lurk value judgments grounded in philosophical and empirical principles which can seem very abstract, but usually turn out to be very practical in what they imply for a busy professional's work. We should welcome this situation. Teachers' professionalism depends on their holding to their own values rather than meekly submitting to those of others. It is, of course, always possible for government reformers to earn the professionals' compliance so that state-sponsored values come to equate with those of teachers. It is possible that practitioners will buckle under political pressure, temporarily sacrificing their beliefs for the sake of professional harmony, and if this were to be shown as already happening, the wilderness years for progressivism might stretch far into the next millennium.

When we turn to research telling us how far teachers' beliefs have or have not resisted pressures to change during the closing years of the twentieth century, we find that although progressivism certainly survives as an English primary school movement, it does not survive unscathed. It is becoming, on some reports, a spent force, declining in numbers of teachers who profess it (Pollard et al., 1994), sidelined by the statutory demands of the National Curriculum (Francis and Grindle, 1998; Webb, 1993), growing defensive and covert in operation (Silcock and Wyness, 1997). Its slow decline was, earlier, dated as beginning at around the time of James Callaghan's 'Ruskin speech' (Batteson, 1997) when anxieties that the United Kingdom was starting to fall behind in industrial production and competitive international trade persuaded politicians to look to countries which appeared to be successfully building up their industrial base. Such worries have continued to interrupt our educational thinking to the present day (Alexander, 1998). They helped maintain, for example, John Major's 1994–7 'Back to Basics' campaign which floated the idea that the economic success of the so-called nations of the 'Pacific Rim' is owed in part to the whole-class, interactive teaching methods used by teachers to ensure their pupils learn formal skills (Reynolds and Farrell, 1996).

The matter of progressivism's survival in the hearts and minds of teachers, nationally and internationally, is a topic of importance in its own right. But it is also significant for what it tells us about the ideology's potential for resurgence. Both nations and continents become ever smaller places in which to live. Teachers cannot cut themselves off from other professionals, working in schools and in related occupations, with whom they will increasingly have to communicate and liaise. Assuming we can discern general educational trends at all — internationally and

New Progressivism

domestically — it is likely that these will impact on teachers' views and upon each other sooner or later. It is worth looking a little more closely at the fortunes of the broad progressivist movement in both international and local contexts.

International comparisons

Drawing unambiguous conclusions from cross-national comparisons about the effectiveness of one type of classroom methodology over another, or the general potentiality of a form of curriculum organization to achieve its ends, is beset with difficulties. Alexander's review of various studies (1995), and Galton's (1998a) verdict on what cross-contextual comparisons can ever tell us statistically, suggest that it may in the end prove quite impossible to detach a country's educational policies from the broader ambitions of governments and favoured values. Morris (1998) makes this point in the first of a series of articles in the journal *Education 3–13* outlining the educational lessons we can learn from countries on the 'Pacific Rim', asking whether it is possible to deduce from a nation's education service reasons for its industrial performance. The fact that the 'tiger economies' have quite recently experienced an economic collapse no more than highlights his case. As Morris says, 'in comparing features of schooling across societies, it is vital to understand them in terms of their social, economic and political contexts, and the associated value systems' (p. 5). We can only assess the success of the way teachers teach or pupils learn by linking that success to the actual aims being sought, which, themselves, must be understood in terms of the cultural 'codes' (Panel, 1997) these enshrine.

What is instructive is to notice the sorts of directions in which governments and educationists across the world seem to wish to travel, in value-terms, and recognize the types of educational process they are harnessing to their ends. A society's real ambitions for itself and its schools may not be as clear as we think. Morris (1998) addresses this clash between reality and aspiration in his review:

> ... while the orderly disciplined classrooms of Asia may be viewed as idyllic by someone from an urban school in say Chicago or London, they may be viewed as problematic in the host country. In Taiwan, Singapore, Hong Kong and Japan the orderly and disciplined classrooms are often viewed as manifestations of the school's failure to encourage creative, independent and critical thinking. (p. 5)

In Taiwan (a country illustrating Reynolds and Farrell's tie-in between classroom methodologies and industrial performance), reformers seek not to strengthen what its government believes is a proven educational approach in terms of its cultural output, but to 'raise the standards of the teaching profession' by allowing teachers more time to cater for individual students' needs, thereby focusing on the development of the 'whole person' (Murphy and Liu, 1998, p. 15).

Trying not to distort Reynolds and Farrell's case: they know that the effectiveness of any teaching is not determined by method alone, but is tempered by the cultural values which enhance or do not enhance the method's effectiveness. This is not too removed from Murphy's argument, and is given credence by Gipps and Tunstall's (1997) finding that even young children (around age 7) will respond differently to the feedback they receive from teachers about reasons for any failure. Whether they believe that failure is owed to lack of ability or lack of effort (a distinction which is, in Gipps and Tunstall's view, culturally grounded) will, evidently enough, affect their attempts to improve. In short, what all seem to agree on is that the association between teaching method and learning outcome isn't a straightforward 'process–product' one, but is facilitated by culturally influenced beliefs about the nature of the learning process itself. Yet we still have to decide what sort of classroom/cultural circumstance we would like or can even tolerate in the United Kingdom which will help us to fulfil our purposes. And even in those very countries Reynolds and Farrell put forward as models, strenuous efforts are being made to relax, not tighten, central controls.

If we try to glimpse the flow of reform within other countries, while remembering that generalizations about large territories such as continents are inevitably selective, we are as able to detect a gathering tide towards more liberal and democratic systems as anything else. And although the democratizing of schools may not always be progressivist in inspiration, it often is — as Harber admits (1997) in his extensive review of nations where the process is under way. In Holland (Sleegers and Wesselingh, 1995), parts of eastern Europe (Cerych, 1997), parts of the United States (Elliott et al., 1997), as well as in many countries across western Europe (MacLean, 1993; Ranaweera, 1989; Rohrs and Lenhart, 1995) and in some parts of South America, Africa and Asia (Harber, 1997), innovators are looking for ways to 'humanize' their educational systems as fast as their counterparts in England and Wales have been trying to tighten up what (presumably) they feel is too lax and diverse an education service. To take a single instance: in Finland, the retreat from a state-regulated National Curriculum and subject-based teaching towards more locally decided, child-oriented teaching is being managed with minimal stress (see Hakkinen, 1997; Webb et al., 1997). Teachers quickly become committed to the curricula they write for themselves (Hakkinen, 1997) — in salutary contrast to the problems of curricular management which have greeted reforms in Britain.

By nature, trends are never wholesale shifts of opinion. Webb et al. (1997) record that in Finland, where (as exemplified) reformers seem to be copying the English progressivist model, there are simultaneous moves towards educational marketing and managerialism which would, in this country, please supporters of the 'New Right' more than progressivists. Probably, the safest generalization to make about international trends is MacLean's (1993) observation on the state of education across Europe: he points out that there are both 'centrifugal' (diversifying) and 'centripetal' (centralizing) forces, reflecting the political struggle between these two factions within Europe as a whole. As he observes, what typifies British educational politics is an attempt to hive the UK off from the rest of Europe through dictatorial (practically wholly centripetal) policies.

Few believe that we can detach school practices from their cultural context and think that they will work in the same way outside as within it. But what we can

New Progressivism

learn from international comparisons is something about what motivates reformers at the most general level (that is, apart from the actual effects of policies). All national systems of education have challenges in common, owed to the fact that we are all human beings with common capacities and limitations which schools (as one type of institution) exist to cater for or improve. Where other governments adopt measures similar to our own, it is always worth looking at outcomes. For instance, in America earlier this century, a conflict judged by Stevens and Wood (1995) to have undermined progressivist education is one that successive governments there and in the UK are still struggling with. This conflict partly explains the to and fro of policy movements between ideological positions within these two countries. Nations, Stevens and Woods say, are 'torn . . . between the ideal of meeting the legitimate needs of every individual and the goal of securing the national welfare' (p. 303). Wesler (1990) counts this conflict among the most important challenges of the modern state — simply because every government has sooner or later to resolve it.

Progressivism in English primary schools

When we look back to the UK scene, the situation is on the face of it more clear-cut than that we find internationally. A protracted onslaught on progressivist ideals from politicians and academics during the 1980s and early 1990s cleared the field for radical reforms. It used in its cause almost any means to hand, from wilful misrepresentation to ridicule (see Ball, 1993; Sugrue, 1997). As Ball reminds us, it was not only progressivist teachers who were the butts of political rancour, it was the so-called 'trendy' academics who had supported them, producing a general distrust of theoretical discussion and a devaluing of educational research (1993, p. 206). Evidence reveals that during the early 1990s the educational establishment as a whole experienced a sort of sea-change in what it regarded as its 'received' wisdom. Whereas, earlier this century, progressivist influence was spread within schools by school inspectors sympathetic to it (such as Tanner, Blackie and Schiller: see Alexander, 1994; Lee and Fitz, 1997), present-day child-centred teachers know that the new OFSTED inspectorate is generally unsupportive of their beliefs (Lee and Fitz, 1997; Silcock and Wyness, 1998). When OFSTED inspectors are in school, teachers are likely to teach more formally than they otherwise would (Brimblecome et al., 1996; Webb et al., 1997).

What we cannot judge from national fluctuations is how far reforms of classroom practice and policy married to apparent reversals of attitude indicate deeper rifts in teachers' values, and therefore in ideology. Teachers have to comply with what are, after all, legally enforced rulings and, being professionals, they will seek to make the reforms work for sake of their pupils. But when we look beneath their surface compliance, we find the seeping down of the more 'traditionalist' beliefs justifying reforms slow to penetrate, despite their marked side-effects. For example, some teachers seem to have suffered a sort of collective schizophrenia, whereby they will readily admit the gains from being able to plan, together, for a National Curriculum, while, at the same time, protesting that its hard-line prescriptiveness contradicts their more basic conceptions of 'good practice'. Tendencies to 'teach to test' and to cover complex ideas superficially ('skating over the surface') conflict with what they believe *should* be happening (Campbell and Neil, 1992; Silcock, 1995; Silcock and Wyness, 1997; Webb, 1993; Woods, 1995).

On such grounds, it is perfectly possible to claim that primary school teachers' values are not changing fundamentally and that a 'manufactured consent' (Menter et al., 1997), while coercing teacher behaviour in fairly obvious directions, is leaving deeper beliefs virtually untouched. The PACE research (Primary Assessment, Curriculum and Experience Project: Pollard et al., 1994), carried out at Bristol, which is a main source of evidence for the way the National Curriculum's implementation is accelerating a general progressivist decline, takes interview data from teachers who, year by year, teach older and older groups of children (the same cohort of 54 children studied longitudinally), and we would expect a fading away of support for child-centredness as we move from the early Key Stage 1 to the late Key Stage 2 levels. This artifact of their research design would — in itself — account for the declining trend Pollard et al. detect. In a later survey of teacher views (Francis and Grindle, 1998), where responses to identical questionnaires sent out to teachers in equivalent areas in 1982 and 1996 were analysed, a strong shift of attitude towards traditional teaching styles was observed (e.g. a belief in firm discipline, regular testing, following a strict timetable, teaching through rote learning, correcting spelling and grammatical errors: p. 275). Yet when the two researchers looked for a parallel loss of confidence in progressive styles, they found 'five of the seven items selected to characterise progressive teaching styles were rated by similar proportions of teachers in 1982 and 1996 . . . In 1996 less importance was given than in 1982 to adopting an integrated day, and to integrating religious and secular studies' (p. 274).

What Francis and Grindle's findings demonstrate is the 'hybridization' of methodology which has happened as a result of the implementation of the National Curriculum (Silcock, 1992, 1995). Formal methods are being 'grafted on' to the informal, rather than replacing them as, in some sense or other, better or more appropriate ways of teaching. Recognizing that a National Curriculum requires a degree of formality for its implementation, we are hardly amazed by an increasing use of formal techniques or some, consequent, erosion of integrated work. Nor are we shocked that today's teachers 'follow a regular timetable, correcting spelling and grammatical errors' and so forth. What we cannot deduce from such research is that, if curricular demands were different, teachers' beliefs wouldn't be different. In short, what primary school teachers would or would not consider 'best practice', outside of any given curricular situation, is still very much an alive question.

Where teachers at both Key Stages have been interviewed regularly through the period of reform, the child-centred language they use to uncover their professional beliefs bubbles up through their discussions from whatever is at the heart of their professional philosophy (Silcock, 1990, 1992, 1995; Silcock and Wyness, 1997), just as it did in earlier times (Alexander, 1992; Biber, 1972). References to the needs of individuals, the 'whole child', the 'seamless' web of knowledge, beliefs in teaching for independence and autonomy and encouraging pupil involvement in curricular decision making, the value of following children's interests, the preference for informal over formal modes of instruction and so on still articulate at the level of curricular management and organization what progressivism means for teachers. It is useful to remind ourselves of their utility as elements of discourse. Teachers do need to talk about practices in ways which link their commonsensical pragmatism to secure principle. And, although links between beliefs and actions are seldom overt, it is unthinkable to suppose that statements of intent, born out of child-centred beliefs, play no active part in a teacher's professional life.

A selection of quotations from interviews with teachers, taken from a recent case study (Silcock and Wyness, 1997), will unearth the belief systems informing the answers teachers give to questions about their changing practices. These have proven remarkably stable over the period, and, it will be concluded, what has insulated them against wholesale revision is a trust in their reliability. The teachers interviewed actually see them as a knowledge-resource taking precedence over imposed policies as banks of professional wisdom. What we cannot know from interview data is the extent to which any responses quoted are typical (statistically speaking) of primary school staffroom exchanges: samples of views picked for research purposes are not randomly acquired. Chances are that the undoubted rise in formal teaching methods in primary schools is accompanied by a loss of informality within the profession as a whole. But the responses given by these few teachers are indicative of the the views they represent, and they are responses to questions meant to discover how far changes of practice are superimposed on more fundamental changes of belief and value. Of 20 teachers interviewed in depth, 11 leaned towards 'child-centredness' to some degree or other, though the content of their stated beliefs varied widely. Views reported are taken wholly from this group.

An illustrative case study (data gathered by Silcock and Wyness, 1997)

Alexander's (1992) judgment that the 'whole-child' concept is central to primary school progressivism is quickly confirmed in discussions with 'child-centred' practitioners. When a Key Stage 1 teacher (female) overviews her own philosophy, by harking back over decades in terms of its progressivist ancestry, her defensive posture hints not at any uncertainty about her beliefs, only that she knows it is not fashionable to hold them.

> I firmly believe that you need to start from the individual child... I'm concerned... with getting at the individual... [Teaching] them a skill, teaching them to read, to write, as a teacher that is my job. I know that it sounds woolly and very 60s-ish, but I would hate to think that was all I was there for. I didn't come into teaching just to do that. I'm not going to change the world but I feel it is more important to try and get a rounded whole person...

It would be rash to suppose that we can identify exactly what a teacher such as the one quoted means when she uses concepts such as 'the individual child' or 'a rounded, whole person', but it would be equally rash to assume that these are either superficial expressions of poorly grasped ideas or examples of empty dogma. They certainly have a pivotal place in any child-centred lexicon, as others say (Alexander, 1992; Biber, 1972). In anticipation of a closer study of these ideas, we can agree with Biber (1972) that the notion of a 'whole child' is meant, on the face of it, to resist a reduction of individuals to constituent abilities and skills. Teachers of young children treasure the relationships they form with their pupils as whole persons — not only because it is an enjoyable relationship for both partners, but because it helps teachers to get to the source of many learning difficulties. For instance, as children move between environments, their social and school experiences act in a unified manner to influence their classroom behaviour. A lower school head-teacher (female) stresses this when searching her mind for the mainspring of her own professional life:

> I *care* very much about the individual child. You know, if the child has got problems at home, they do show in school. So you have *got* to know the child.

Such statements illustrate the very broad, child-centred stance many primary school teachers take towards their pupils, which at some level or other dignify their professional beliefs in comparison with others. It is not that the National Curriculum doesn't channel their work significantly, it is that we cannot suppose from its effects a corresponding shift in values. Given the amount of time primary school teachers have to spend with their classes, their 'person-centred' attitude is, as Silcock and Wyness say (1997): 'not only unremarkable, it is probably ineradicable from the lives of those whose expertise is bound up with a strongly caring ethic' (p. 135). Many teacher beliefs and practices are transient. But we can judge from what these practitioners say that changes of belief are occurring against a backdrop of value stability, not as symptomatic of wholesale ideological shifts. The following quotation, again taken from an interview with a Key Stage One teacher (female), is not at all an admission that her basic attitude to curricula has changed, as an evocation of past times used to mourn the loss of interest-based learning.

> I remember donkeys years ago . . . I didn't have to worry about where the hell did it fit with the National Curriculum . . . You [organized] your teaching to get the inspirational bits . . . that you used to enjoy. Like it's a nice summer's day, let's just go out. You don't get that flare of teaching now . . . that buzz of excitement (p. 136)

A long-term government drive towards standardizing classrooms has affected these teachers' motivations and of necessity altered practices, but without completely transforming the values of those teachers who admit to being child-centred. Such modifications of attitude and belief in order to protect values rather than remould them as discovered from the analysis of interview data speaks of the resilience of child-centred ideology in its capacity for transmutation in the face of attack. To assess the evidence for this resilience, we can look briefly at the two

New Progressivism

slightly different ways (identified by Silcock and Wyness, 1997), that teachers' lived ideologies have responded to pressures for change. It is then possible to hazard some prognosis about the ideology's options for further adaptations — assuming (as seems virtually certain) that politicians press ahead with their standardizing policies.

Type 1 (pessimistic, defensive): a subversive 'child-centredness'

Some teachers have responded to attacks upon their belief systems by hiding their misgivings behind a defiantly subversive position. Because their very professionalism is bound up with what they believe childhood education demands, they adopt the mantle of expediency (e.g. teach the National Curriculum) as far as they have to, while continuing to invest their energies into achieving other educational ends. They will not always admit what they really think (note the cautious note in the quotation below), but there is little doubt that what is stated as a matter of principle is not lightly or frivolously held, indicating what this first school headteacher believes fundamental to the aims she sets for her school.

> The National Curriculum has meant that they [i.e. her staff] are not spontaneously reactive to ideas from the children. [One] of my hardest jobs is to talk them out of that and say (is this going to be public?) . . . to hell with the National Curriculum because the work that comes from the children . . . it will fit the National Curriculum and its requirements . . . You can push the work the way you want it to go [and] maintain the child-centred approach. (p. 136)

A rearguard attempt at maintaining quality provision in the face of reactionary policies is not wholly confined to Key Stage 1 teachers. A Key Stage 2 teacher discussing the effect of standardized testing (SATs) on her work recognizes that she has a battle to fight.

> . . . Will the tests — particularly at Key Stage 2 — influence our teaching style and jeopardize our philosophy? I think . . . that in the back of our minds we know that we are going to have to modify our approach sometimes, but by golly we are very mindful that we need to fight it! (p. 137)

This siege mentality is exacerbated by attacks from politicians who seem to have a poor grasp of the realities of classrooms. A male junior school headteacher tells us, bluntly, why — in his view — teachers have little choice but to teach as they do.

> [The] proper way to teach these children is child-centred. This class-teaching is absolute nonsense. I feel like wringing the necks of these people, because we have double age groups in classes . . . an ability range which is enormous. We could have a non-reader and a reader with a reading age of thirteen in the same class. Well you can't class teach to that! Well you could do: most would be bored to tears and the others wouldn't bloody understand you.

It isn't that this head is mounting a last-ditch, pig-headed defence against the inexorable advance of whole-class teaching, he is simply saying, as strongly as he is able, that in the circumstances of his school such teaching does not represent a real option. One is struck when studying interview transcripts of discussions with teachers by the knowledge that the accusations against them occasionally made that they have been indoctrinated by 'trendy left-wing' rhetoric or have a poor hold on classroom realities cannot be substantiated in the 1990s. Teachers are palpably aware of the way public opinion has been shaping up over recent years and of the enormous weight of adverse judgments arraigned against their beliefs by academics as well as by politicians. It is no longer remotely fashionable to claim to be 'progressive' or child-centred.

Listening to what teachers say about their beliefs impresses an interviewer not with its dogged addiction to practicalities, but its deep-seated reliance on experiences which have taught teachers what does and does not work in their relationships with children. For example, one of the fundamentals of child-centred work has been the enjoyment of learning shared by teachers and pupils: this enjoyment has always been a major feature of child-centredness — connected with beliefs in the intrinsic motivation of child-initiated activities and the value of the 'whole child' concept. One of the most depressing findings from interview research over recent years has been that teachers do not enjoy the job as they once did (Campbell and Neil, 1992; Silcock, 1992, 1995). In the following quotation, taken from an interview with a lower school headteacher, it is not simply the sincerity of the emotion which is striking, as its evident truth. If enjoyment is disappearing from primary school work, something of immense importance is disappearing with it.

> [We] have got youngsters coming out of college who will never know what I know of the joys of teaching very young children and ... oh dear, how the nation will be that much worse off for lack of flare and creativity ... I remember with joy teaching ... when you used to love it and look forward to it and it would be wonderful (with) the children waiting for you to be doing ... whatever it was ... And we have lost that, and I think we have lost it forever. (p. 135)

What is revealing about these child-centred practitioners is their firmness in their philosophy in the face of pressures to change. They tolerate the reforms with which they have to live, but do not particularly relish many of them. They know that a prescribed curriculum does not lend itself well to a child-centred philosophy — so much the worse for a prescribed curriculum.

Type 2 (offensive, optimistic): a 'new' child-centredness

By contrast to members of the first group, other teachers are anxious to distance themselves from the idea that their philosophies conflict at all with any legislation meant to give their curriculum more regularity and coherence. Child-centredness is not seen as bound up with an exclusive 'interest-based' methodology or as antipathetic to whole-class teaching. It is a general guide to help teachers choose their primary-oriented way of meeting demands over and above others. A JMI headteacher tries to be unequivocal:

> Our philosophy is to maximise the potential of every child. [And] by child-centred, you mean the child is in the middle of the process . . . at the centre of everything that I do. (p. 137)

This global judgment is so generalized it seems almost banal. One would be hard put to imagine any teacher disagreeing with it. But the head is keen to retain her 'child-centred' label, despite her staying with the relative safety of generalizations about 'maximizing children's potential'. Some teachers are not so much retreating from formerly entrenched positions as strategically reinterpreting them. A Key Stage 2 teacher separates her 'child-centred' philosophy from 'child-directed' learning, which, she knows, would be incompatible with modern educational trends.

> We define [child-centredness] as what we feel is in the best interests of the child . . . I don't see it as totally child-directed. I would hope that we have a happy medium, the teacher and the child learning together. (p. 137)

Again, what is noteworthy is the teacher's guarded revelation that her practices aren't 'totally' child-directed. She knows that they could not be in a present-day classroom. But nor has she given up on child-directed teaching, she is simply trying to be clear about its role in her curriculum. For this second group, the political scene is regarded as by nature fluid. The direction of reform has always been towards a gradual relaxing of restriction, and there seems nothing to prevent teachers continuing to teach informally, using integrated topics if these are desired. The National Curriculum prescribes content not method. Subject orders characteristically identify 'process' as well as content aims (e.g. those for History and Science).

Some teachers are quick to point out that the requirement that they 'differentiate' tasks — that is, they match their demands of pupils to individual levels of ability and maintain individual progress records — justifies their individualistic approach to teaching. There would seem little point in — for example — keeping individual diagnostic records if these were not going to reflect back upon the way pupils are actually taught. In response to a question as to whether his philosophy will have to yield ultimately to the demands of the National Curriculum, a deputy head of a lower school answers:

> No, I don't think the National Curriculum has made me feel that child-centredness is out because . . . it gives the teachers some sort of yardstick on where they're going, and what children can do, and where they are now.

When pushed, these teachers are apt to react angrily to suggestions that they ever believed children should take full charge of their learning. A male Key Stage 2 teacher confesses to the resentment he feels about the sorts of misconceptions that abound about his way of thinking.

I'm a teacher of the much maligned sixties, and Plowden, and I have to say that I don't know where these sixties folk are who let their children do what they want, because I've never come across them!

In many ways, members of these two groups (as discussed by Silcock and Wyness) have more in common than there are differences between them. The reason for separating them at all is to reinforce what is believed to be decisive in guiding educationists towards ideological revision — that some practitioners are themselves looking for such a clarification. They want to bring their beliefs into line with the centrally inspired practices which they all know are part and parcel of belonging to a modern teaching profession. They want to do so because their professional *raison d'être* hasn't altered, even though the curriculum has: that is, there is still believed to be real value to working in a child-centred manner, whatever the written curriculum asks of them. What unsettles progressive practitioners, as discovered in interview, is not that confidence in their own beliefs is shaken but they are uncertain about how far the reforms (and especially the English/Welsh National Curriculum) compromise their stance. Members of one category, as defined above, are very pessimistic about recovering their preferred approach within rigidly standardized frameworks; members of another think the terms set by ideology and standardized curricula are not necessarily incompatible. As discussed, these latter teachers appear to be adapting their ideologies to changing times, thereby encouraging academics to work towards equivalent ends.

Alternative classroom ideologies

It would be misleading to suggest that child-centredness, although the easiest ideology to uncover in discussion with primary school teachers, is the only one to be found there. Primary school progressivism survives in a broader ideological context with some stable and some relatively unstable elements. What seems stable is a general lacklustre enthusiasm for the standardized curriculum — i.e. for the traditionalist position. This is a point worth making, for one might otherwise believe that the imposing of a National Curriculum in 1989, being an obvious instance of political policies relying on traditionalist beliefs, symbolizes the ideology's triumph. It doesn't. It is true that teachers realize the importance of what are sometimes called 'traditional methods' or styles (see Francis and Grindle, 1998). What is queried is whether such features of methodology (e.g. of believing in the importance of firm discipline, marking spellings and grammar) are — in isolation — reliable indicators of a deeper value system.

In fact, the most stable element of a value-system tapped into during interviewing is that which is sometimes called neo-elementary (Richards, 1998) — the sanctifying of basic skills, especially reading. In the 1997 research (Silcock and Wyness), practitioners were asked to prioritize their aims: they were asked whether they believed their main task was to teach basic skills, teach the National Curriculum subjects, attend to the personal and social development of their pupils, or something else. Of those who agreed to differentiate between these (and most didn't), few placed the teaching of the National Curriculum subjects as central. Some thought that more 'process'-oriented developmental issues take priority:

> Until the social aspect is sorted then the curriculum is not going to work with that particular individual. Order and discipline is vital in a school like this, to function. Then comes the curriculum. (p. 139)

Most believed: '[if] you can't read you're lost . . . I'd choose basic skills' (p. 139).

The overwhelming conviction of primary school teachers that to teach basic skills 'is what our job is' (p. 139; see also Campbell, 1993b) might hint at a closely prescribed — i.e. traditionalist — model of what it means in our society to be educated. It probably doesn't mean that — though for some teachers the belief can have such a connection. What is more obviously construed from responses is that the reason why basic skills are thought vital is that they are the means to other ends: 'if you can't read you're lost' implies that many important future doors are closed, not that being able to read is in itself what makes for an educated person. Being literate and numerate and able to converse with others are foundations for any ideal — i.e. they are ideologically neutral. It would be a very strange ideology which doubted the importance of our main means of entrance into worlds of knowledge and skill.

Ideological questions which do hinge upon a preoccupation with basic skills are questions about methodologies to be employed teaching them, for they reveal the further aims associated with such a preoccupation. Teachers who question the imposing of a 'literacy hour' or 'numeracy hour' upon schools might do so because of their wish that pupils see their own skills in a positive light. In short, squeezing basic skills teaching into set frameworks makes difficult further timetabling to take account of smaller group or individual needs. Since initiatives about teaching basic skills in scheduled periods are only just being introduced in schools, we have no hard evidence yet as to what their drawbacks might be for those with 'child-centred' aims. Only, in principle, prescriptions of the sort discussed always carry with them the dangers of inflexibility, the fact that by nature they are very difficult to accommodate to the circumstances of a school or the preferred forms of curricular organization that a staff dedicated to child-centred ideology might have worked out in some quite imaginative ways.

Some primary school teachers are pragmatists. How tenuously or firmly pragmatic beliefs are taking hold in teachers' minds is impossible to know (as said: we don't, yet, have reliable statistical evidence), but qualitative data establishes at least their existence.

> It's horses for courses . . . pattern, fashion, idealism doesn't come into it . . . styles will suit the conditions of the room, numbers of pupils, how you are feeling, the work you've got to cover. (p. 138)

As a 'statement of intent' the above by a Key Stage 2 teacher (male) has a slightly cynical feel about it since it doesn't instantiate pragmatism as an ideal, but as an alternative to ideals. And this is its difficulty. For teachers to believe that they are nothing else but pragmatists is to become enmeshed in the 'horses for courses'/ 'goodness of fit' contextualizing of their jobs which, as already pointed out, doesn't give them new values to work for but diverts them from the value-decisions they still, actually, have to make.

Summary

Progressivism does continue to exert a powerful grip on practitioners' imaginations. Qualitative research shows how some English teachers hold subversively to their beliefs, being either unwilling or unable to abandon them, while others struggle towards a 'new' ideology fitted for the times. One might argue that both groups should be encouraged by trends in other countries where reformers appear to have very different aims from those followed by this country's reformers over past decades. A general, worldwide march towards the democratizing and humanizing of educational systems is not always 'progressivist' in inspiration, but 'person-centred' values of some sort are usually behind it (Harber, 1997).

In England, it is difficult to find anywhere in the educational literature a major ideal which has, yet, superseded child-centredness as a lived ideology. Attempts by UK government agencies to win English teachers' hearts as well as minds has notably failed: teachers are more likely to say they feel demoralized by reforms than inspired by them (Harber, 1997; Campbell and Neill, 1992; Pollard et al., 1994; Pollard and Broadfoot, 1997; Woods, 1995). This does not mean that teacher values are unchanging, but it does make hazardous any attempt to plot long-term ideological trends.

During periods of transition, we have to take seriously what the teachers themselves say about their own notions of good practice. For some time, child-centred values have provided a form of protection against ideas which may be seen as reactionary and regressive. These values provide a shared conceptual defence against the market doctrines primary school teachers commonly regard as alien to their work, hinting at reasons why many (possibly a majority) do, still, cling to their older philosophies, if only in part (Francis and Grindle, 1998; Holmes, 1995; Pollard et al., 1994; Silcock, 1997; Silcock and Wyness, 1997). This persistence of child-centred values in the minds of substantial numbers of teachers gives some impetus to the closer scrutiny of the social and educational benefits potentially earned by their continuing to hold fast to their belief systems. Following chapters are dedicated to such a scrutiny, which begins with a review of the central principles with which any study of the ideology must come to grips.

Chapter 5

New Progressivism: Principles to Be Reviewed

In re-examining principles of progressivist ideology, there is no expectation that these will, somehow, be judged outdated. It is the abiding power of these principles which makes a review worthwhile, since we intuitively recognize their potential. They are the cornerstones on which educationists can erect structures of beliefs, which members of a modern teaching profession can unashamedly profess, without their feeling that the rest of the educational world has absconded long ago to firmer ground. It is the way principles are translated into practice which are expected to need rethinking, alongside — often enough — a clarification of what a progressivist principle might actually mean. It is not difficult to superimpose onto a sophisticated concept its caricature or an over-simple outline based on surface features. Where this happens, it is essential to retrieve the principle itself, and remind ourselves of the issues which are at stake.

A review of principles will establish the ideology's academic, political and practical viability as both interrelated and independent areas of study. It would never have been enough to concentrate on a theoretical rationale at the expense of the practical or vice versa. The educational literature is full of meticulously devised curricular models which lack political and economic realism, while accounts of educational policies satisfying all main contenders on the scene, but without theoretical verisimilitude or practical credibility, are not hard to write. By keeping in touch with progressivism's core rationale, the review will admit the ideology's shortcomings in its dealings with — for example — standardized curricula and imposed accountability systems. But it will also keep faith with its own deepest values, in order to be clear about the contribution progressivist thinking might, again, make to fulfilling contemporary expectations. In a very real sense, innovations in primary school provision shaping our present-day educational system have been bought at the expense of progressivism's decline, hastened on by a series of ongoing critiques. These critiques have tended to feed off each other's misconceptions as well as raising questions inviting detailed answers, so some of them betray not only errors of perception regarding progressivism but weaknesses at the very foundations of the newer policies. It is justifiable not only to mount a defence of ideological precept but to show as part of that defence what could have been (or could still be) more workable policy innovations if the relevance of a progressivist rationale to the contemporary scene were admitted.

New Progressivism

A first shot at putting together the rationale (Chapter 3) claimed that it has an internal validity (it hangs together as an argument), external validity (it can be applied to contemporary classrooms) and historic credibility, in that its starting point is the 'Plowden' progressivism to which commentators interested in modern child-centred beliefs usually turn for guidance. Its values have been recognized as humanistic, linked to conceptions of learners whose status is underpinned by a 'new' developmentalism and whose rights and responsibilities are identified as democratic. A new progressivism takes from each of these areas those perspectives (unique to the areas themselves) which give us a full definition of the role in schools, *vis-à-vis* culture context, of individual learners. New progressivism (like the older varieties) is person-centred. It is individualistic at its core. But this individualism has many facets — it is not a naive individualism (i.e. one ignoring social responsibilities). Conceiving school pupils as individual learners is to imply a developmental, ethical and democratic integration of accounts, which — while sporting their independently won validity — become 'progressivist' in combination. Child-centred teaching should not be confined to methodological techniques (e.g. one-to-one teaching) or single aims (such as reaching for individual autonomy), a particular form of learning (e.g. learning through play or through activity methods), or a democratic school or classroom ethos (based perhaps on whole-school interactions and relationships). Its multi-perspective skeleton is important. Progressivism has suffered much through criticism from those who have singled out one perspective as central and proceeded to probe related weaknesses.

Four themes present embryonic issues for review, arising from the rationale mentioned, in the light of public critiques. These themes take as their starting points curricular questions which give them their educational bite. This curricular orientation accepts that an educational text must not become so side-tracked by theorizing as to forget its main purpose. To fix this orientation, we can simplify the themes in terms of those questions of school curricular design listed earlier as always addressed by educational ideologies (this is why the ideologies were thought, themselves, to exist). The questions are recapitulated as: what is education for? how do pupils learn and develop/and how should they be taught? and what kind of accountability system do we need with which to track outcomes? Anyone revising ideological beliefs will find, as unavoidable, questions about educational aims, about the nature of learning and cognitive development, about teaching methodologies and about the forms of democratic process by which teachers, themselves, will expect to be brought to account. Each of these questions, taken as a theme, is examined separately.

The first theme to be visited is not — as logically one would expect — that of aims and values. It concerns developmentalism. And there is a reason why this theme is seen as a broker for the rest. One of the facts we can be sure of regarding professional teaching is that its relationship with children's development is direct. One educational purpose is indisputably to bring about learning and to foster children's intellectual growth. No study of teaching or classroom organization can be taken seriously which is not sensitive to whatever we do know, factually, about learning and intellectual change. It is true that empirical soundings are never enough to generate school curricula, and value-statements take precedence over them. But it will prove, in the event, more straightforward to demonstrate progressivist values on the heels of establishing our factual knowledge than it would if we delayed dealing with such matters. It is not accidental that many educational beliefs have altered following empirical discoveries. Rousseau's eighteenth-century notions of how children might develop outside of corrupting social influence have been superseded by more psychologically reliable theories.

There is a sort of rule here. The cognitive progress which progressivism acknowledges will be shown as crucial not only because of the significance of developmental theories but because of their social/cultural links. Developmental theories are, now, known not to be value-free. The educational recommendations which will follow from both sorts of discussion will be seen as born from the same joint decisions about values. But we only become convinced of this by following through the developmental arguments first — for it is these which, in this case (i.e. concerning the value-basis of developmentalism), are most contentious. Another very tangible reason for beginning with empirical study is that this is likely to begin to raise practical matters from the outset. What we think may or may not be practicable is always a major player on any education stage, where practicalities so often dominate. There would be no benefits to be gained from deciding on lofty ideals for primary schools which were too problematic for teachers or politicians to countenance.

The rule broached asserts the primacy of developmental studies in educational theory, not because the empirical does have primacy over the philosophical, but because it is easier to approach the latter from a position where factual matters are already clear. It is worth remembering that it is because of the privileged position held by theories of learning and development in educational study that some modern writers have looked disapprovingly at child-centred rhetoric. By contrast, influential writers in primary school curricular studies, such as Blyth (1984) and Blenkin and Kelly (1981, 1996), have situated their child-centred stance within developmental accounts for good reason. We cannot alter the innately given cognitive processes by which children's minds function, and in so far as we know, factually, what promotes human improvement we have to take due account of such influence in our classroom planning and policies.

However, we should not forget that the logic of school curricula gives value-statements precedence over the empirical: teachers have to know their aims before they can properly decide anything else. An eminently practical form of teaching may, still, be undesirable. It would be a rational conclusion to reach that child-centred teaching is an enjoyable business for teachers and pupils alike but is not one an educationist should go to the wall for. Insofar as progressivist values need rethinking, these will either be seen as relevant to a modern, pluralist, technologically-driven state or they will not. And, because our society has evolved in special sorts of ways, there is always the chance that our usual ways of preparing children for it need recasting in different moulds. If, for example, it turned out that child-centred beliefs underwrite the development of aesthetic sensibilities but do not provide the best framework for teaching technological skill or managerial expertise, we might conclude that these beliefs helped us understand an earlier phase of social history, but should be adopted in today's classrooms only by educators specializing in the teaching of the creative arts. So, the second theme to be worked through concerning personal and public values is at the heart of progressivist ideology. If argument doesn't convince us about it, the rest is lost.

The third theme discussed is that of informality of teaching method. Perhaps more than any other topic, it is the likelihood of progressivist teaching methods achieving curricular aims which has worried academics and policy makers, with doubts about their effectiveness regularly surfacing in research reports. Teaching is a pragmatic business, involving the routine resolving of dilemmas rather than the strict application of ideologically driven ideas. It would seem a matter of common sense that teachers, as professional people, should avoid making commitments which will, as a consequence of their being made, automatically prevent certain options appearing within their skill repertoires. In other words, if an ideological stance restricts a professional's behaviour in any way at all we have to question it: an imaginative teaching style is one where, presumably, 'inclusivity' is as elastic as it is feasible. To assume 'exclusivity' at the level of classroom action is to predetermine the outcomes of almost any empirical comparison between an ideologically limited teaching process and one which is freed from constraints.

Lastly, the involvement of learners in their own learning — regarding them as autonomous agents — is studied against the backdrop of a totality of reforms assuming that teachers, not pupils, are responsible for pupils' achievements. Beliefs defending pupils' rights as individuals might be seen as weakly acquiescing to the will of those who, by definition, are too immature to wield democratically given powers. A modern, 'humanistic' progressivism, like prior versions, mandates teachers to respect the rights of pupils in those matters which most concern them, but it will not ignore the complementary roles of teachers. Nor can teachers, in turn, ignore the views of parents and politicians on how far learners should be free to decide their own futures, just as they can't overlook the practical difficulties 'liberationist' policies might raise for curricular planning and public agendas. School inspectors will look askance on any school which liberates pupils' powers of judgment without building in safeguards against the same pupils' possible abuse of such powers. Anticipating the details of the review, it is to be accepted that improving children's minds can never rely wholly on judgments about the abilities and preferences of the pupils themselves.

If answering three central educational questions (couched within four themes) provides the content of the review, the review process is also tripartite in form, involving three distinct kinds of exercise. There will be points of clarification, points where principles are defended against attacks, and points where change is — as a result — accepted, involving a reworking of ideas. The art of revisionism is to know when to bow to just criticism, when to retrench and when to innovate! These three exercises are supplemented by a regular summarizing of points and a final stocktaking. Because the themes which are tackled represent studies founded in quite substantial bodies of literature, usually of a multidisciplinary sort, issues will sometimes be raised which cannot be taken to a conclusion since to go too far into an argument deviates from the main debate and reduces its effect. Those who would wish to pursue these issues further are helped in a final chapter, which isolates main points by reference to key texts and writers. This chapter is also meant to bring together ideas which people of a contrary frame of mind might wish to take cognizance of when preparing their own critiques. Stripping the flesh from the bones of what is a fairly complex case should show either its naked strength or its plain vulnerability.

Chapter 6

Developmentalism

Because ideologies are belief systems, they rely on research for supportive evidence. Our beliefs may or may not be true, and it is obvious enough that any beliefs reckoned to be false on empirical grounds should be abandoned. Piaget's association with the progressivist movement began when his ideas about children's thinking appeared to coincide with those of child-centred teachers. In recent years, his influence has waned and critics (Alexander, 1994; Bennett, 1987, 1992; Mackenzie, 1997; Richards and Light, 1986; Wells, 1986) find Vygotsky's (1962, 1978) proposals more in keeping with the routines of modern classrooms. 'Social constructivism' (where pupils need a structured support for their learning to guide its progress) is orthodox doctrine now on teacher education courses, replacing the older, Piagetian 'constructivism' (where pupils progress intellectually through following their own, self-monitored activity: see Pollard, 1990, for a comparison of constructivist and social-constructivist approaches to school learning). It gives some theoretical sustenance to those who believe that teachers need to structure pupil learning in a strongly directive manner.

However, it is still worth asking how far Vygotskian notions *are* superior to the Piagetian in explaining school success? And, in so far as Vygotsky's ideas do take us further than Piaget's, what kind of classroom practices do they actually support?

Piaget and Vygotsky

In their twentieth anniversary appraisal of the Plowden Report, Halsey and Sylva (1987) accuse Piagetian psychology of a 'myopic focus on the physical environment whilst ignoring the social context in which the children grow' (p. 9). Having exposed Piaget's Achilles' heel, they are able to pronounce how 'the gradual demise of Piagetian theory leaves Plowden without a theoretical base' (p. 10). As part of the same review, Neville Bennett condemns the 'constructivist' position which Piaget pioneered because, he says, it does not treat social context seriously. Bennett goes on to deride progressivists for their 'flabby and erroneous conceptions' linked to 'ill-digested Piaget' (p. 75).

The judgment that Piaget miscalculated the role of social influence remains widespread and is pervasive. Actually, he had a detailed theory of how children access the views of others for the sake of their mental improvement, as commentaries lately acknowledge (Cole and Wertsch, 1996; Kitchener, 1996; Smith, 1996;

Valsiner, 1996). It is no longer a question of deciding whether Piaget or Vygotsky is correct about the role of adult intervention in children's development (black and white verdicts of this sort are nowhere justified by the evidence to hand) but of realizing how two major developmental traditions, together, explain some key features of teaching and learning. These traditions have been compared repeatedly in the literature (see Cole and Wertsch, 1996; Kitchener, 1996; Tudge and Winterhoff, 1993; Bruner's 1997 appraisal of the two writers is especially revealing). They can be summarized briefly.

In Piagetian psychology (Piaget and Inhelder, 1969), infants do not see themselves from other people's viewpoints without their first having explored the natural environment, coming to recognize their worlds as stable and interesting places as well as acquiring sense–motor and coordination skills. Challenged by those around them, children become more and more aware of flaws in their own thinking and eventually modify their 'egocentric' beliefs (i.e. derived from unique perspectives) to discern wider and more flexible views of situations important to them. It is this social phase in the growth of mind which brings with it the greatest conceptual changes, and Piaget dignifies it as such in his general theory. What Vygotsky makes us question is Piaget's belief that it is the early (sensory-based) achievements which explain the later, social expansion of intelligence — not the intrinsic importance of the latter. The message of Piaget's work is that young learners are from the outset 'competent' agents for their own progress, whether within or outside social environments. It is their self-generated activities and interests which press them forward. He opposed his views not to those of Vygotsky (whose work he admired: see Van der Veer, 1996) but to the relatively passive conceptions of learning favoured by 'Behaviourists' who were popular when developmental psychology was in its infancy (Piaget, 1970).

By contrast, Vygotsky saw that we do not really improve mentally until we have learned important lessons from others. He used the term 'internalization' (1962) to fix the way patterns of social relationship are, somehow, 'swallowed' into our minds where they pattern our thinking also. Bruner (with Haste, 1987) echoes Vygotsky's ideas in his accounts of how toddlers learn social-interactional skills through the games parents play with them, and then simulate the to-and-fro of these skills internally, to aid their reasoning and problem-solving. Vygotsky's claim that social context always contributes to intellectual progress has become accepted wisdom, as has his recognition that social intervention (e.g. good teaching) can take children further than they might otherwise go (within the so-called 'zone of proximal development': Tudge and Winterhoff, 1993). These ideas make sense. We readily accept that socially valued 'higher order' skills, such as those associated with self-regulation and abstract, critical thought, are essential for long-term personal improvement — at least in modern societies.

Where theorizing outstrips what we really know are the speculations of some neo-Vygotskians that children's mental processes are either owed virtually exclusively to their interactions with others or are so reliant on interventions it is difficult to separate children's individual from social identities (Cole, 1996; Cole and Wertsch, 1996; Rogoff, 1990; Rogoff and Wertsch, 1984; Wertsch, 1979, 1991; Wertsch and

Smolke, 1993; Liverta-Sempio and Marchetti, 1997, review and discuss these theories). Such beliefs have the effect of removing from children the main responsibility for their own minds and gives it to those who have care over them. At bottom, as Lucariello complains (1995), an 'enculturalist' thesis — where cognitions are thought of as culturally transmitted — does not articulate a role for individuals in their own progress and almost certainly goes beyond what Vygotsky himself wished. He knew that children's personalities are as much a foil for their social learning as social context constrains individuality. To exemplify: Moll (1994), in an attempt to reinsert Vygotsky's work into mainstream empirical child psychology, subjects the following phrase from one of Vygotsky's papers to detailed consideration. He reasons that it really does mean what it says — learning from others follows on developments which have occurred 'naturally', through children's employment as individuals (i.e. apart from anything they might have learned from others) of innately given processes.

> Cultural development does not create anything over and above that which potentially exists in the natural development [of] the child's behaviour. (Vygotsky, 1929, p. 418)

Moll (1994, p. 334) introduces us to what he calls the 'paradox of Vygotsky'. Whereas social inputs are needed for some developments to get started at all, it has to be children's natural capabilities which make their encounters with these possible. Innate capabilities (the 'natural line') complement, in that they make accessible culturally endowed capabilities (the 'social line'). It isn't that the social line determines the individual or vice versa, but that two types of developmental process facilitate each other.

The concept of childhood we can take from Vygotsky is a reverse image of the Piagetian picture of children being competent learners from the outset, but it complements rather than contradicts Piaget's vision. To represent, fairly, the intentions of people trying to calculate the social origins of cognition, their efforts, often enough, are an attempt to recoup ground sometimes lost sight of when we start exclusively from a child's point of view. In education, we nonetheless need the two (individual/social) perspectives, and although not everyone yet believes we can unite Piaget's work with Vygotsky's in a satisfactory manner (most notably Bruner: see 1997), there are a growing number of developmentalists who see the merit of combining the strengths of the two schools of psychology rather than attacking one from the position of the other. And the way they are pushing ahead with a new developmentalism which mines our two main strata of knowledge about children is instructive.

Reconciling developmental traditions

Bruner's attitude towards the issue of theoretical reconciliation is ambivalent. In an article celebrating the work of the two giants of child psychology (1997), he salutes the seminal contribution made to our understanding of human cognitive development by each but concludes, pessimistically, that there is an 'incommensurable gap' between the stances they take to their subject which bars any attempt we might make to bring both together within a single theory. Piaget, Bruner tells us, tries to 'explain' causally why children structure their minds as they do, while Vygotsky's approach supports a hermeneutic or socially interpretative study of children's improvements through time. Bruner knows that both causal/explanatory and interpretative views have a place within developmental studies, but supposes that as they depend on distinct research paradigms they cannot share a unified account (see also Bruner, 1995). He concedes by implication that the two approaches are complementary. A first conclusion, therefore, might be that Piagetian and Vygotskian theories, though complementary in major respects, cannot coexist within a single framework in order to give us a fuller description of human intellectual development.

Nelson et al. (1998) contest this conclusion. They test out the hypothesis that the social knowledge which Vygotsky saw as basic to children's progress is gained through children's self-managed experiences, and that this fact presumes an integrated experimental/explanatory paradigm. What they are saying is that it is not only possible to enquire into the causes of children's culturally gained interpretations of the world but essential that we do, in order to discover how these interpretations are actually assimilated into children's lives. In their own words:

> We believe that a new understanding of how children come to understand actions in the social world through adopting the explanatory genres of their culture can be attained through an explicit *experiential* interpretation of social cognitive development. The experiential approach attempts to explain development in terms of the cognitive resources available to the developing child in interaction with the world as experienced. (p. 11)

As Nelson et al. argue, Bruner has to be right, as a matter of principle, when he deems impossible the *simultaneous* enquiry into developmental issues, experimentally and interpretatively. But it is quite possible to comment on Vygotskian hypotheses from a Piagetian perspective, and Piagetian ideas from a Vygotskian standpoint, thus bringing the two traditions ever closer together. In Nelson et al.'s (1998) view (also Astington and Olson, 1995), an experiential discussion of the way in which 'Vygotskian' skills and concepts are acquired takes our theories beyond the purely descriptive. They reject as false alternatives the ideas that children's social knowledge has to be seen either as a product of enculturation or of 'individual autonomous minds constructing theories on their own and testing them against data' (p. 11). Children's interactions with both material objects and (culturally agreed) symbols support each other. One of Nelson et al.'s points, which their research supports, is that this hypothesis nowhere contradicts Vygotskian thinking, in that it accepts the role of social context in intellectual development, yet, through its reliance on children's cognitive resources as constructive mechanisms, it does chime well with a neo-Piagetian paradigm.

Jaan Valsiner (1992, 1996, and with Lawrence, 1994) plugs the same gap between the two types of theory. Valsiner's dominant idea is that experiences become part of us through a process of mental 'transformation' — as opposed to a process of cultural 'transmission' (with Lawrence, 1994). Human beings develop by interpreting what they are taught, not by internalizing it directly in the way we might ingest food, that is not by somehow 'swallowing' ideas whole as these are presented by others. Even educationists taking a more or less unqualified Vygotskian approach accept that a straight 'transmission' hypothesis is not feasible, and realize that individuals make sense of socially given knowledge through a form of mental transmutation (Tharp and Gallimore, 1993). Just as Piaget thought (e.g. 1954, 1978), we can only explain qualitative intellectual change by supposing that we do not store information gleaned from events directly but abstract from it what suits our purposes, resynthesizing (i.e. 'constructing') what we believe, think, know in terms of those purposes.

Silcock (1994b, 1996) describes, much as Valsiner does, how we bridge between different experiences via the perspectives channelled through reflective transformations. It is because we can alter our own thinking by recursive perspective-taking (moving backwards and forwards from one viewpoint to another) that experiences are combined in novel ways and we create new meanings. For example, what a child learns happily via a self-chosen pursuit (perhaps some understanding of the role of construction materials learned during constructive play) helps academic topics (e.g. engineering, building) to be interpreted in terms of the pre-existing positive attitude and experience. A 10-year-old studying a Van Gogh painting of a chair, from the viewpoint of his or her own efforts to paint the same object, will learn something about the technicalities involved that no amount of direct instruction could achieve. New concepts are created through transformations grounded in perspectives which will have individual purposes.

The idea of a 'bridging perspective' explains something of the complex transactions between self and environment which must occur when children move from one level of understanding to another. It is easy to oversimplify such processes and suggest that there is some sort of one-to-one relationship between human experiences and what we are capable of understanding. This isn't the case. It isn't children's experiences, as such, which control their development, it is the sorts of perspectives they are able to take from those experiences. Two children sharing the same social background may for instance (for reasons connected with their personal ambitions — i.e. the way their experiences have become structured) have completely different attitudes towards schoolwork and adult guidance. It is the availability of relevant, informed perspectives which decides how children meet their classroom assignments. This is the basis of what is sometimes called 'constructivist' teaching (Bidell and Fischer, 1992; Driver, 1983, 1989; Driver and Bell, 1986; Duffy and Jonassen, 1992; Hand and Treagust, 1994; Keiny, 1994; Littledyke and Huxford, 1998; Summers and Kruger, 1994; Sutherland, 1992; Von Glaserfield, 1989, 1995).

At the simplest level, Piaget's groundbreaking theories explaining how children 'construct reality' (e.g. 1954) are complemented (not contradicted) by Vygotsky's work on verbally mediated interactions. Early childhood educators find that this complementarity gives impetus to recent attempts to tighten up the curricular structures of learner-oriented classrooms (French and Song, 1998). Others see

New Progressivism

it as justifying educational interventionism at both primary and secondary level, provided that the interventionism respects both 'top-down' and 'bottom-up' factors: Vygotsky's work is helpful in pointing to the form the (top-down) teacher interventions must take, while Piaget sets the unique (bottom-up) cognitive scene into which interventionists must intercede if they are to be effective (Adey and Shayer, 1994; Biggs, 1992a and b; Gaskins et al., 1992; Resnick, 1977; Resnick et al., 1992).

All educationalists addressing questions about teaching and learning benefit, to some degree, from the 'marriage of Piaget and Vygotsky' achieved by neo-Piagetians (Adey and Shayer, 1994; Resnick et al., 1992; Silcock, 1996; Valsiner, 1992, 1996). For progressivists who have come to rely on the Piagetian tradition to justify their beliefs, this reconciliation is bedrock for the rebuilding of their ideology. It is, therefore, important to follow through the implications of a new-look developmentalism by searching within relevant corners of progressivist thinking to discover what modifications to practices are required and what approaches can be retained in their older guise. The question 'how far must we change "child-centred" primary school teaching in the light of a Vygotskian modification of Piagetian theory?' is raised by many writers, but it is seldom broached for openly ideological purposes.

On a first analysis, there are four themes which seem unavoidable given what we know about progressivist practices. These themes are: (a) the proactive involvement of individual learners in their own learning (reflecting on the nature of individualism itself); (b) the role of first-hand experience in general cognitive development; (c) the nature of developmental 'stages' (the developmental 'scene' into which teachers will intervene); and (d) the links between cognitive and sociocultural experience which most obviously mark out the purposes for a child-centred education.

The proactive involvement of learners in their own progress: the developmental role of individuals in their own education

Progressivist teachers insist that learners must be actively engaged in their own learning. The idea of 'active engagement' does not mean they are always physically active as some have believed (Antony, 1979; see Blenkin and Kelly, 1989, and Silcock, 1993, for discussions), but nor does it mean that learners need only comply with a situation to make sense of it. An involved learner is one who is voluntarily committed to a task and who approaches it with both understanding and purpose. In the sense that the processes discussed above as responsible for cognitive development are directed by individuals for personal reasons, what is verified is that learning and development *are* accomplished as outcomes of individual transformations, implying a background of related experiences (a relevant perspective) and a degree of task-involvement.

The 'Vygotskian' modification of this Piagetian precept recognizes that constructive processes do not occur in a value-free manner. In short, what we learn determines, to an extent, how we learn. This was, as said, not Piaget's belief. In a basic text (1971) he considered whether individuals construct their minds in order to achieve equilibrium (i.e. a balanced, structured accord with environmental circumstance) or, simply, to create relationships with the world: he questioned whether 'equilibrium' or 'construction' was the fundamental arbiter of cognitive development. He opted for equilibrium, on the grounds that this acceptance united human development with that of the rest of the biological kingdom, while to reject it would place human beings apart from the natural world. Few would, now, accept that the whole weight of developmental progress can rest on one regulatory mechanism (see Fodor, 1976; Haroutunian, 1983; Meadows, 1993). Many developmentalists (not all) are moving towards the 'humanistic' model of adaptation Piaget himself toyed with which *does* set us apart from the rest of the animal kingdom: we simply do not seek self–world equilibrium consistently. People can be attracted to challenges which lead them into very disequilibrated situations. A mountain climber or polar explorer is hardly seeking to maintain a comfortable accord with his or her environment!

This is not to say that the 'equilibrium' concept has proved wholly redundant — Adey and Shayer (1994) suppose that it is the overcoming of 'cognitive conflict' in order to retrieve a balanced self–world relationship which motivates their students to learn science. But it is difficult to see all human striving as owed to a desire to retain an even state of mind. It seems more plausible that we make relationships with the world according to our own purposes, rationally decided (i.e. for sake of our ambitions and aspirations), and for no 'scientific' reason external to those purposes. As Adey and Shayer (1994) discuss, cognitive development is linear and progressive, but 'blind' — i.e. it does not head towards any predetermined goal. Another way of putting this is to say that each time individuals take charge of events they are asserting a personal value — they are implying that one action is in some sense, for them, 'better' than another, for reasons engaged by their purposes, not because of interference from an underlying biological law.

Vygotsky's work exploits the same principle from a socio-historical point of view. For Vygotsky, development could not be value-free because it has to follow set pathways if human beings are to reach culturally valued ends. However, the recognition that development is not value free does not imply that it *can* only follow culturally signposted routes. Each time an infant intentionally chooses to reach for one object rather than another, or engage in one play activity rather than another, he or she is asserting a personal value, and values selected for personal reasons may or may not match ones that are socially agreed. The educational challenge is to help individuals fully appreciate those academic values intrinsic to curricular aims: but, we must remember, this has to be effected by individuals for sake of individual purposes. On the basis of such a conclusion, education (at least of the progressivist sort) is defined as a self-managed, or personally achieved, cultural transformation. Learners, entering educational institutions, should find in them opportunities to construct their own minds in ways reckoned by others (and understood by themselves) to be beneficial. Because the restructuring of minds does not happen through either direct or indirect transmission (it cannot be predetermined, except in a very general sense), individuality is as much a starting point as an end point for teachers. It is constrained through culturally measured experience, but it exists (and, logically, has to exist) prior to that experience.

As soon as we examine educational processes, we find two poles of learning which teachers have to take into account (the individual and the cultural), and the term 'co-construction' (Cole and Wertsch, 1996; Verba, 1994; Nelson et al., 1998) is used to conceptualize these. The term becomes misleading only if we imagine that the roles played by individuals and social context in cognitive change are, somehow, equivalent or symmetrical. Although we are aided in our adaptations by what we learn from others, we each stand in a different place in our relationships with the world because the world of our variously labelled experiences is one we have constructed uniquely. This brings into view the 'humanistic' approach which psychologists and educators like Carl Rogers (1983; also Brandes and Ginnes, 1986) use to justify their notions of 'student-centred learning' and 'learner-centred' teaching. As well as contextual factors dictating the form and significance of what is publicly given, and those variables hidden inside experience and personality, there remain influences unique to situations channelled by individual purpose. We change ourselves for good reason, *vis-à-vis* what we perceive as happening in our immediate lives.

Self-conceived purposes and intentions, giving rise to aspirations and ambitions, are not 'positivistic' (i.e. we determine our own purposes, they don't determine us). Nor will they merely reflect other people's purposes, though, again, no one can wholly cut themselves off from their communities. Cole and Engeström (1995) touch on ways in which we achieve this by citing Leont'ev's two levels of intentionality, the modular (the level of individual consciousness) and the molar (at the collective level, often working unconsciously). While our most common purposes are never 'borrowed' from those around us, they gain meaning and significance from the manner in which they are publicly received and fulfilled. Education has to ensure that we express and expand our individuality in worthwhile ways. What we must not lose sight of is the fact that because education is a cultural transformation (not delivery or transmission), becoming educated is something all students must achieve for themselves. And just as there are many good reasons why school pupils should accept what schools offer, there may be a number of other reasons why they believe they should not. There is after all a natural tension between individuals seeking to preserve their existing relationships with their environments and those social imperatives insisting that they change.

What this enormous complexity implies is that, for their own reasons, whatever anyone else might wish, individuals can resist change, including what is apparently most in their interests to accept. Maybe we all resist radical alterations to an existing self-view. Alternatively, we can distort what we learn, minimize its value, overstretch its significance. If they so wish, pupils can set up barriers to their own education by rejecting a school's culture and what they disclose within it. What matters, ultimately, are the *relationships* children form with their knowledge, their tasks, their teachers, within the cultures that are meant to transform them — i.e. the particular perspectives they are able to take *vis-à-vis* this knowledge. It is common enough for children to memorize their lessons for school-centred purposes in ways which thereby disconnect these from other experiences, making it impossible for such lessons to cast the illuminating perspectives upon life which education exists to provide. Because progressivism acknowledges that school learning is managed by individuals for their own reasons, its promise is that by respecting pupils' individualities their achievements will both enhance their present lives and be a basis for future developments.

Transforming the physical: first-hand experience

'Child-centred' teachers like to arrange first-hand encounters with the world. Their rationale is that children come to know what the physical environment consists of before they learn to understand it. There is an intuitive logic recommending this idea: it does seem a matter of common sense that if we wish children to grasp concepts of the world they must, first, meet objects to which the concepts refer. Challenges to this belief are, now, familiar, though they have to be met afresh with each problem-area, for the arguments related to them alter through reapplication. Regarding first-hand experience, the questions are, firstly, whether such experience is possible at all (isn't the physical world always seen through conceptual spectacles?), and, if it is possible, whether or not it is basic to all conceptual development, as Piaget believed that it was. By answering these questions, it becomes possible to review what teachers' attitudes to this area of educational practice ought to be.

Firstly, as Wertsch (1991) tells us, a major theme running through Vygotsky's writings is his claim that human action on both social and individual planes is mediated by tools and signs. Cognitive development is the coming together of natural processes of maturation (the 'natural line') and a gradual understanding of symbolic processes (such as language). Words, along with their meanings, are used by people in concrete situations. Even knowledge of our physical environment will be channelled through those symbolic systems we build up through our interactions with others. It is by employing our culturally given skills that we make sense of the physical. As Wertsch puts it:

> [a] sociocultural approach to mind begins with the assumption that action is mediated, and that it cannot be separated from the milieu in which it is carried out ... the main criterion is that the analysis be linked in some way with specific cultural, historical or institutional factors. (p. 19)

Since all our understandings of the world arrive as products of the actions we take upon it, knowledge is from the start situated within a milieu — an environment localized in time and space. What we discover in our physical environments is, to a degree, pre-shaped by context both in content and in the ways the knowledge functions for us.

We have to see what Wertsch is not saying and cannot say. Believing that the physical world is labelled symbolically, and that we are forced to submit to that public way of dealing with it in our thinking, does not mean that individual perspectives upon it have to match predetermined views. Wertsch, like Vygotsky, rather ignores the role of individual choice because that is not the point of his study, but he doesn't deny its existence outright. There are distinctions to draw between the cultural labelling of objects and properties (sets of agreed meanings concerning the world) and individual recognitions of these (our perspectives on the world). We all have to find our own ways towards publicly credited ideas, and while doing so we will interpret such ideas in a (potentially) infinitely variable manner. We will do this because although signs and symbols, properties, functions are 'given', the purposes within which symbolic systems are employed are not: the experiences giving rise to our purposes concern all aspects of our lives and not, just, those which are mediated symbolically. If that were not true, we would have to believe that our lives, too, conform to culturally drawn blueprints, planned for us by those who had gone before. No one would wish to believe that.

Another reason we give for our liberation from pre-set ideas is that physical environments are — by definition — not culture contexts. The physical world is that source of meanings which, being universal, gives human beings a common area of interest. Yet our knowledge of it has to be constructed, like any other, and it is usually thought to be constructed early in life. One of Piaget's 'startling' discoveries (Greenberg, 1996) was that children develop 'object concept' rather than it being, as Kant (1781) and many others thought, innate. Contemporary debates tend to wonder at the age when this concept is established, and the precise mechanisms establishing it, rather than the fact of it (e.g. Siegler, 1991). We structure a physically permanent and stable framework within which to locate our more mature ventures and this achievement usually precedes others.

Cole's interpretations of Vygotskian principle (1996, with Wertsch 1996) and those of Wertsch (1979, 1991; Wertsch and Smolke, 1993) cast doubt on such presuppositions by pointing out that even the most familiar objects have cultural meanings attached to them. Cole claims that all human activities are mediated by artifacts (and he includes, as artifactual, symbolic and semiotic systems such as linguistic representations, verbal narratives and discussion): bottles, cans, knives, forks, plates, cups, etc. are more than domestic utensils, they are cultural tools, and their use implies a much larger network of ideas and associations on which we draw unconsciously and which contextualizes our thinking in a general sense. Our world is culturally ordered, and we cannot understand it except through ideas taken from shared experience.

As said, although this contention picks out the way our lives rely on verbal mediation, it is misleading to conclude from it that physical reality is, in fact, wholly 'socially constructed', and that unmediated first-hand experience is some sort of delusion. It is very much the pre-existence of objects on which the pervasiveness of cultural influence depends. Piaget recognized early in his career that without our becoming aware of a stable physical and sensory world we could never acquire that flexibility of thought which typifies adult reasoning and which crowns our cultural efforts. Meanings are not somehow buried inside objects and thereby inseparable from them; they resemble, more, labels which we attach, alter, rethink, abandon, according to our purposes. All psychological representations are publicly agreed — even the iconic and enactive: we have to decide what are appropriate outcomes of practical activity, and what are the significant physical features of objects to isolate. But this does not mean that children must sanction such agreements before they can begin to grasp physical parameters. They will reach their understandings in their own ways, and for their own reasons, stressing some features more than others, possibly detecting properties others ignore or discovering novel uses for the objects they play with. Nelson et al. express this as follows:

> [the] dialectical semiotic mediation theory of development proposed by Vygotsky ... does not assume one-way traffic from 'culturally normative beliefs' to the child's mind. Rather, through participation in social and cultural activities the child interacts with material and symbolic forms that instantiate cultural norms and beliefs. The child must still do constructive work to *make sense* of those social meaning structures for her-/himself. (p. 11: italics in the original)

It is children's active enquiry into both the physical and symbolic environments which leads ultimately to their differentiation and control of each. Because children are able to divide social from non-social experiences (they do not blend into some sort of experiential mush), they discriminate the physical dimensions of objects and events from the verbal meanings we attach to them. It is true that we cannot think about anything without the mediation of representations (which are socially structured), but this does not mean that our thoughts are moulded by the type we employ (as Cole and Wertsch occasionally appear to believe). The ubiquity of human perspective-taking is such that we are well able to fashion and refashion our concepts endlessly: that is, I can take perspectives from one idea upon another (e.g. reframing an empirical discovery within a formally agreed concept or vice versa). We think about our own thinking — alter it, redraft it, confirm it, reject it. Our own viewpoints are often the things we most criticize. Karmiloff-Smith (1992) decides that this ability to 'take ... representations as objects of cognitive attention' (p. 30) is special to human beings. We are never, somehow, buried behind or within our own thoughts, but are able to distance ourselves from them, using cross-perspectives from one area of experience to another, guided by that special organization of experiences which is our individuality.

Returning to the matter of physical objects: it may turn out that our awareness of the sensory is learned tacitly in a way we never have to test out against publicly determined positions (see Reber, 1993). Piaget's analyses of human transactions with the physical (1954) would partly support such a conclusion, as he proposed that we develop 'schemas' of relationships between ourselves and objects which become, gradually, part of our memory store but do not always operate through symbolic representation. Gibson's theorizing that sensory perceptions feed directly into cognitive structure would fit with such a theory (cited and discussed in Reed, 1997), and would further explain why human beings don't, as a rule, confuse the physical parameters of objects with their symbolic identities. After all, the point of a 'symbol' is that it represents something other than itself. A mirror, which can attain many sorts of meaning, including the metaphorical and aesthetic, has symbolic powers precisely because it is an object of a particular shape and constitution, to which an infinite number of conceptual labels might be attached. If its status as an object apart from its symbolic meanings were in doubt, we would lose altogether the creative control we actually have over the way we exploit and apply such meanings.

To summarize: we do not confront our mental and physical worlds passively. We are masters and mistresses of our own thinking, just as we are in command of our own actions. Indeed there are limits to what we can learn from others. Most evidently, children begin to understand their physical environments, at some level, by interacting with objects directly. This has to be true because of the way we define the 'physical': something of what we mean by it is that physical parameters *are* distinct from the meanings we attach to objects. Such a realization confirms the existential fact of a universe of separate objects to ourselves, to which a host of possible (including mistaken) meanings can be attached. If objects did not have physical identities which were distinct from any cultural labels attached to them, we couldn't argue about the detailing of these labels.

Coming to the second question asked about first-hand, primary experience: whether 'first-hand' experience is *necessary* for cognitive development involves less friction with Vygotskian theory in that it has to follow from the idea that development is value laden that all forms of development, grounded in experience, are possible. We have to accept this, even though it might appear a strange sort of argument. For the reasons stated, it would seem highly unlikely that anyone can escape learning about the physical universe altogether, but it is not unusual for people to concentrate their minds on experiences filtered through books, video, film or whatever. Practically, as said, it seems a fantastic idea to suppose that children in a primary school might not acquire a handy repertoire of sense–motor capabilities. Yet, one suspects that, already, there are notable differences between the way children organize their early experiences. For some people, dominant ways of thinking may well be owed fairly exclusively to second-hand contacts with television, computers or films — rather than being grounded in primary contacts.

We must value first-hand knowledge. Without it, we cannot embellish the physical world aesthetically, scientifically or socio-historically. And the minds of people whose ideas are predetermined largely by what they have read or have been told will be very different from those of people with a rich sensory experience. Although we must all comprehend our common physical universe at some level, this does not mean we will choose to apply our understanding to other areas of our lives. If ever the 'virtual' reality generated by computers comes within everyone's reach, it might happen that the fantasy lives of those regularly visiting their virtual universes become alternatives to, rather than imaginative mirrors of, concrete reality. Sooner or later, we must decide the extent to which we value the developmental ends entailed by such a possibility.

The question of the relevance, educationally, of first-hand experience is bound up with questions of value, and we must as unflinchingly as possible assent to the role of such experience. Historians, geographers, scientists, artists (and so on) refer back to the 'real' physical environment in much of what they do. But people can, as said, develop alternative forms of thinking which might be justified within their own terms. This possibility should not tempt teachers to ignore first-hand experience. Quite the reverse: the fact that individuals can develop in ways which bypass a thorough grasp of the sensory makes it imperative for teachers to watch that such a bypass does not occur — insofar, that is, as they accept the virtue of our comprehending the physical as a rich source of pleasure as well as providing a base reference for academic concepts. Most primary school teachers are 'child-centred' enough to try to guarantee that children do benefit from such experiences, though this is no longer quite so true as it was. The demands of the National Curriculum are such that teachers have been forced to cut back on teaching methods which are by nature resource-heavy. Organizing 'trips out' to the seashore or walks in the country, preparing construction, manipulation and play activities or resourcing practical hypothesis-testing in science and technology sessions are time-consuming, and it has lately become tempting for teachers to abandon them in favour of simpler forms of knowledge transmission.

First-hand experience is as essential to mental growth as early childhood educators believe, once we accept the value of traditional forms of knowledge such as science, geography, literature and so on which assume a grounding in sensory experience. However, this doesn't mean that other sorts of experience matter less. We have moved a little way on from the classic Piagetian picture. Separating the physical features of objects from their symbolic features analytically does not imply that we can or should separate them educationally. The neo-Vygotskian contention that what young children need to aid their thinking is a great deal of talk (Bennett, 1992; Tizard and Hughes, 1984; Wells, 1986) has to be agreed for the reasons which have been argued: what should be uncontroversial is the idea that these two worlds of experience (the worlds of the sensory and the socio-cultural) coexist, and that teachers must thoroughly organize for both in their teaching.

Transforming minds: phases of development

The qualitative growth of mind, beginning with the structuring of actions and objects and terminating with mature thought, describes the stage theory assumed by developmentalists to be a progression from practical skills and concrete understandings to abstract operations. Such a progression is tethered immovably within school curricula: usually, concrete and practical activities are the stock-in-trade of primary teaching and more abstract and generalized problem solving engaged with routinely in secondary schools and institutions of higher and further education. This sequencing makes possible, for example, the staging of National Curriculum levels. Almost all subject levels betray in their 'level descriptors' the stages described, although, to be accurate, the National Curriculum does not prescribe that levels of understanding occur in any special sequence. In fact, lately, a stress on formal symbolic skills in primary schools conflicts with the belief of primary school teachers that practical and concrete activities should normally accompany the symbolic. Child-centred teachers, especially, respect the approximate sequencing of developmental stages partly because of the arguments made above about the role of the sensory in cognitive change, and partly because sense-based and visual activities usually, quickly, attract learner involvement.

The thing to remember is that classic stage descriptions are no longer believed universally necessary, given that there are cultural values built into them: we have once more to apply the Vygotskian rule. Otherwise, developmental progress would be wholly 'natural', in the way Piaget once tried to show. Research studies tell us that people do not advance unerringly, and across all knowledge domains, towards the type of thinking he described as 'formal operations'. This progression is limited to areas in which individuals have interest and experience, and to cultures which value abstract ways of thinking (see Sutherland, 1992). To put this educationally: the extent to which students progress in a stage-wise manner (which school curricula demand) will be influenced as much by personal and cultural choice as by individual ability. What this conclusion does not deny is the utility of developmental schemes: only that we have to be aware of the value-judgments residing within them.

For example, it is not self-evident that abstract thinking is of greater import than a mechanic's 'lower level' practical problem solving or a designer's visual preoccupations. A community might for its own reasons decide that they are. Similarly, when children become sidetracked by practical or visual pursuits to the extent that they find it hard to 'progress' developmentally, we need not regard this as somehow deviant or educationally questionable. J. B. Biggs (1992a) believes that one of the points of education is to persuade learners away from a reliance on knowledge 'grounded' in their own idiosyncratic experiences towards the more universally valid forms of declarative, procedural and conditional knowledge — that is, they should ultimately have a principled grasp of ideas, and be able to reason out why some problem-solutions work and some do not. Yet, the refinement of skills grounded in experience, such that we can apply them 'non-logically', is now considered important for much skilled, professional behaviour (see Schon, 1983). This point does not make Biggs' view incorrect: we just have to recognize that it would be a mistake to settle on a single model of educational excellence in advance of any arguments proposing alternatives.

For progressivists, who will tend to be 'interventionists' in the sense that they seek to enhance pupils' developmental progress rather than determine it (Adey and Shayer, 1994; Blyth, 1984; Blenkin and Kelly, 1996), it is a knotty issue as to how directive their interventions have to be: yet, the point of a Vygotskian revolution is to show us that if teachers are not directive in how they teach, someone else will be. There is no 'natural' end-point for cognitive growth — we are not plants or creatures with a programmed maturational cycle. We are whatever we decide that we are: if we believe progress towards 'higher order', formal operational skills is desirable, then we have at some point to nudge learners through 'Piagetian' stages. We have no choice but to do so. Usually, educational curricula, such as the English/Welsh National Curricula, do assume a fairly consistent developmental climb through stages of understanding and skill. And, given the way in which academic disciplines have developed, it is hard to see how such a climb can be ignored by teachers who value such disciplines. Yet we have no absolute grounds for believing that this upward climb is universally normative — it is almost certainly culturally normative in western societies (i.e. what we normally decide should be true). That is different.

Socio-cultural developments

From Vygotsky's work, we learn that some meanings we take from cultures are crucial. While resisting the idea that individualism is wholly inconceivable outside of culture, it is prudent not to deny the enormously powerful social forces which insert themselves into everyone's experiences. Nelson et al. (1998) put this cogently:

> What the child encounters in the world of experience, always from the child's perspective, is scaffolded and guided, and eventually linguistically labelled and described, by other people who are critical to the child's very existence. In this sense the child's knowledge is from the beginning co-constructed with social others, and after a few years, it is co-constructed explicitly through linguistic forms in many cases. (p. 13)

The 'co-construction' of mind is marked in educational contexts, since learners are expected to take the chances presented by schools to convert their immature understandings into the more sophisticated and mature. Insofar as they climb upward through intellectual 'stages', they will do so because they see that it is in their interests to do so. But this type of progression isn't attractive to everyone. There are many sorts of culturally situated forms of learning — some of which are harmful, even destructive of those who submit to them. Children can become easy prey to indoctrinators and to others with political and ideological axes to grind. The social partner implied by the idea of the co-construction of mind does not always have the interests of learners at heart.

Persuading learners that certain types of pursuits are in their best interests, is the job of teaching. Education (if progressivists are right) is a transformation learners must work for themselves, by accepting those 'co-constructions' which are most easily managed in school-organized settings. But there is more than one viable concept of education, even within fairly narrow institutional terms. To suppose that all pupils must climb a developmental ladder is one thing, to suppose that they must climb that particular ladder which a National Curriculum erects is to accept a rather overworked blueprint for state education. Progressivism rejects such narrow conceptions, and in doing so it recognizes both the diversity of outcome that a pluralist society can tolerate and the diversity of possibilities for personal fulfilment built into learners' own unique relationships with the world. Human beings seek to go beyond the given and stride forward in all their endeavours. In doing so they engage with many different value systems.

Summary: a 'new' developmentalism

Blyth (1984) writes that Rousseau's contribution to education (and Rousseau's contribution is usually thought to mark the birth of progressivism) was that he noticed how a theory of education had to take note of the way children develop. Blyth also points out that the frailty of Rousseau's educational ideas (see also Darling, 1994) does not detract at all from the view that developmentalism has a crucial role to play in education generally, and progressive education in particular. If we agree with Blyth's opinion, we must become as sure as we can be of our developmental explanations. What has been argued is that the dichotomy favoured by those who once rejected Piagetian psychology and thus rejected the progressivism it shored up was always a false one. It was never a question of whether children are best conceived as 'lone scientists' making their own way in the world or as 'social beings' improving largely through interactions with others (see Bennett, 1992, Littledyke, 1998, Mackenzie, 1997). Both conceptions are recognized as in some sense or other correct (and have to be recognized as correct if we are to understand the bi-polar nature of important cognitive processes), depending on how we interpret the Piagetian and Vygotskian positions, respectively, which generate them.

From one point of view, the 'new' developmentalism which has been described is not new at all. Nelson et al.'s (1998) idea that children's minds are products of their own experiences resembles Blyth's (1984) adding of 'experience' to 'development', when he qualified what he took to be the progressivist stress on individual action with an equal stress on the effects that actual experiences (especially social experiences) have on learners. He was harmonizing 'internal' and 'external' factors and reaching equivalent conclusions to the ones reached here. An even longer time ago, Dewey (1976) offered us advice much like Blyth's — telling us that it simply isn't possible for teachers to ignore either learners' personalities or wider, public expectations, since these were both part of every learner's everyday experiences.

From another viewpoint, the realization that children 'co-construct' their minds is very new. For what it implies is that the integrity of individual and cultural forces each have to be respected whenever we bring children to a classroom task. This is, in the end, neither to accept culturally determinist beliefs that individuality is socially artifactual nor the 'Plowden' type of progressivist views of childhood which relied fairly exclusively on classic Piagetian theory. We do not have to be adversarial developmentally or educationally. On any count, the factors which the two great developmental traditions — the Genevan and the Russian — describe figure in children's day-to-day learning in ways which teachers can't bypass. They have little choice but to refer in their teaching to students' own personally motivated actions alongside attempting to persuade them to pay regular attention to other people's views. It is hardly a coincidence that this conclusion reflects the difficulty cited earlier which governments experience when struggling to reconcile the legitimate needs of individuals with the national welfare. It underlines, from the viewpoint of empirical research, issues which have anyway become unavoidable on the political stage.

As educationists, we are often over-hasty in letting new ideas push out the old, without properly assessing the profit from our doing so. It was once common to think that adult interventions in children's learning — teaching them to read, write or whatever — could not work until the children themselves were, somehow, 'ready' for them. We overstressed what was already present in children's experiences, as Robin Alexander warned (1994). During the 1980s and 1990s, the opposite danger has threatened. There has been a tendency to imagine that skills such as problem solving depend largely on the 'internalizing' of socially given experiences, that assuming we get the curricular context right everything else will follow, and we can to a large extent ignore children's existing attitudes and states of mind. The proper course for us is to opt for neither extreme. The bipolar idea of 'co-construction' does not deny an often irresistable push parent cultures give to an individual's beliefs and attitudes, abilities and ambitions. But it does articulate how the unique experiences pupils bring to a learning situation not only impede or facilitate this influence, they are needed to make it happen in the first place. No one can grasp a circumstance they are not, in some sense, mentally prepared for. As J. L. Biggs puts it (1992), children and cultures create each other.

Chapter 7

Curricular Values: The Relationships between Learners and their Knowledge

The problem with traditional values

Two sets of demands pattern every child's education — the knowledge and skills which a society asks of its citizens and those more personal aspirations and qualities which regulate individual impetus and drive. By approving both sets, we might justly decide that the flight from primary school child-centredness over past decades has gone too far towards prescription and has not achieved the equitable system which reconciling public demand with personal aspiration suggests. It is never easy to achieve a fair balance between competing factions. And just as some teachers might want to try out a 'new' child-centredness in schools, believing that by doing so they are conceding reasonable ground to public expectations about standards and skills, others might reckon that a centrally structured, closely monitored policy stays the best bet. With the older Victorian types of traditional education long behind us, a benevolent didacticism avoids the perils of too much coercive drudgery, tedious recitations and rote learning which filled the lives of young schoolchildren a century ago.

But there are problems with traditional values as these generate educational aims and school curricula, infecting traditionalist ideology at its roots, arising as they do from two essentials which together structure the 'classical' traditionalist ideal. These essentials are: its oversimple concept of how values are to be learned (that is, its concept of the nature of learning and learners) and its flawed, even dangerously flawed, beliefs about what they should learn (its value specifications: or the concept traditionalists have of culture itself). An examination of developmental theory has begun to tease away faults within both of these concepts, and we we can check them further by studying the traditionalist beliefs which seem to have informed much policy making recently.

There is nothing ignoble, facile or inauthentic about the traditionalist model of what it means to be an educated person, and there need be nothing wrong with educational aims derived from it. Whether there are or not depends on how the model is interpreted and applied to practical issues. Antony O'Hear's views are quoted as exemplars of traditionalist thinking because as well as fitting the paradigm stipulated earlier, they are not over-rhetorical as are some of the 'New Right's publications (probably encouraged by 'Black Paper' writers' success in influencing government policy during the 1960s and 1970s: see Cox and Dyson, 1971). For

New Progressivism

instance, if 'real' education means teaching long established ideas in direct ways, all modern primary school teachers are tarred with the same brush:

> [A primary] school is no longer a place to learn, but a place to play, to enjoy oneself and perhaps, by the way, to pick up a smattering of what is, in many cases, useless knowledge. (Yeo, 1994, p. 130)

O'Hear's words are more measured. When he writes (1987) that:

> the proper and effective use of reason must take place against the background of inherited forms of thought and experience . . . there is a sense in which all true education has a strongly conservative aspect. (p. 102)

he is recommending a traditional form of education not because he believes tradition must be honoured for its own sake, but because of what it can teach our age. So:

> an immersion in the disciplines of history and literature . . . (an) understanding of the classical and Homeric worlds as if from within [will] bring out the continuities between these worlds and our own, which is their cultural successor. (pp. 104, 105)

He is convinced that we will cope better with our lives through familiarizing ourselves with our own knowledge traditions. He is especially drawn to established studies in the humanities, as embodying our highest cultural ideals:

> An education focussing on history, literature and the arts will provide the best way of developing the sort of understanding and sensitivity to our lives and experience that will enable us to cherish what is higher, more complex, better-ordered and ultimately more fulfilling. (p. 109)

His sideswipe at 'Deweyan' progressivism (p. 108), that it is superficially preoccupied with transitory topics, follows on his belief that, like much he finds 'barbaric' about modern society and its education (p. 106ff.), its pandering to whatever is current is not in the best interests of the learners themselves. It cannot achieve the 'wisdom that comes from seeing things in a wide human context, in their full complexity and interconnectedness' (p. 109).

Such justifications for an ideology make sense given O'Hear's assumptions — i.e. that we have through past ages accumulated an unassailable body of knowledge which we should all possess, and that, accordingly, we should not stray far from studies sanctioned by that knowledge. But they do rely heavily on beliefs about how educational aims can be achieved which, ultimately, derive from out-of-date conceptions both of learning and of culture itself. There is both a psychological and cultural naivety underlying this modern-day version of traditionalism which it is revealing to expose.

Firstly, from a developmental perspective, education as a form of 'transmission' is untenable, given the conclusions reached in the previous chapter. No developmentalists think that individuals 'receive' knowledge, rather like a radio receiver receives messages sent out by a transmitter. It isn't that such a model cannot approximate in some settings to what happens when — for instance — learners memorize information or rehearse ideas to some state of perfection, but teachers usually set their sights on more sophisticated goals. The transmitter/receiver conception of learning conforms to what Popper calls 'the bucket theory of mind' (1979), which is derided by psychologists as well as philosophers because it takes no account of the active role of individuals in their own learning (see Swann, 1995). A belief in learning as transmission has to be part of traditionalist ideology for the good reason that as soon as one prescribes *particular* sorts of knowledge, skills and qualities as suitable for all within a society, one implies that these can, indeed, be learned by everyone in a fairly undiluted fashion. There would be little point in setting knowledge targets and then saying that many learners can only reach these in some watered-down manner, or argue that teachers should be able to select subjectively from them.

The question of whether many learners in a western society can make sense of the sorts of classically founded subjects traditionalists fall back on to instantiate their beliefs (i.e. whether or not traditionalist curricula are inherently elitist or not), was recognized as a problem by T. S. Eliot (1948), who is sometimes regarded as a spokesman for traditionalist values. But we have to superimpose onto this very real difficulty the question as to whether anyone *should* acquire their values through a process of transmission, even if it were to be thought practicable for them to do so. If I really desire to share my love of Shakespeare with a class of children, I might shrink from teaching about his plays didactically, even if I believed I could, because I sense that knowledge which is not freely chosen as a personal pursuit will not serve as a personal value and will not illuminate one's life. There are ways of teaching which give learners a participatory role in their own education, and anyone who sees education as the initiation of learners into what is worthwhile might well prefer those ways.

The 'transmission' concept of school learning complements an equally inflexible concept of culture. The ideal which O'Hear invokes specifies a *particular* body of knowledge, values and beliefs as constituting a culture. For him, there must be no compromising on whatever is decided to be at the core of our heritage. This static concept is inadequate even as a description of the way of life of a fairly homogeneous state, and, significantly, those who hold it often resort to specifications of their own personal beliefs. O'Hear writes that in Britain it is '*our* history and *our* artistic traditions' (p. 109) which deserve study, because 'things matter to us and affect us in unequal ways' (p. 110). Recognizing the contentious nature of such statements, he decides that, in practice, people who live in a society will appreciate what is worthwhile about it, and will naturally wish to share their appreciation with others. Yet even simple cultures (let alone those found in pluralist societies) are not finalized bodies of knowledge, values and beliefs, they are *fluid contexts* within which we all have to find our niches. As contexts, cultures are by nature ever-changing and under dispute, not solidified and settled: we have all to find our places within our own cultures, but there is not, just, one right place for us to be. To complement a dynamic concept of learners as individuals in a transformational relationship with their societies, we must pose a dynamic model of the cultures potentially able to transform them.

Dr Nicholas Tate, when he was chief executive of SCAA (the School Curriculum and Assessment Authority), might have approved of O'Hear's paper in preparing his 1995 brief that 'pupils of all cultural groups in Britain should be taught what it means to be British and helped to develop a strong sense of British identity' (cited Burtonwood, 1996, p. 227). He employs a culture concept which is detailed and finalized. He must believe, as does O'Hear, that what he proposes has value for everyone in contemporary British society because our traditions demonstrate that it has; and he must also believe that every child in a British school can, potentially at least, make good sense of a concept of 'what it means to be British'. There would be little point in someone heading a state education quango arguing that only a select proportion of state school pupils could really benefit from such knowledge.

Burtonwood (1996) attacks Tate's views by citing Karl Popper's (1966, 1994) rejection of culture as a 'superorganic entity' — i.e. as a singular framework within which everyone has little choice but to reside. Burtonwood opts for a 'transformational curriculum which goes beyond culture' (p. 227). His notion of both our culture and school curricula is that they are contexts within which learners of all kinds, from diverse parent groups, should be able to realize their own ambitions, even if this implies their rejecting a specific model (such as the British). Burtonwood is not saying that there is anything 'wrong' with our being British or of schoolchildren learning about a British way of life: he is doggedly opposed to an educational system which promotes any set of contested ideas exclusively. That is: he is disputing the principles underlying traditionalist ideology.

Problems with traditionalism show themselves in the hardships experienced by anyone trying to teach a standard (knowledge-based) curriculum. To some extent, progressivism originates in a dissatisfaction with forms of teaching which can alienate many and only serve the interests of a few. It is not suggested that modern traditionalist teachers always use didactic forms of teaching, but if we affirm that many learners really cannot cope with abstract 'classical' ideas which anyway sit uneasily with some non-indigenous values, it is also a fair assumption that teachers may find that their only ruse, if they are to survive as classroom authorities, is coercion. So traditionalist curricula, despite their high aspirations, can degenerate into the Dickensian caricature which sees pupils as learning whatever they are told to learn just because they are told to learn it. Such curricula become not vehicles for achieving the lofty ends aimed at by a Matthew Arnold, a Leavis, an Eliot or an O'Hear, but become mechanisms of control — means of keeping pupils (who would otherwise reject their schooling as oppressive) in their place. In modern times, this possibility led Blenkin and Kelly, faced with what they saw as the National Curriculum's coercion of young children into learning situations unsuited to their immaturity to herald the 'Death of Infancy' (1994).

It is easier to criticize an existing system than to propose alternatives. There are problems trying to invent a new language which will deliver the values progressivists seek. Traditionalist curricula have the merit of at least being clear about aims. For example, Tate and O'Hear are able to point to measurable outcomes, gained through testing in examination, which might show that their own values have been realized. When progressivists come to design 'open' and 'dynamic' curricula, the very diversity of content implied makes for difficulties of assessment and evaluation. In the past, some solution to this difficulty of knowing what criteria to apply in judging progressivist classrooms has been found by considering the role of 'processes' in curricular management. Kelly, who has written much about process-model curricula (Blenkin and Kelly, 1981; Blenkin, Edwards and Kelly, 1992; Kelly, 1980, 1986, 1989, 1994), is guided by the child-centred values of many primary school teachers.

By taking pupils' learning and developmental needs as deciding factors, teachers discover that it is learners' relationships with their own knowledge which matter rather more than the teaching of a specified content. Such a finding is lent validity by 'constructivist' beliefs that we have to put ourselves in the shoes of the learners themselves to judge the extent to which school knowledge, truly, becomes known (von Glaserfield, 1995). But the 'process' concept stipulates more about curricula than a few necessary features of learning. And, on first acquaintance with it, it seems ill-defined, in that it isn't altogether clear what does or does not count as a curricular process, just as it isn't altogether clear how the outcomes of a process curriculum can be best assessed. If we are not to use formal tests, how are we in the end to know that a child-centred teacher has been successful? The process idea needs reanalysis if it is to be reintroduced as a conceptual device for designing and assessing school curricula.

Processes

The process-curriculum model idea was a brainchild of Lawrence Stenhouse (1983; Rudduck and Hopkins, 1985), who was responding to his own aversion to curricula designed around behavioural objectives. He found that the listing of objectives as the first step in planning curricula tended to bind a teacher to rigid procedures — like 'an intellectual navvy' as he put it (Rudduck and Hopkins, 1985, p. 85). Teachers became slaves to goals which were either too precise to be achievable or were so trivial as not to merit attention, while the goals learners might actually achieve within less straightened circumstances were not easily stated. For Stenhouse, education is not an instrumental exercise whereby teachers can target their aims in a well defined manner. It is better seen as a family of procedures which, because they have features in common (they can be thought of as a family), usually lead to desirable learning outcomes. By identifying what marks the procedures themselves as educationally successful (i.e. their 'process' features) Stenhouse thought that teachers could, fairly uncontroversially, ensure that what school pupils accomplished would be worthy and commensurate with normal social values.

However, the difficulty with specifying 'processes' in place of the objectives which traditionalist curricula require, is that unless these are carefully stated they can appear too tenuous to guarantee that learning will transcend superficiality. This isn't only a matter of definition, it is also one of usage — i.e. of how we believe the concept can or should function in educational discourse. The notion of a 'process' supposes that there are observable patterns in classroom activities which betray underlying social or psychologically significant changes (such as changes in learning). But these patterns can be of many kinds. And adherents of process-model curricula (Stenhouse: Rudduck and Hopkins, 1985; Blenkin, Edwards and Kelly, 1992; Blenkin and Kelly, 1981; Blyth, 1984; Kelly, 1980, 1986, 1989) refer to three very different sorts, without clarifying the links between them. Firstly, the manner in which teachers and learners approach tasks (procedural principles) has process dimensions. Secondly, the relationships learners form psychologically and socio-psychologically with their activities can be talked of in terms of processes; and thirdly, the epistemological relationships learners make with what is learned — that is, the form understandings and skilled behaviour ultimately take — are also discussed in terms of processes (such as the application of learned concepts to real-life situations, and their capacity for stimulating new ideas).

Taking these in turn, a first grappling with the process dimension of curricula as listed above involves what Stenhouse and Kelly call 'procedural principles'. They are naming the general attitudes or approaches which teachers adopt and to which learners respond to ensure that education proceeds in worthwhile ways. The word 'procedures' is associated with the behaviour of teachers or learners — depending on how these are described. For Kelly (1989), it is the *manner* in which teachers teach and learners learn which signals whether a situation is educational or not, rather than whether these situations lead to any publicly set goals. Procedural principles are 'intrinsic, guiding . . . principles [which are] part of education as a continuous lifelong process' (p. 106).

The second way of studying processes is discussed differently by different writers. For Stenhouse, 'understanding' appears paramount — evidence that pupils thoroughly understand what they learn would correspond to evidence that important cognitive processes are being tapped into by a programme of study. Alan Blyth (1984) refers to skills and concepts which pupils need to 'enable' them to manage their own progress: following his fairly exclusive interest in primary education, he argues that there are a number of strategies teachers can deploy to liberate their pupils as learners at a fairly early stage, helping them to manage their own school activities with cumulative success. For Kelly (e.g. 1989) important curricular processes are those which reflect developmental change. Successful schooling is that which regulates learners' general improvement throughout their lifecycles.

A third way of conceiving curricular processes pinpoints those longer-term goals thought by Stenhouse to determine criterially the proper grasp of any subject (he instances from humanities work 'cause, form, experiment, tragedy'). Although these criteria are firmer in what they say about content than those linked to teaching methods, Stenhouse loosely categorizes them as 'procedures, concepts and criteria', which he believes are not to be taught as objects of mastery, but are better thought of as themes recurring in many topics teachers organize, rather than being found in any singular objectives achieved. He gives an illustration:

> The infant class considering the origins of a playground fight and the historian considering the origins of the First World War are essentially engaged in the same task. They are attempting to understand by using the concept of causation; and they are attempting to understand both the event and the concept by which they seek to explicate it. (Rudduck and Hopkins, 1985, p. 88)

So a classroom teacher might adopt methods which focus on a theme like causation because pupils can reapply what they learn in various situations. When looked at in this way, process indicators open doorways to the transferrable and 'higher order' skills which are becoming increasingly prioritized by writers in terms of their educational significance.

Although these three types of curricular 'process' are not always distinguished, a preliminary examination of their use within curricular design shows that they can be thought of as having connected functions. The first (procedural principles adopted by teachers) embodies the stance which teachers will take towards their daily job: in an analysis of primary work, this might be a 'child-centred' stance whereby teachers would check — for example — that procedures engaged learners actively with classroom tasks. The second encapsulates the process aims teachers are trying to achieve through adopting the stance. Again, in an informal or 'child-centred' classroom, one might expect to see pupils showing a high degree of enthusiasm or interest in what they did, and seeking to apply what they learned to their own real-life situations. The third formulation reveals longer-term indicators of those values which are guarantors that schooling has worked and aims have been achieved.

To stipulate all three categories of process is beneficial in starting to expel from the term confusions which its very generality attract, as well as predicting benefits from using it. Sometimes, to discuss processes is to discuss ways of behaving; sometimes, it is to discuss signs of the quality of a learning or teaching situation; and sometimes it is to discuss curricular outcomes. We should always know which meaning is being employed so that we don't fall into the trap of believing that it is some 'catch-all' concept able to replace all others entailed by curricular design. For instance, sets of relationships pupils make with their own knowledge marks out the quality of any learning which results. But — when expressed in this way — they do not imply that knowledge content (as opposed to learners' attitudes towards it) is unimportant. The reason for paying attention to this somewhat technical point is that one of the most frequently made assaults on progressivist curricula is that they polarize process to product or content. Certainly, progressivist beliefs about 'best practice' take us beyond the business of pre-specifying content, because progressivists do wish to make sure that whatever is learned in primary schools is understood and makes a difference to pupils' lives. Yet, however the 'process' concept is defined or used, to stress it, as Vic Kelly does, is not to leave product unstressed, or to propose that the content of a curriculum is unimportant. Dewey's (1976, p. vii) very similar proposals were unfairly attacked in the way modern progressivists' theories have been attacked and Stenhouse's formulations of humanities curricula were attacked — critics reckoning that they assumed a 'false dichotomy' between what is learned in schools and the manner in which it is learned.

To repeat: in Kelly's 'process' model (1989), as in the 'enabling' curricula of Alan Blyth (1984) and Stenhouse's humanities curricula (Rudduck and Hopkins, 1985), processes (i.e. the ways in which pupils learn controlled pedagogically by teachers obeying set principles of procedure and leading to certain general sorts of outcomes) are a stable component standing in place of aims, whereas taught concepts are variable. But both are vital. Writers only question whether it is possible at all — especially in an increasingly pluralist society — to reach agreement on prescriptions of content, and whether when we do we are setting a realistic task for teachers. No one denies that knowledge is *in general* valuable. The contention is that knowledge prescriptions *alone* do not produce educated citizens.

What process statements do is help teachers bypass difficulties of curricular planning which arise from the very fact that reaching a consensus about content is well nigh impossible. The attempt to impose such a consensus in England and Wales in 1989 provides a rare case study testing out whether it can or cannot be done. Since we are — currently — experiencing a revision of the third version of the curriculum within a ten-year period, and each revision relaxes, further, legal obligations on teachers to teach the written programme, this is hardly evidence that the pre-specifying of content works. The jury may still be out on whether a standard curriculum (comprising content statements) can ever be mounted successfully, but present observations suggest that Kelly's (1994) riposte to its first inception that it would not work has been justified. The only real alternative to lists of statements of content (broken down as objectives or targets to be achieved) are usually thought to be process criteria allowing teachers to judge whether one topic or another is suitable for any particular class or class group. Some National Curricular subject orders include 'process' statements (see, for example, the Science and History orders), indicating that there is some public consent to Stenhouse's formulation, but — in the absence of a full-blooded application of process criteria to the school curriculum as a whole — it can be counted as no more than a faltering step down the road he wanted curricular designers to travel.

The job remains of explaining what might be written into newly revised progressivist curricula and of showing how processes can replace curricular aims or stand as indicators of appropriate content. We need more than a clarification of terms to persuade us that teachers can organize their work so that each type of process does lead to the others, and that outcomes are culturally valued. The first category — those procedures which define a contemporary 'child-centred' stance — are so fundamental to a progressivist rationale they require full treatment in a single chapter (Chapter 8). The second and third, concerning learners' relationships with their work and process criteria for worthwhile content outcomes (i.e. reflecting the value of what is learned), fall within this chapter's orbit of concerns. They will be tackled next.

Learners' relationships with their knowledge

Primary school teachers occasionally refer to the 'whole' person or 'the whole child' (Alexander, 1992; Biber, 1972; Blatchford and Blatchford, 1995). When they do this, in the way that Dewey did (Tomlinson, 1997), they can mean many things, but one interpretation says how our central capabilities unite around our personal qualities. We relate, as whole persons, to our knowledge and skills, through interest, ambition, application, commitment, making links experientially in ways which constrain the capabilities themselves. 'Constructivism', as discussed in the previous chapter, assumes human 'constructors' actively shaping events from the viewpoints of their own lives and thereby achieving personalized ends, *en route* to the cultural transformations which educational institutions prize. What we sense, because of the very open-endedness of the idea of sustaining learners' positive attitudes to school knowledge, is that it may not be that easy to detect with surety those who approach schoolwork in ways likely to benefit them in the longer term and those whose attitudes are such as to lead to school failure (however this is measured) or terminal alienation from academic study. We suppose that there are behavioural indicators to help us, otherwise child-centred teachers could not retain the approach that they take.

The clearest sign that children's learning is occurring in ways valuable to the learner is, perhaps, that they appear 'interested' in it or are motivated by it. Enjoyment has always been a staple feature of child-centred classrooms, and the fact that a number of teachers do not enjoy the job as they once did (Chapter 4) is noteworthy. For the value of enjoyment lies not, simply, in its motivational power, but in its signalling (as a process indicator) that learners are taking an appropriate perspective from their own experiences upon the task in hand. There is, in other words, some chance that they are making sense of what they are doing. So to believe that 'school is no longer a place to learn but a place . . . to enjoy oneself' (Yeo, 1994) is to miss the point about the role of pleasure in learning. Signs of pleasure in a child's expression may be taken as signs of learning.

But they aren't always. And they aren't the only signs which matter. The notion of 'interest' is a relatively gross term, signalling a passing fancy as much as a lifelong pursuit. It is insufficiently revealing of what must happen when we are willing to persist with difficulties and struggle on despite temporary setbacks. Having accepted that children may not, naturally, be interested in subjects they nonetheless must study, progressivists must conceptualize the 'process' relationship actually preferred. Otherwise, the very foundations of the ideology are at risk. Also, we must query, as did Richard Peters and Paul Hirst (1970), whether the relationships children form with their school subjects can be separated from subjects themselves. Hirst (with Peters, 1970) argued that the qualities we value in ourselves as educated people are intrinsic to distinct bodies of knowledge and can only be gained through disciplining ourselves to the specifics of the subjects. The very term subject *discipline* implies that what is involved in learning to maintain our intellectual progress is our subjection to a specific form of study. As Darling points out (1994), both Hirst and Peters turned against progressivist ideology because they believed its approach was intellectually lax.

Developmentally, it was argued that learners must be able to take perspectives from existing experiences on what they are doing to allow them to make sense of it. If we decide that the school knowledge has to be more than superficially retained (and sometimes simple memorization is all a teacher is aiming for), then we do need to be able to describe learner perspectives in fair detail. Educational and cognitive psychologists who have studied the conditions required for learning transfer and the application of knowledge (see Désforges, 1993, 1997; Meadows, 1993; Resnick, 1985; Salomon and Gibberson, 1987; Voss, 1987) pinpoint those psychological conditions which lead to a thorough conceptualization as 'mindful' or 'metacognitive'. A 'metacognitive' overview can be described as an ability to place ourselves in relationship with our own activities, such that we monitor what we do and, potentially, see any implications for related areas of life (Cardelle-Ellewar, 1992).

Such mindfulness may not always accompany interest, as said, but it will show itself in learners' secure engagement with task and, over the longer term, in their emotional commitment to a programme of study. For such reasons, Blyth (1984) decides that it is pupils' 'engagement' with curricula which tells us the curricula are working — once we look beyond performance outputs as the main end of teaching. Blyth is aware that while we are content to measure success by looking at performance only, then teachers might achieve their ends through well-planned teaching and careful instruction, but once we set our sights on learning of a different quality, then we have to monitor more closely learners' attention to task.

Désforges' (1997) idea of 'personal commitment', and Woods' use of the term 'strategic interest' (Woods, 1980, discussed in Wallace, 1996) also bypass interest as a single motivator to the need for pupils to channel their enthusiasms into those pursuits which will be socially and vocationally 'in their interests'. While wishing to avoid the trap of ideology, Woods (1994) suggests that the secret of good teaching lies in the imaginative ways teachers make learners feel in charge of their learning, rather than their being discouraged at any lack of progress. Whatever terms are used, the key would seem to be *at the very least* to keep learners on task by encouraging them to form commitments, at the expense, sometimes, of curriculum coverage.

Possibly the most stunning illustration of the key role played by pupils' self-monitoring of their own progress is that provided by research projects informed by constructivist and neo-Piagetian psychology (Adey and Shayer, 1994; Driver, 1983, 1989; Driver and Bell, 1986; Hand and Treagust, 1994; Resnick, 1979, 1985; Resnick et al., 1992; for reviews of some of these see Sutherland, 1992; Littledyke and Huxford, 1998). What characterizes these projects are learners being helped to approach tasks from the standpoint of familiar experiences. Providing curricula are organized so that pupils' existing intuitions about what they learn are built on, 'quality' learning should be assured. In terms of primary schools, then, to infer from constructivist and/or neo-Piagetian programmes (similar enough to classify together) their 'process features' is to discover something about designing progressivist curricula. A brief consideration of these, beginning with a more in-depth account of one of the best known, will illustrate the conclusions which follow.

Adey and Shayer's (1994) Cognitive Acceleration through Science Education (CASE) experiments with 11 and 12-year-olds followed the interventionist model of teaching which assumes the developmental outline above. It should perhaps be said that although the project was organized with young secondary age pupils, its principles apply to all forms of teaching and have been generalized to work with younger pupils (see Littledyke and Huxford, 1998; Resnick et al., 1992). CASE project leaders 'intervened' in students' learning rather than engaging in formal 'instruction'. That is, they matched their teaching to whatever ideas were proferred. Nothing was introduced which didn't have a fair chance of latching onto concepts which were already known. For example, project managers made sure that any new terms were adequately understood before their students' thinking was challenged scientifically. Once learners had grasped these new terms, they were challenged to solve scientific problems and asked to discuss their own solutions freely among themselves before reaching final conclusions. Most importantly, students were led, through encouragement and a sensitive scaffolding of their interpretations, to see the principles lying behind their discoveries. This followed what Adey and Shayer call the 'high road' to metacognition (echoing Salomon's proposals). Students' 'accelerated' cognitions hung on their abilities to overcome the 'cognitive conflicts' resulting from having their ideas challenged, and to continue to monitor and reapply improvements in their own learning.

What teachers using this approach do not do is present to their classes problem solutions as already worked out in advance of learners' own thinking. Certainly, anyone following Adey and Shayer's method would need to prepare students for the specialized nature of scientific tasks (mathematical, historical or whatever: see Littledyke and Huxford, 1998) by familiarizing learners with a subject-specific language, but this is to make sure that there is a smooth transition from students' own knowledge to the newer concepts. They will take most care in guaranteeing learners' 'mindfulness' (as Adey and Shayer describe it, their ability to 'think about their own thinking': 1996). By testing out existing beliefs and hypotheses experimentally and in discussion with others, learners come to realize what is involved in dealing with (in this case) scientific problems, so taking themselves forward to knowledge application and the transfer of skills.

Constructivists and neo-Piagetians teaching younger children follow similar procedures to those of Adey and Shayer, though these are adapted to the age of the pupils. So in Resnick et al.'s (1992) teaching of arithmetic skills to children of infant age whom they describe as not 'socially favoured', they elicited children's own informal knowledge and insisted that the children trusted such intuively gained knowledge before proceeding with any new teaching. When Resnick et al. introduced formal notation and standard mathematical ideas they did so by linking these to pupils' intuitive understandings, helping children apply their growing knowledge in everyday problem solving. Ultimately, even very young pupils took part in mathematical discussions — i.e. they did not just 'do' arithmetic. Like Adey and Shayer, Resnick et al. achieved quite dramatic success with children of all ability levels. J. B. Biggs (1992b) judges that the success of their teaching is owed to its tackling problems from two directions together — 'top down' and 'bottom up'. While new knowledge is securely linked to pupils' existing ideas, mathematical terms are introduced so that pupils make the best use of their own growing understandings and apply their new mathematical perspectives to self-generated issues.

A way of highlighting the 'process' dimensions of constructivist teaching and learning is to reduce the model to its essentials. Without oversimplifying it, and accepting that, within education, not every instance of a category conforms to type, one would suggest that there are three dimensions to a constructivist model of learning in so far as it is taken as implying a model of teaching. There are emotional, cognitive and contextual or socio-political dimensions. Children must be committed to their learning (emotional), they must understand tasks they meet (from the perspectives of their own experiences: cognitive), and they must have the freedom within their classes to interact with others, test out their ideas and check these against relevant alternatives (contextual/socio-political). These three 'process' conditions invariably occur in constructivist projects such as those described (though they are seldom explicated in this way by constructivists themselves). Motivation and pupil commitment are often thought to arise naturally within a constructivist framework (Littledyke, 1998). But teacher 'interventions' only work because students comprehend the problem situations they face: that is, in Adey and Shayer's programme, not only were the students' own experientially generated ideas invoked but those characteristics of scientific methods which were inevitably new were painstakingly introduced by project managers at the start of their teaching. On top of that, pupils need sufficient freedom from coercion and competition with 'correct' answers to believe that they are in charge of their own activities.

Student commitment, comprehension and control are watchwords of constructivist teaching, and though each condition interacts with others, each has independent status. It is possible for learners to be committed to tasks they don't understand; they may grasp situations they have no control over; and they may feel in control of situations to which they are not committed and poorly recognize (often happening when teachers relinquish too much managerial authority). All three conditions are needed for curricular aims to be achieved. Interestingly, when teachers are introduced to constructivist teaching, recognizing that eliciting experiences ensures comprehension and preserves interest is quickly grasped: it is the idea that pupils must be seen as 'in control' of their own progress which is hardest to come to terms with (Hand and Treagust, 1994). Teachers by the nature of their profession believe that they should be the ones who are directing affairs. Hand and Treagust separate the role of teachers as 'managers' from their role as 'controllers': it is possible that teachers manage classrooms in ways encouraging pupils nonetheless to remain in control of what they do.

There are other, more general conclusions to reach from a study of constructivist projects. We can split the relationships learners form with their own knowledge from the curricular subjects themselves and decide that both deserve independent consideration. No psychologist or educator wishing to foster conceptual knowledge and application believes that subjection to a 'discipline' is a natural or necessary outcome of subject application alone. A student's willing subordination of time and energy to schoolwork presumes that certain sorts of commitments are brought by learners into classrooms, and the extent to which they are making such commitments depends not so much on the knowledge content of the activity as on a learner's preparedness to tackle it. Over time, engagement with academic work becomes in itself pleasurable and self-motivating, but this very fact recognizes that a relationship (i.e. the overview gained through the achievement of a match between cognitive and knowledge structure) between learners and their knowledge makes a fundamental difference. It is this relationship which can be seen as the prerequisite for continuing advance.

Perhaps most critically for progressivists who seek to learn from constructivist experiments, these demonstrate how teachers, through their organization and styles of teaching, can help pupils stay in touch with their own thinking in order to take themselves forward. Giving learners opportunities for self-determination is essential to any progressivist scheme, corresponding partly to what Blenkin and Kelly (1996) mean by a 'developmental' curriculum. Psychologists, too, studying metacognition (Cardelle-Elewar, 1992), propose that side by side with teachers developing problem-solving skills they have to watch for opportunities to foster personal autonomy and self-confidence in their pupils, since self-monitoring is not, merely, a psychological skill. It is a state of mind which accompanies our own recognition that we are in control of events and able to oversee matters.

It is always tempting for teachers to think that once we have settled on an educational requirement we can teach it as ideas to be memorized or behaviours to be instilled through practice. All of us from time to time are tempted to resort to didacticism as the surest means of guaranteeing a knowledge transfer. Progressivists suppose that a mindful commitment to subjects cannot be taught formally, since it is incorporated within pupils' changing values. Values are, by definition, ways of knowing and thinking we have freely chosen. They are certainly fostered in classrooms — and, indeed, they have to be fostered interventionally (they do not, naturally, accompany ageing or persistent study). But they are not to be confused with learned facts or actions made routine by training.

Progressivist teachers use all means at their disposal to encourage pupils to feel 'in charge' of what they do, who can then develop through 'strategic' choice (to borrow Woods' 1980 term) a value-relationship with their school subjects. To be honest, none of the writers cited discuss this latter aim but it is implicit in every 'learner-centred' technique they use. In Resnick et al.'s (1992) research, key mathematical ideas were introduced into pupils' discourse quickly, but they were introduced in such a way as to allow pupils to supply their own self-chosen applications imported from outside the classroom. What we learn from these reports is that the committed, 'mindful' engagement with task, which psychologists have noted, is not to be taught as a set of skills. It is part of the relationships with subjects which pupils make when they are free to make them. These relationships can be facilitated or fostered, even 'scaffolded', using techniques such as those Adey and Shayer advocate, but they still rely on students' own voluntary commitment to task. This conclusion underwrites the well-known child-centred maxim that pupils must participate in curricular decision making, but, beyond that, psychologically based studies highlight it by stressing how features of 'process' at issue, grounded in pupils' assimilation of new learning to their existing lives, are not mere 'extras'. Aiming for them is not icing on the cake of general education. It is the cake itself.

Process outcomes

Processes which pattern pupils' relationships with their own learning and those which signal a quality of outcome are, often enough, the same processes, separated through evaluation rather than their having a distinctiveness of content. We can see why this is so. There are two complementary dimensions to a 'process' relationship: pupils will appreciate and feel in control of what they learn within a pupil-centred environment, but the knowledge gained has its own independent role (i.e. learners transform cultures in order that cultures should transform learners!). I may learn mathematics because puzzling over numbers interests me, but the mathematical skills I acquire should serve my interests in broader ways. They have instrumental value for me — separate from my attitude towards them.

They may even serve communal interests. Students who are committed to classroom tasks rethink these as sources of personal achievement and esteem, but, hopefully, what they ultimately learn will be seen as relevant to the life of the wider community. The simplest example to give is the one which concluded the previous section: while pupils are progressing through self-monitored study, they will (as a matter of course) see the relevance of their studies to their lives and will recognize the applicability of what they learn. Given that knowledge application is linked to understanding (by writers such as Désforges, 1993, and cognitive psychologists such as Salomon and Gibberson, 1987, and Voss, 1987), it is also publicly desirable, in that the worth of studies to a community must, somewhere, include how far they can be applied to real-life problems. But there is a difference between a sign of quality learning (part of methodology) and the process dimension of outcomes (what methodologies are designed to attain), so it will prove useful to discuss, briefly, process outcomes separately from the part they have in day-to-day teaching.

To formulate curricular processes as outcomes is to formulate them as criteria for the effectiveness of a course of teaching. We look at what will tell us that our 'process'-oriented curricula have actually worked. Recognizing that we are looking for sure signs of progress in the acquisition of knowledge and skills, teachers will usually conceive their broader child-centred purposes in developmental terms. They will oversee not only children's learning of facts and skills, but their pupils' broader intellectual, social and personal growth. And one approximate way of parting process outcomes from other sorts of attainment is to note the former's developmental status: insofar as 'processes' are seen as emotional commitments and attitudes, controlling perspectives and conceptualized knowledge, they are likely to be related to developmental change rather than the straight learning of topics. Earlier developmental analysis was meant to reveal the conditions for pupils ultimately achieving 'higher-order' skills which will serve their interests as lifelong learners. So it is worth reviewing process outcomes, interpreted as cognitive, social and personal achievements, in the context of the new-look developmentalism which has been introduced and check how far the progressivist values underwriting process statements might also need revision.

Cognitive outcomes

Standing firm on his neo-Piagetian beliefs about teaching and learning, Martin Shayer (1992) writes that the main improvements he finds in children's learning, when they have undertaken a programme such as that designed to teach Science reported above (Adey and Shayer, 1994), are changes in cognitive structure. Children progress in ways detectable through the sorts of clinical testing Piaget made famous, rather than it being so easily measurable through the more usual academic pencil-and-paper forms of testing. The latter progress happens, but, unless developmental change is accompanied by teaching geared to a school syllabus (as in the Adey and Shayer project), it is typically delayed for around a year or so. As Shayer says, where a programme of teaching takes a written syllabus as its object of study, immediate gains will be in that course of study, but it will be clear to anyone reading about these projects that they are not accomplished quickly, and if it were short-term formal gains we were looking for we would probably turn to a different kind of teaching.

There may be a cost to pay for wanting children's achievements to transcend their learning, simply, to give set answers to set questions. Progress may be neither rapid nor easily measurable. To repeat what Shayer takes pains to clarify, this cost is not inevitable, since teachers can use National Curriculum materials in their lessons, and they can help students, directly, to 'bridge' between subject areas, achieving learning transfer (Adey and Shayer, 1996). But, once we accept a teacher's time limitations, it may well be that achieving one set of goals makes rather less likely their achieving of another. Fortunately, the cost described is one that teachers are probably willing to meet. One doesn't have to look far into interview research with teachers to find that Shayer's reasoning about outcomes based on an empirical review has echoes in many practitioners' reasoning based on their experiences of trying to maintain a quality provision in schools. When asked about changes they have observed occurring because of their implementation of the National Curriculum, a number complain about 'not going into any depth' and being forced to 'skate over the surface' of subjects (Silcock, 1995; Silcock and Wyness, 1997). What they are complaining about is that as soon as they are impelled to conform to a transmission model of teaching, there is a loss of 'in-depth' learning. Teaching aimed at process goals takes time. And in so far as teachers do try to help learners make a positive relationship with their own learning (in order to guarantee worthwhile outcomes), they can only do so by pacing their teaching to ensure that children continue to understand what they learn and stay committed to task.

This does not mean that children taught in a pupil-centred way will always suffer in public examinations by contrast with their more traditionally taught peers.

It is just that they might appear to make slow progress in the short term. Relevant to this general issue is Galton's (1998b) revisiting of his ORACLE research (Observational Research and Classroom Learning Evaluation: Galton et al., 1980) to assess the effects of the National Curriculum during its first ten years. He believes he finds evidence for a lowering rather than a raising of standards evident over the full period. He partly blames such a situation on the tendency of teachers to focus on the formal delivery of subjects rather than concentrate on ways of making sure that children actually understand what they learn. Galton's belief reinforces Shayer's connecting of developmental improvement to formal test results: it is tacitly proposing that although slower-paced, informal teaching may not 'deliver' the goods so immediately and obviously in the first instance, it does so over a lengthier period.

The positive point to glean from empirical studies based on neo-Piagetian principles (such as the ones described), aligned here with a 'new progressivist' ideology, is that they do produce *developmental* gains: pupils are incorporating their school experiences within their expanding personalities. One would hazard that if we are serious about achieving 'quality' outcomes we might move to the sorts of profiling schemes used, for example, in many parts of Australia (Brady, 1997). It is unfortunate that in England we do place a heavy reliance on the summative testing of performance outcomes — rather than on trying to uncover more basic changes by assessing the ongoing, formative effects of teaching. Few would argue that education is solely concerned with test and exam results. Yet the way educational systems tend to be evaluated relies heavily on results which can be ordered into form or class tables, exam scores and school league tables.

If we are not careful, within such systems the 'performance' tail comes to wag the 'educational' dog. For example, presently, in primary schools, teachers are encouraged to teach literacy and numeracy skills in periods devoted centrally to standard exercises and procedures. No one doubts the importance of teaching children to read. But we need to remember what reading is for: its value lies in its function as a way of accessing information for a wide variety of purposes (including the pleasurable). Once we detach it from its accessing function, we may appear to set its performance characteristics (how well children demonstrate reading skills) above the others, giving pupils confused messages about why they are learning to read at all. Since it is perfectly possible for someone who is learning to read skilfully for their own purposes not to 'perform' quite so well when their skills are formally tested, this confusion of messages can inhibit not assist learning. Making our value-messages clear to learners is fundamental, given that there are no actions teachers take which do not have value-implications.

This is, partly, why the outcomes which progressivist teachers press for are characterized by 'process' terms such as understanding, commitment, applicability, relevance and the extent to which they help learners make sense of their own particular life-situations. By focusing on these, teachers are advertising to their pupils what they believe are the true ends of education and that the performance aspects, though useful indicators of progress, are subsidiary. They are committing themselves to one sort of teaching rather than another because they believe that such teaching will be effective over a long period. What evidence we have suggests

Curricular Values

that they are right in thinking that outcomes related to lifelong achievements have to be gained through specially designed curricula (i.e. acknowledging and fostering relationships between learners and their knowledge).

Social outcomes

Were it demonstrated that progressivist teaching produced long-term developmental gains at the expense of very specific outcomes we might have to modify child-centred practices, for what was advised earlier was that children need to learn highly specific skills to access academic knowledge. Children taught within 'process' curricula benefit, it seems, in an all-round intellectual sense, so the question asked — as it is asked — does not arise. It is developmental progress which opens the way, for example, to the learning of 'higher order' skills, such as the ability to apply one's ideas critically. But it does arise in a slightly different context. Process curricula are geared to the states of mind and attitudes of learners, not to the achievement of limited objectives (that was Stenhouse's starting point for designing them). And, from time to time, teachers do have a responsibility for teaching material whether or not learners seem prepared to assimilate it — this might depend on many sorts of circumstance, but most often it will depend on what is happening within a parent society.

Progressivism is individualistic in its approach. And individuals may not naturally want to combat any prejudices or biases expressed in the attitudes of people around them. For this reason, critics have suggested that progressivism's enhancing of the role of individuals overlooks the fact that much learning considered obligatory in primary schools originates from socio-economic circumstances found in contemporary life (Boyd, 1989; Brehony, 1992; Epstein, 1993; Lowe, 1987; Lawton, 1992; Onore and Lubetsky, 1992). Lawton's (1989, 1992) slight distaste for progressivist teaching is owed to his belief that it encourages the self-seeking inertia in all of us at the expense of socializing learners to their wider public duties as citizens. Epstein (1993) and Walkerdine (1994) offer more or less the same objection, though in the former case, the culprit is adjudged to be a particularly doctrinaire view of child-development: Epstein (1993) thinks that once child-centred teachers accept that even the youngest children can come to grips with socially potent issues and acquire critical perspectives, progressivism can become appropriately politicized. Walkerdine (1994) is more pessimistic. Her tendency, like that of the 'new left' in general, is to go 'beyond progressivism' (Cole and Hill, 1996; Jones, 1983; Brehony, 1992). Many socialists and egalitarians are impatient with classroom policies which indulge the wishes of individuals at the expense of the common good.

It is not hard to accept criticisms concerning the dangers of teachers overindulging children's natural biases. After all, progressivist teachers elicit and respect pupils' existing views, whereas in order to become fully fledged citizens, pupils must become aware of their own civic responsibilities and have a due respect for the dignity of others. This may mean their rejecting an ingrained prejudice towards another group which they bring with them to school, and such a rejection goes beyond that of modification or gradual change. It is important to accept the strength of this criticism: a teacher may be looking for some immediate reversing of a pupil attitude in situations where, for example, racist harassment has occurred.

But, while accepting the criticism, we still have to demarcate progressivist ideology from the ambitions of the reconstructionists (Lawton, 1989) or socialists (Brehony, 1992; Cole and Hill, 1996; Jones, 1983) who wish to liberate the political purposes of schools. The sort of socially transformative role for schools which socialists urge may be an outcome of the culturally resourced self-transformation which child-centred teachers look out for, but it is not its inevitable complement. Teachers who want to 'change society' may claim to be progressivists (as did the staff of William Tyndale school), but the empowerment of pupils implies for them a democratic not a subversive role in a contemporary state. Child-centred teachers may wish to right social wrongs, but that aspiration, as it is stated, is not integral to progressivist thinking.

Certainly, all teachers are gatekeepers for their larger communities, and they have in modern times acquired or had ascribed to them a role which may mean their organizing lessons in highly structured ways, since these do not always arise out of pupils' normal experiences (they sometimes do of course). Equal opportunities issues have reminded teachers over recent years of their dual responsibilities — towards a wider community and the personal ambitions of the individuals they teach. Not coincidentally, what characterizes modern progressivist teaching is exactly the willingness of teachers to undertake the social responsibilities outlined. Because the concept of individual child development is not value-free, some degree of 'framing' or 'scaffolding' of children's progress will always be justified within primary classrooms.

A difference between the teacher who favours a 'process' curriculum and one who delivers prioritized knowledge in a more direct manner is that the former will maintain pupils' personal commitment to whatever they must learn, even though this may involve a more diverse and laborious effort than if teachers just teach set lessons. And recognizing that the learning being discussed is basically ethical (entailing a sense of responsibility and respect for others' differences), one would presume that it is only through a sincere commitment that ethical concepts can, in fact, be properly applied to social situations. In the absence of such a commitment, pupils soon become as skilled as adults at producing token gestures or reproducing slick answers to expected questions. At least, within curricula where pupils' attitudes towards their own knowledge are seen as securing the importance of the knowledge itself, it becomes possible to make sense of issues of individual respect and responsibility for, at bottom, teachers are showing pupils the very respect they are trying to teach.

A more routine difficulty for progressivist teaching arises from any conflict existing between what teachers might see as a desirable learning outcome and what interests learners themselves. As argued, schools are places where pupils have to climb from a personally structured value-system to a more publicly referenced one, and this transition is unlikely to be achieved easily. It is hardly a novel insight, but it is worth reminding ourselves that teaching can be smoothy managed and professionally enriching, but it can also be very tough and frustrating! And what makes all the difference is that invisible gap between individual and public value. If the gap is especially large, it may be impossible to bridge and education fails. Fortunately, the bridging process is, usually, routinely managed and, where it is not, the problem posed for teachers is, at least, made manifest so that various ways of resolving it can be tested out.

When Marilyn Osborne (1997) tried out some observational research as a way of evaluating her own science teaching, she noticed that a daily rivalry between individuals and the larger group stimulated progress rather than hindering it. She concluded that individual children reporting their efforts faced verbal challenges, or would realize that they hadn't altogether succeeded in ways appreciated by their teacher or by the rest of their class, but they wouldn't suffer from more than a mild or temporary loss of esteem. More usually, they sought to improve what they did in order to gain approval. Her judgment on her research was that although there was a gap between individual and group values and purposes, it was the tensions created by this gap which, in part, encourage children to greater efforts to improve in their work.

Personal outcomes

It has to be true that the paramount gains for individuals within a child-centred classroom are those following on teachers' respect for learners' personal values. Once we acknowledge that even the youngest child is (and has to be) an agent for his or her own learning, we are put under an obligation to ensure that whatever is studied has not only the compliance of pupils but is learned in ways that make sense to them. We find ourselves within the 'neo-Piagetian' paradigm which invokes learners' viewpoints as a preliminary to introducing new ones and look for the process indicators which tell us that in-depth or quality learning is occurring. In short, we become progressivists. The qualification that Richard Peters (1966) once pithily stated, that simply affirming children's interests may not be in their interests, is always at the back of a modern schoolteacher's mind, but what this qualification doesn't say is that children's interested commitment to learning doesn't matter. To know what is in the interests of learners does not tell us how we should teach valued knowledge — to discover *that*, we have to look at what we know about learning and cognitive development, and rediscover how intellectual change is always self-managed, though it has to be managed within a value-laden context.

If we are honest, much of what children learn in school becomes hived off from what they learn outside the institution as 'school' knowledge and, up to a point, there is nothing wrong with knowledge learned instrumentally; pupils also discover that to memorize topics in this way may make these accessible for exam and interview purposes. What progressivists suppose is that methodologies which engage learners' activities do have a chance of achieving more fundamental ends — as well as allowing examination passes. They seek to develop pupils' minds so as to enrich their personal lives. Developmental theory shows us that even the youngest infants are 'whole' people, as deserving of respect (within the terms they themselves establish) as those of any other individual. Because they are young, they have needs transcending their own personal interests and attitudes, but it is no less true that their lives are of as much intrinsic value as are the lives of an adult. Progressivist, process-oriented teaching is geared more to that essentially humanist realization perhaps than to any other.

Progressivism and educational humanism

Re-establishing the personal commitment of learners to school knowledge as a first aim for teachers repositions progressivism within the mainstream of humanistic movements in education. Humanistic educators, like progressivists, as perceived by Hall and Hall (1988), are:

> ... concerned with the whole person, [aiming] for the full development of the individual. (p. 16)

Humanism, like progressivism, has evolved over centuries. It has existed since classical times in the views of those who have insisted that respect is owed to any persons solely because they are human. The idea of personal 'dignity', which is central to debates about human rights, implies that our very humanness should be a guarantor of our respectful treatment by others. This notion inspired Kant (1781), as it did Rousseau (see Lukes, 1973). What has changed historically, in ways affecting both progressivist and humanist movements, are our perceptions of the sorts of creatures we are, and the nature of the forces which are trying to subdue us. There are many sorts of humanness, as there are of the tyrannies which threaten it, so there are many sorts of educational humanism, and for some writers, the term 'humanism' itself is no more than an umbrella sheltering beneath it the humane viewpoints of many otherwise very different people (Davies, 1997; Southern, 1970).

Traditionally, the humanist movement has allied intimately with science (see Blackham, 1976) in its long war against religious dogmatism. During the period of the philosophical Enlightenment, Rousseau's humanism (Grimsley, 1973; Tarrant, 1989) pitched him at odds with what he saw as a corrupting society: he championed the rights of individuals to break free from the chains of social tyranny. What he did not believe was that individuals could learn, unaided, how to defend themselves against social corruption while being shielded from it within rural settings, as has been suggested (e.g. by Dewey: see Darling, 1994). The 'horticultural' metaphor for child-centred teaching is usually blamed on Rousseau (Alexander, 1994; Dearden, 1972a; Sugrue, 1997) but it isn't the only way to interpret his writings, and it isn't the most relevant one for teachers. Plants do not interact with each other or with their 'gardeners'. Darling (1994) to an extent rehabilitates Rousseau's ideas within progressivist literature by explaining to us how the philosopher was in his own way an 'interventionist'. In Rousseau's descriptions of Émile's education (1762/1911),

Émile's tutor leads the boy towards insightful ways of judging the world, in a gentle and considerate manner, using strategies not easy to detect but which thereby leave his student ruler of his own mind much as modern constructivists and child-centred teachers seek to do. As Darling comments:

> pedagogical power is deployed so discreetly that Émile is unaware that many of his apparently chance experiences are in fact engineered by his manipulative mentor. (pp. 28–9)

Moreover, the point of Émile's education was not to shelter him forever from social influence, but to ensure that his rationality, gained through a lived experience, would allow him to cope with his society when he rejoined it (Darling, 1994; also Tarrant, 1989).

More recently, scientists' desire to subordinate reason itself to physical, psychological or sociological 'laws', i.e. to assume that human beings are explicable in terms of wider social and psychological forces, has provoked the strongest humanist counterblast. And it is this conflict which reverberates within education, for as soon as we regard our own minds as subject to empirical laws we are on the road to developing technologies which will exploit those laws for 'transmission' purposes. For an educational humanist, it is unacceptable to deal with others purely in terms of those behaviourist, cognitive, socio-cultural and psychoanalytic models which constrain our minds and personalities within rule-governed systems. It is of course permissible to allow psychological and sociological approaches to inform our thinking, as teachers and theorists, but we have to guard against regarding our students as 'no more than' bundles of behaviours to be conditioned, 'inputs and outputs' of information to be managed, unconscious drives sublimated in ways they do not understand, organisms unknowingly seeking equilibration or as self-deluded, culturally strung puppets.

Human reason is irreducible to fundamental processes (which is not to say that we cannot discover the conditions which foster it). And it is because we are rational that we are able to decide our own futures for ourselves. Sartre (1948) anchors existentialism to the idea that human beings have no choice but to create their own existence from their own self-awareness: 'man', he says, 'is what he makes of himself' and 'man *is* freedom' (p. 34). He does not find this situation in the least upsetting, but acknowledges it as the foundation for our most precious ideals. The fact that we are responsible for ourselves is 'alone compatible with the dignity of man ... it is the only [fact] which does not make man into an object' (pp. 44, 45). Popper's (1994) denial that societies are 'super-organic' entities somehow controlling our lives, and Isaiah Berlin's (1969) warning that our social institutions can usurp our freedoms as well as defend them, explore the same belief that human reason should not be subordinated to anything more meaningful than itself. We (not our parent societies, governments or cultures, or our social institutions) are responsible for ourselves and our destinies.

A belief in the irreducibility of rational thought does not suggest that we have no responsibilities towards others as well as towards ourselves in both our social and educational lives. And just as a humanist commitment to the rights of individuals has always been tempered by the recognition that social responsibility accompanies such a commitment, so must that same recognition inform the work of progressivist teachers. Otherwise, some new 'humanistic' form of education could defeat the progressivist cause before it becomes fully prepared for a third millennial upsurge. This has already happened in Japan where, according to Abiko (1998), a progressivist phase of educational policy was succeeded by an academic or 'essentialist' phase and, now, by a 'humanistic' phase. Because humanists know that individuality has to be expressed within a community (Blackham, 1976), a divorcing of progressivism from humanism occurs the moment progressivist teaching becomes individualistic in the sense of it being geared to the purely personal. In this country, interviews with child-centred teachers (Silcock and Wyness, 1997) reveal a widespread contrary assumption — that pupil individuality is inextricably bound up with its expression within a cultural context. Blatchford and Blatchford predicate a largely 'progressivist' text called *Educating the Whole Child* very much on this assumption (1995).

The most frequently made distinction between a positivistic and humanist approach within education is that which divides statistically based research methods from qualitative forms of data analysis. Both have validity. Yet it isn't accidental that the statistical investigations which most hurt progressivism did so by 'reducing' the ideology to some observable forms of behaviour — such as teaching style. Both the 1976 Bennett research and Galton's ORACLE project (Galton et al., 1980) — which contributed to the discussion paper of Alexander et al. (1992) meant to discredit progressivist methodology — used 'objective' observations as raw data. Humanistic studies holistically connect teachers' ideological intentions with their values and practices, which can then be assessed in terms of the interactive relationships between parts and whole (examples are Sugrue's 1997 case studies). These are more likely to convince us both of the existence of child-centred practices and of their efficacy.

As argued, many (though not all) kinds of individualistic approaches in education are rooted in the humanitarian ethic which underwrites much contemporary humanistic philosophy and social science (see, for example, Gauld and Shotter, 1977; Harré et al., 1985; Pring, 1997), including the scientific humanism of Karl Popper (1977, 1994; with Eccles, 1977). This moral position recognizes children's rights for no other reason than that children are human beings and, because they are, will have a unique point of view on the world which can, and should, be respected. Children are thought to be true individuals from birth, with rights of ownership over what they do. Their rights are never absolute, as children are minors. But, to teachers, it makes sense to be cautious about any strategy which potentially excludes any one child's personal interests.

Once children are regarded as 'formed' human beings, whatever their age, their relationships with teachers can be seen as transcending set curricula and the practical tasks in hand. Teaching a subject effectively is not to be founded on teaching skill, the intrinsic quality of texts and teaching materials, or even the cognitive abilities of learners. It is the relationships between the various elements in the educative process which will determine outcomes — i.e. the extent to which each element responds sensitively to the others. That relationship is contextualized by a teacher acknowledging pupils as fully contributing partners in the teaching/ learning process. For a progressivist, as for a humanist, teachers and learners are part of an undivided community, committed — as a community — to the advancement of knowledge (eloquently put as a credo of educational humanism by Richard Pring, 1997). School learning is seen as a voyage of discovery for all involved rather than as an apprenticing of ignorant children to knowledgeable adults (Pring, 1997; Deci and Ryan, 1994; Patterson, 1973; Richards, 1988; Rogers, 1983). Similar explorations of the links between learners, knowledge and task have dignified the writings of successful teachers such as Stephen Rowlands (1987) and John Holt (1975, 1994), as well as the views of modern advocates of 'creative' teaching (Woods, 1995).

To summarize: when teachers speak warmly of their 'child-centredness', they often do so because they assume that longer-term intellectual, social and personal gains only happen through pupils' emotional investment in tasks, as 'whole' individuals, signalled most obviously by learner commitment coupled with a sense of their being in real charge of their own progress. Such a belief finds justification in the humanistic principle that educational values arise out of individual commitment, freely made. If education is a cultural transformation, that transformation — for progressivists — has to be self-managed; it follows from individual learners accepting what is 'on offer' in contexts where their existing motivations are respected and evoked. Along with Pring (1989b), child-centred teachers believe that personal 'empowerment' is not an optional aim for educators, but has to be a conduit for the achievement of any educational purpose which transcends a surface level of teaching.

Chapter 8

Informal Teaching Methods

A formal/informal division between styles or approaches to teaching is used interchangeably with traditionalism/progressivism by many commentators. Teachers themselves have always claimed to be 'formal' or 'informal' in approach. In his appraisal of progressivist achievements, Robin Alexander's (1994) main caveat is that the ideology's antipathy to traditionalism polarizes formal against informal, process against product, whole-class against individualistic methods and so on, restricting teachers' choice of practices unnecessarily. Such polarizing has been already admitted as fatal to effective teaching (Alexander, 1994; Carr, 1988; Mackenzie, 1997; Sharpe, 1997). Because it is, empirical comparisons of whole-class, small-group and individualistic teaching bolstered the government-sponsored 'three wise men' report (Alexander et al., 1992) which was meant to be a watershed in converting primary school teachers from their child-oriented follies. The present HMCI (Chris Woodhead) berates progressive primary school teachers for insufficiently using whole-class teaching. Even the Prince of Wales chides traditionalists and progressivists for their 'fatuous' arguments (1997), implying, presumably, that classroom techniques should be chosen for their effectiveness not their ideological credentials.

In the past, it may well have been true, as one of Jim Callaghan's Yellow Book advisers told him, that 'some have allowed performance in [formal skills] to suffer as a result of the uncritical application of informal methods' (cited Chitty, 1989, p. 75). A few teachers might never — on principle — have taught pupils as a single, whole class. Yet, today, most teachers (if not all) use mixed methods. Many will admit — somewhat paradoxically — to an informal approach while, at the same time, wedding formal to informal techniques. The Plowden Report, commonly seen as a progressivist manifesto, recommended a judicious mix of whole-class, group and individualistic teaching.

At issue is what divorces a teaching method or technique from a broader style, approach or stance, and how the two ways of discussing teacher behaviour actually connect as pedagogic skill. It isn't only that the terms 'formal' and 'informal' have meanings which vary according to usage (although they do), it is that varying usage easily leads to uncertainties about meaning — for instance, a clear indication of informality noticed when the term is used to designate teaching style becomes diffuse when it indicates the particular steps a teacher takes to realize his or her style.

To clear up confusions, by seeing better how and why they occur, we need first of all to agree some basic definitions.

The nature of formal and informal teaching

Formality relies on prescription. Anyone who attends a formal occasion, such as a formal dance or dinner, knows there are rules of dress and etiquette to follow. If I make a formal speech or strike a formal pose when addressing an audience, I am falling back on conventions of some sort to add meaning to what I do. Teaching formally means obeying pre-designed rules or conventions. Informality, by contrast, is the abandoning of prescription in favour of adapting behaviour to situations as they occur. To act informally is, on this definition, not to worry about given rules but to take soundings from whatever happens and try to 'fit' actions to changing atmospheres, evolving scenarios or whatever. Informal teaching methods are used by teachers who adapt actions to circumstance, and it is quite proper for teachers of any ideological persuasion to teach informally.

What suits informality to progressivism is that its flexibility allows teacher actions to be matched to learner need. Learner needs — in progressivist curricula — can be summarized as whatever is entailed by ensuring that school pupils not only develop valued concepts, skills and qualities, but acquire these in self-managed, personally committed ways. A good way to understand child-centred informality, then, is to say that teachers teach pragmatically, as John Dewey recommended (1916/1899; also Kelly, 1986; Tomlinson, 1997). Although the needs of learners are tied in with circumstances, the accommodations of each to the other are not mechanically achieved. Teachers have to strive to maintain an honest allegiance to both, and they are most likely to succeed where they refuse to be bound too closely by pre-set curricula.

Naturally, where child-centred teaching suits actions to need, this does not stigmatize whole-class teaching. Teachers might train whole groups of children for progressivist reasons (perhaps as preparation for autonomous peer-group study: Cooper, 1993), while others might instruct individuals in a specified skill or concept (sometimes called 'direct' instruction — see Galton, 1989a). In these circumstances, we find ideological differences in the stated justifications for methodologies, not in their physical features. Empiricists who compare methodologies without checking teacher justifications cannot make the ideological points they think they make — they are using 'positivistic' research methods to assess 'humanistic' pedagogies. And those who condemn progressivists' informality or who wish to convert teachers to more whole-class teaching are attacking chimera. They need to examine more closely the rich detail of classrooms to see, better, the poor teaching, which is ideologically neutral, that should be condemned.

Now, any teacher who wants to guarantee the quality relationships between learner and knowledge suggested above will, often enough, teach individuals and small groups. The overt tell-tales of progressivism are curricular and pedagogic diversity. But, to restate: 'whole-class' instruction has its honourable place in any curriculum — how much is used depends on what are judged to be learner requirements. One can hardly condemn this rule of thumb — of selecting methods to suit whatever is taken to decide effective teaching. But we have, again, to cut off child-centred pragmatism from the present-day educational slogan of 'goodness of fit' or 'fitness for purpose', mooted by Alexander et al. (1992). As noted earlier, this phrase, which was perhaps meant to supersede ideological principle, is either a catch-all for any potentially successful technique (depending on what is being fitted to what) or is — more worryingly — itself an ideological slogan.

Relatively little attention has been given to pragmatism in the educational literature (Richards' 1988 discussion is one notable exception). So it is worth extending an earlier introduction to it. Educationally, the term 'pragmatism' is used in three main ways. It is linked thematically to modern versions of the philosophical movement called pragmatism (see Mounce, 1997), and in that guise (as earlier discussed in Chapter 3) it promotes a view of educational decision making as having to use criteria situated in — and validated by — context. Secondly, it is an essential characteristic of the job of teaching owing to teaching being an essentially practical enterprise — the vast majority of classroom decisions have a pragmatic dimension of some sort, in that these decisions will take into account contingencies of circumstance and resource. Thirdly, it is a useful way of defining an informal teaching method: to be pragmatic is to avoid pre-set (formal) rules. On the basis of this analysis, we find that although all teachers are pragmatists when they take account of circumstances they cannot ignore, some are ideologically predisposed to pragmatism, believing 'goodness of fit' solves all main questions. Child-centred practitioners stay mid-way between the two camps in that they make methodological decisions pragmatically to achieve their ideological aims.

It is likely that many confusions which arise when we discuss teaching method arise because the very profusion of possibilities in classrooms is not reflected by a rich language, so we are forced to over-use the terms we do have, and risk misclassifying a complex scene. Yet we do need to grasp the nettle of complexity if we are to be sure of our educational policies. Any approach to school curricula which is not traditionalist or progressive is likely to be pragmatic, in that criteria are required to help curricular designers choose from one set of beliefs or another, and the only criteria existing outside value-orientations are those respecting the effect of circumstances. An educational 'third way' has to be that of pragmatism. There are many versions of pragmatic decision making in contemporary educational literature, and it is educative to examine some of these as, often enough, they are thought to supersede the more overtly ideological. Firstly, each of the main types of pragmatism identified relates in a loose but nonetheless direct way to a contemporary approach or policy towards good teaching which is considered ideologically neutral.

Pragmatic methodologies

Technical rationality identifies beliefs about teaching held by those who see it is as essentially a practical business, and that a close study of what good teachers 'do' will reveal a number of constituent components (sometimes called 'competencies') which can be understood and taught to others (including apprentice teachers). Good or effective teaching is known to be good because it matches up to a public blueprint thought to be exemplary by those who have studied it. *Reflective practice,* on the other hand, is a term used by a number of writers who find teaching to be a complex judgmental process, entailing rapid decision making made by professionals who have discovered what works through long experience. The virtues of quality teaching derive from the implicit theories and ideas of teachers that are built into their actions rather than it matching up to some publicly agreed criteria. Debates revolving around these two models of what is or is not 'good teaching', though usually contrasted (Carr and Kemmis, 1986; Schôn, 1983), are mirror images of each other in the way they both occupy territory thought to be ideologically neutral, theoretically speaking, though for very different reasons.

Those who look at what does or does not make for good educational practice in terms of measured outcomes are resolutely committed to showing how some practices are more effective in achieving pre-set aims than are others. It is a matter of teachers selecting the appropriate technique for a circumstance and, providing they get this 'formula' right, they will (by nature) be teaching well. The very existence of an OFSTED (Office for Standards in Education) presumes that some system following rules of technical rationality can apply to teaching. That is why OFSTED's handbooks (e.g. 1995b) sometimes list effectiveness indicators, borrowed from empirical research, to signpost criteria lodged in the OFSTED framework by which teachers are judged during inspections. Admittedly, OFSTED inspectors use their professional judgment to discern more than one 'model' of good teaching. When they enter schools, they are meant to leave their personal biases behind them, so that they can apply their framework to all possible expressions of excellence. 'Effectiveness' research, too (Caldwell and Spinks, 1988; Sammons et al., 1995; Mortimore et al., 1988), underwrites teaching competencies, pointing to what turns them into good practice by qualifying them valuatively (teachers are 'motivated and capable', 'highly involved' in decision making, resources are 'adequate' and headteachers 'supportive' of staff needs, and so on: Caldwell and Spinks, 1988, pp. 31–2).

In other words, both OFSTED and effectiveness researchers are careful not to step on the ideological toes of practitioners (though there may be ideological biases colouring both the OFSTED framework and empirical research agendas); they do not venture far beyond very general descriptions and consider the professional insights actually used by different teachers to direct their actions (the beliefs they hold about how pupils learn for example) in specified circumstances. This sets the outer limits of the technical-rational approach to the design of good teaching, which is not that we cannot discover at a very high level of abstraction a common blueprint, but there will be very many ways to interpret that blueprint (because it is so general or abstract) and it is in its interpretation that much of the meat and drink of good teaching lies.

What we have in teaching are a number of competencies which all teachers will deploy in some way at some time or other, depending on their interpretations of the circumstances concerned, matched to their broader purposes. It is worth knowing what these competencies are: but simply looking for them in a teacher's behaviour will never allow us to predict whether outcomes will be achieved or not.

The primacy of a teacher's purposes (that these focus on more fundamental matters over and above the competencies themselves) mean that even the most general statements cannot always guarantee good practice. Caldwell and Spinks (1988), in their search for 'the effective school', admit:

> not all [effectiveness criteria] will be found in any one highly effective school and ... some schools which are considered highly effective may have some characteristics which are in fact the opposite of those listed. (p. 30)

Teachers who turn to the literature on reflective practice for guidance on how to use their skills would find themselves in exactly the same quandary as those who, faced with a classroom dilemma, turn to OFSTED handbooks for informed help. There are many detailed accounts of how professionals 'think in action' or 'converse' with situations (Schön, 1983), solving problems rapidly through creating 'theories of the moment' and so on. But there is nothing in process descriptions themselves which help us to stretch our minds beyond a grasp of what is professionally competent. Long experience and routine expertise do not, in themselves, make for excellence in teaching: practitioners may 'reflect' consistently and show extraordinary pragmatic expertise without achieving the sorts of outcomes we would normally expect to find in a successful school. For example, a highly autocratic teacher, or someone with dubious political motives or who intends to indoctrinate pupils with an unsavoury religious fervour, may be mentally astute and pragmatically gifted.

To be fair to those who write about reflective practice, few see it is a comprehensive statement of what it means to teach well, and a number add their own theoretical slant to mainstream accounts (Griffiths and Tann, 1992; Pollard, 1997; McIntyre, 1992; Zeichner and Liston, 1987), sometimes proposing hierarchies of reflection which teachers might develop, from the most intuitive to the most critically penetrating (Zeichner and Liston, 1987; Griffiths and Tann, 1992; McIntyre, 1992). Obviously, we have to recognize practical skill, and to realize that there is more involved in it than the triggering of conditioned actions. Conceiving pedagogy as reflective practice is a real step forward in our coming to grasp the sociopsychological processes involved. What we must add to the repertoire of the skilled practitioner is a sufficient control of his or her skills to allow them to deploy these in ways which are known to be developmentally sensitive and socially responsible (in the long as well as the short term), coupled with a clear-sightedness about aims.

The lesson to be learned from this short exploration of two well-known approaches to pedagogy is that if good teaching is not a wholly technical enterprise, neither can it be judged as solely the imaginative deployment of professional skills. Teaching methods have to be applied dexterously, in obedience to whatever rules operate, in context. Yet neither in its operation nor in its objectives can teaching escape being fitted to the premises built into some ideological conception or other. As 'model' approaches to our studies of good practice, technical rationality and reflective decision making provide the best examples we have (practically paradigm cases) of the way two competing pragmatic philosophies might persuade us that a liberation from ideology is possible. Technical rationality assumes that we can always link technique to circumstance (in the way that a craftsperson following craft rules achieves) and that doing so is the high road to quality teaching. Schôn's version of reflective practice, in its preoccupation with teachers' contextually focused artistry (akin to musicianship), makes pragmatic skill itself an end rather than a means to an end. For progressivists, pragmatism is without question a means to an end, and is eschewed both as a sole criterion for classroom decision making and as an ideal of performance.

It is probably laudable to wish to conceptualize teaching capability as a technical enterprise or as a set of contextually refined professional skills. Insofar as these efforts succeed (and — to repeat — they both succeed at a fairly general level), their ideologically 'neutral' viewpoints certainly escape the possibilities of bias and a narrowing of ambition which can be linked to value-commitments. But they only do this by missing out within their schemes the requirement at the heart of good practice that teachers direct their skills in line with their values. This omission is not a trivial one: it tells us what might make the crucial difference to success in teaching and hints at why teachers tend not to personalize their own professional skills with the language of either technical rationalism or reflective practice, but stick with terms such as 'formal' and 'informal'.

Technical rationality and reflective practice are the best known pragmatically based ideologies on the contemporary scene, but they aren't the only ones. Anyone who seeks to avoid a commitment to an existing value-orientation, but who wishes to establish some consistent policy towards curricular management, must follow a pragmatic line. So Billig et al. (1988), when imagining alternative guidelines to the progressive and traditionalist, pin their colours to an ideology they call 'dilemmatic', since teachers need to draw on any approach they can to solve their day-to-day practical difficulties. They refer to other interactionist studies (Berlak and Berlak, 1981) which reconcile opposing theoretical tendencies (e.g. focusing learner need or subject demands) within every teachers' desire for practical solutions to practical problems. Billig et al. (1988) recognize that although teachers often enough have to find a place for both 'progressive' and 'transmission' methods in their teaching, 'it would not appear to be a simple matter to define precisely what that place should be' (p. 50). Similarly, there is a fundamental problem confronting any teacher who feels drawn to a child-centred ideology: '[h]ow do you get children to invent and discover for themselves precisely what the curriculum pre-ordains must be discovered?' (p. 50).

Unfortunately, a 'dilemmatic ideology' (p. 54) does not tell us how a teacher confronting the 'forked path' of a dilemma can choose which direction to take. To say that all options should be open is to miss the point that if they are all 'open' at the level of value-commitments, a teacher will have no criterion by which to choose how to proceed. A true dilemma is a dilemma precisely because alternatives press equally upon our minds unless we have prior duties to guide us. Accordingly, teachers trying to decide on either a formal or informal technique, or whether or not to 'scaffold' children's problem-solving towards a known set of outcomes (perhaps written into a National Curriculum), have to resolve their dilemmas by reference to their professional values. Being open-minded in itself is no help to them. Certainly, teachers have to be pragmatic. But they are pragmatic in the service of other aims — otherwise their pragmatism is dulled into a sameness, a mediocrity.

Galton (1995), too, banks on a close empirical study of classrooms as the guide for teachers' practices. Having decided that empirical research shows how 'progressivist' teaching (e.g. children being 'provided with individual assignments') is less effective than interactive 'whole class teaching' (p. 16), he reduces the findings of his ORACLE studies (Observational Research and Classroom Learning Evaluation: Galton et al., 1980) to a few salient lessons. He decides that it is not the styles of teaching themselves which matter. Neither class teaching nor individualized instruction are to be blamed for failed learning or offered as reasons for success. What matters is the opportunity methods provide for teachers to engage in 'certain types of exchange . . . or interaction' such as the asking of 'challenging questions', and for ensuring that pupils 'pay greater attention and concentrate on their work' (p. 17). Galton's studies find that whole-class teaching, on balance, gives teachers more opportunities to engage in these valued sorts of exchange. He goes on to speculate that different methods might be appropriate at different stages in children's education, allowing increasing pupil independence as they internalize more basic skills and capabilities.

Once again, the difficulty with this approach is that we cannot reach the kinds of conclusion Galton does from a study of external circumstances alone (what might be called the pragmatic fallacy). In terms of his discussion of 'whole-class teaching', it is not the exchanges, as described situationally, which he believes follow from the employment of this method that we should be valuing. For one thing, it is very difficult to categorize interactive whole-class teaching as a single method — it can be organized in many ways to achieve different sorts of purposes (see Higgins, 1997). More pertinently, we have no way of knowing through observation what a 'challenging' question is or whether pupils 'paying attention' is likely to lead to learning or not, outside of applying another set of criteria to the pragmatic. Challenging questions are challenging when they engage a learner's current thinking in ways leading to a better understanding of some topic or other. Pragmatic circumstances (of any sort) do not tell us whether that condition is present — we have to look behind behavioural features to that developmental/psychological state of mind supposed, here, to make the difference.

Adey and Shayer (1994) challenged pupils by creating a cognitive dissonance their pupils wished to resolve: this conflict arose in circumstances where pupils' own responses to scientific problems were carefully elicited. In Resnick et al.'s (1992) research, the adults teaching arithmetic were (we can reasonably assume) deploying the sorts of pedagogic skills which OFSTED and 'effectiveness' researchers identify, and of which Galton would probably approve. But they were doing more than that, and any technical descriptions used would not isolate what the researchers themselves are suggesting makes the difference to teachers reaching their educational aims. In the Resnick et al. study, what played a heightened role was the deployment of pragmatic skill to link children's familiar experiences to mathematical tasks and concepts while maintaining these children's value-relationships with their own knowledge. In short, good teaching, on this conception, represents a specialized way of using pedagogic skill. It cannot be reduced to it. The pedagogic model implied in this description, designated psychologically as 'neo-Piagetian', is called here, as an emergent ideology, 'new progressivism'.

Another development in our social life which promises to revolutionize classroom method because of its alteration of the concrete terms within which teaching operates is that connected with the expanded use of information technology. We live in a computer age, and it could be that teachers need only recognize the potential of electronic machines to be able to unlock all manner of possibilities for imaginative teaching. Will not computer wizardry — once its potential is realized — clear the way for new, innovative and reliable modes of teaching? Yet what American studies suggest is that success with IT in the end arises not from the surface appeal or inherent potential of machine technology but from its being wedded to hands-on, 'real life' situations in the 'child-centred' manner (Luban, 1989; Papert, 1980; Weir, 1989). Seymour Papert, creator of LOGO, the computer language used by children, doggedly stays with his Piaget-inspired, child-centred philosophy. His prediction is that, around the time of the new millennium, pupils will, themselves, become 'digitally armed' and begin to succeed educationally through their own efforts, despite the problems associated with western governments' retreat back to an old fashioned vision of education (1980; also Kenny, 1998). Papert knows that computers give teachers a fairly unique opportunity to 'empower' children to take some charge of their own learning, and this is the path ahead he wills us to take.

More general research into the technical features of teaching methods is that of Tomlinson (1995), who delves into the 'learning potential' of our most common teaching strategies, given specified learner and situational conditions. Tomlinson takes us beyond the crudity of 'fitness for purpose' to questions about which kind of teaching will suit which learners in specified situations. As he realizes, what works for one teacher with one set of pupils might not work for another with the same set of pupils. His positioning on the issue of what is or is not good teaching methodology is sound enough. But, possibly, he underestimates the degree of variability he himself introduces when admitting that internal factors, peculiar to teachers and learners, are always likely to intercede in learning. Simon (1981b, echoed by Galton, 1989a) was certainly guilty of that error, criticizing progressivism as stopping the development of a 'scientific' pedagogy, without recognizing that such a pedagogy is impossible, even in principle. The teachers' perennial problem (and the empiricists' limitation) is that the uniqueness of pupil personality can intercede such that prescribed methods may always need modifying to keep faith with aims. No teacher can ever be certain that any one technique will, in fact, work with any one pupil. This is why aims and values are decided prior to method. Teachers must always be prepared to alter their actions to suit their aims (this is the simply stated justification for informality). Much confused discussion in education reduces to an understandable reluctance we all have to disentangle empirical issues from deeper problems posed by disagreements about values and beliefs.

To repeat: because teachers must modify techniques to keep faith with aims, what will separate the pragmatism of teachers with different ideologies will be

Informal Teaching Methods

the sorts of modifications they believe are needed to maintain their stance. If, like many educationists, they are ideological pragmatists believing that it is always a matter of 'horses for courses', and that one doesn't need any other criteria to decide methodology, such a belief will create a 'mixed economy' with the strengths and weaknesses which have already been discussed. The pragmatism of the child-centred teacher can be described in a variety of ways, but it is linked to known value-oriented aims. And it has to be. For teachers to be successful in problem-solving they need more than pragmatic skill, they need a goal outside pragmatism itself at which to aim. This is unavoidable.

Dewey was one of the founders of pragmatic philosophy and also a stalwart American progressivist. He was able to combine pragmatism with a belief in progressivist education, because he believed that any education which was effective had to make sense to the pupils themselves in terms of their own experiences. But this did not lead him into the trap of believing that there were no principles outside of lived experience which we need to guide us. As Pring (1989a) notices, the very titles of Dewey's books (e.g. *The Child and Society, The Child and the Curriculum, The School and Society*) showed that his intention was to integrate individually lived experiences with established social values. The ambition here, too, has been to show that not only is there no contradiction between fostering individual pupils' development and recognizing the social ends of teaching, one presumes the other. That is: if we extend developmental principles so that their implications are properly worked out in terms of the classroom social order which will embody them, what results is a special sort of democratically aligned community. Because Dewey's educational writings centred on the socio-political themes mentioned, it is worth returning briefly to this element of progressivist theory.

Dewey and a democratic primary school classroom

Dewey was the philosopher whose thinking affirmed many of the principles being discussed. He knew that the practical circumstances most pressing on teachers' day-to-day teaching decisions arose from teachers having to reconcile individual children's needs and actions with a school's aims of preparing its pupils to live in a democratic state (Dewey, 1916). These social aims for education didn't blind him to the even more basic condition affecting a teacher's work, that such a reconciliation had to become a part of pupils' daily experiences if it were to be consistently achieved: Dewey's pragmatism (e.g. Blenkin and Kelly, 1981; Blyth, 1984; Darling, 1994) sensitized him to the idea that anything which was not integrated in pupils' experiences would ultimately prove of little value to them.

Dewey's staunch 'bipartisan' philosophy (stressing individual experience and social context equally) isn't always acknowledged. This is because many modern writers can, justly, claim something of Dewey's influence within their own traditions, a fact true for ideological pragmatists, reflective practitioners, postmodernists and cultural psychologists as much as those promoting individualism. For example: in putting together the thesis that culture dominates human development, Wertsch

(1991) cites Dewey's 1901 presidential address to the American Psychological Association in which he (Dewey) argued, against the psychological trends of his day, that the cultural, historical and institutional roles of individuals had to be properly calculated before anyone could fully understand mental functioning (p. 3). For Mounce (1997), too (also Brehony, 1997; Jones, 1983), as well as for Wertsch, the social objectives of children's school learning appear dominant in Dewey's writing.

In some contrast, O'Hear (1991) pillories Dewey for the malignant influence upon education of his progressivist writings which promoted individualized, child-oriented teaching. O'Hear's critique is not without foundation, as it is Dewey's insistence on the role of individual pupils' experiences in school learning which in the past recommended him to British educators fighting the child-centred cause. Both Kelly (Blenkin and Kelly, 1981; Kelly, 1986) and Blyth (1984) used Dewey's writings to promote learner-centred curricula. Alexander (1994), too, accuses Dewey, along with Rousseau, of placing individual experience above the transmission of cultural values (p. 22), and so displaying a rather naive, progressivist 'innocence'. But, for Dewey, individuality didn't at all imply a personal isolation from others. Individualism only makes sense in its relationship with communal life. In commenting upon O'Hear's text, Brehony (1997) offers Dewey's socio-political credentials as proof of how we cannot blame Dewey for progressivists' supposed over-reliance on individualized learning. Dewey (like Rousseau) took the refining of personal experiences as a means to the engineering of a harmonious social order. In other words, it is Dewey's bilateral views that typify his thinking, not his looking in one direction more than another. Mounce (1997) suggests that because 'Dewey tried to have it both ways' his writings are, in the end, not as helpful as they might be on issues such as the educational. However, it is never easy to put together an educational rationale which does give equal weight to individual and social welfare, and we have to admire Dewey for his consistency in at least attempting to achieve this balance.

In his analysis of the self/culture relationship, Dewey reaches similar conclusions to modern developmentalists. Like them, he saw mental development as the outcome of processes where social and personal factors each provided a foil for the other. In discussing *The Child and the Curriculum* (1900), he tells us:

> ... subject matter [is not fixed] ... experience [is] fluent, embryonic, vital ... ; the child and the curriculum are simply two limits which define a single process ... a continuous reconstruction, moving from the child's present experience out into that represented by the organised bodies of truth that we call studies. (p. 11)

His view of individual and cultural experience is that both are unfixed and fluid: children's thinking is under constant revision, governed by a sort of dialogue between personal and social voices speaking sometimes covertly, sometimes overtly, in consciousness. This very modern conception can be interpreted within both neo-Piagetian and neo-Vygotskian paradigms; educationally, it supposes that teachers are always kept on their child-centred toes by having to estimate children's needs

Informal Teaching Methods

from a prevailing social viewpoint and moderate social demands by reference to individual capability.

It also presupposes a democratic classroom climate which depends for its maintenance on the extent to which individually and socially derived criteria are likely to 'win out' within negotiations. Constraints operating in this form of social organization are regulated by the varying ways tensions occurring through individual/social frictions are resolved. These tensions are not just unfortunate consequences of teachers refusing to insist on a hard discipline, but are, as Osborne discovers (1997), points of growth both for children as individuals and as members of communities. Often it is individuals who must moderate their opinions in the light of group commentaries; sometimes groups must heed the advice of an individual. But democracies, arguably, only flourish through debates and argument. It is probable that the 'higher order' processes we call reflective criticism and critical analysis will not thrive except where tensions cause one person or another to look for weaknesses in a proferred view, thus creating cognitive conflicts and provoking reflective adaptations. This sort of climate is the air of democracy, not an ethos of coerced agreement between participants, or one where everyone has a voice but power distributions are such that only one group's view will affect decisions made.

Such power distribution depends on the political enfranchising of those members of classrooms most likely to have least power — i.e. the children themselves. It is integral to the progressivist enterprise in that child-centred teachers seek to 'empower' learners within their own curricula. The democratizing of educational situations has for this reason long been part of progressivist agendas, and it is not surprising to find a review of trends towards democratic education linked (if 'loosely') to progressivist teaching (Harber, 1997). It isn't only linked to progressivism, and Harber (1997) sees the modern resurgence of democratic movements, starting to overturn a preponderance, internationally, of authoritarian regimes, as more widespread than depending on the flourishing of a single ideology. But one has to wonder whether the imposing of a democratic structure on classrooms (or on a teaching profession or educational system) will, alone, create a democracy. Participation depends on the enfranchisement of those who take part — both in terms of the power they can wield and their awareness of the situations which affect them. It assumes the fulfilling of pupil rights to which progressivist educators are dedicated. And it does set some conditions of its own. Democracies might develop naturally in child-centred classrooms, but they are more likely to do so if we become aware of what organizational strategies will help make them work.

Arriving at these conclusions brings into view the teaching strategies themselves. It is perhaps urgent, after much theorizing, to stipulate a set of new progressivist, practical guidelines, embodying the ideas which have been worked out. These are drawn from the books and papers of writers whose work is synthesized on preceding pages, typifying strands of ideological belief. This work includes the research and theorizing of neo-Piagetians (e.g. Adey and Shayer, 1994; Resnick et al., 1992; Biggs, 1992; Nelson et al., 1998; Valsiner, 1992), some neo-Vygotskian theorists such as Bruner (1972), constructivists (e.g. Driver, 1989; Driver and Bell, 1986), Deweyan philosophy and the curricular inventions of British educationists such as Blyth (1984), Kelly (Blenkin and Kelly, 1981; Blenkin, Edwards and Kelly, 1992; Kelly, 1980, 1986, 1989, 1994) and Stenhouse (Rudduck and Hopkins, 1985). Principles listed are classified as discrete ways of achieving twin goals, which, added together, correspond to a modern definition of progressivist education as being a 'self-managed cultural transformation'. Deconstructing this definition, we arrive at two types of general aim, which are: (a) the individual transformation of culture, which makes possible (b) the cultural transformation of the individual.

These highly general aims engage us with procedures teachers will adopt to respect a school curriculum's complementary features — its bridging between the individual and the social, and its starting point within a viewpoint taken from one mode of experience *or* the other. Either teachers focus on helping pupils to meet tasks appropriately, or they adapt prescribed materials to individual requirements. The two types of practice are discriminated for the reasons which have been given. One reason why modern progressivist methods diverge from others (the older more individualistic forms of progressivism, the more traditionalist, eclectic or ideologically pragmatic) is that they follow from a rationale concerning the transformative relationships engineered between individuals and cultures. Both 'bottom-up' and 'top-down' practices are progressivist when they assume that intellectual progress is individually managed.

It hardly needs adding that the procedures stated are meant to be indicative rather than comprehensive, and a limit of eight principles is set, overall, for convenience. It would be foolhardy for any writer to suppose that a comprehensive listing of possible teacher procedures (even at the level of classroom policy) is possible outside of an enormous and rather tedious taxonomy. Each statement is made prescriptively (e.g. 'teachers should . . .'), since it is as prescriptions for a teacher's action that they are meant to be taken even though the direct involvement of pupils may be explicit.

Procedural principles

The individual transformation of culture

1. Teachers should treat pupils as agents for their own learning

That pupils are agents for their own learning is axiomatic for progressivist teaching, and its implications for those committed to the ideology are enormous. Various strategies follow from it, starting with the initial requirement for pupils to understand their own curricula and the demands these make. Consequent on that understanding is the proviso that pupils consent to teacher expectations (in some sense or other) in order that they can fulfil these overtly, having made appropriate commitments. How far a curriculum such as the National Curriculum can become comprehensible to pupils and how far teachers might wish to discuss the legal and resource constraints under which they themselves operate has to be a matter associated with many factors including pupils' ages and backgrounds. It is not suggested that young children are treated as if they are adults who can consent legally to a course of study, and, where pupils have difficulty agreeing to classroom rules (in order to comply with them), parents will normally become involved in negotiating a way ahead. Classroom teaching is, very much, a contractual situation established between learners and teachers whereby the latter have institutional authority and power, whereas the former have the 'whip hand' regarding what is actually achieved (rather like employers and labourers, which hints at the contractual basis of teaching). It is the learning behaviour of pupils (not a teacher's) which is the endpoint. Without pupils' compliance — at the outset — teachers cannot hope to succeed.

Other procedures stemming from this first principle are that pupil activities should, as far as possible, be organized such that they are self-paced by learners with situations maximized where pupils make choices and exercise a decision making responsibility for themselves. If they are to manage their own learning ultimately, they will never do so unless they work in classrooms where they do, really, make some decisions about procedures and policies from moment to moment. It is not that teachers can ever abandon their overall responsibilities for curricula, it is that education must operate within classroom democracies, if learner autonomy has any meaning. How much curricular choice and democratic decision making are possible within standardized teaching situations introduces different sorts of question which do need attention (Chapter 9), and whether or not self-paced work combined with choice inevitably leads to an integrated curriculum depends how it is organized, though, often enough, it probably will. But where pupils are recognized as, ultimately, responsible for what they themselves achieve, and where this recognition is explicit, the teacher's job becomes one of facilitation — though, it is hastily stated, not *only or simply* one of facilitation (Tharp and Gallimore argue, on similar grounds, that teaching can be regarded as a form of 'assisted performance': 1993). Adey and Shayer's (1994) following of a 'high road' to 'metacognition' in leading their pupils towards a principled overview of their own learning is one example of how teachers can both treat children as autonomous agents while empowering that very autonomy through structured teaching.

2. Teachers should at the start provoke as wide a range of relevant pupil perspectives as possible regarding topics to be studied

Neo-Piagetians and constructivists often begin their teaching by inviting pupils to 'import' their own experiences into the classroom setting. This is a way of guaranteeing that personal opinions and attitudes are aired, and can begin to become refocused, regarding the particular aims of a programme of study. The point is not that any or all outside experiences are relevant to classrooms: what matters is that some links are made between the new knowledge to be taught and relevant pupil experiences. What seems inevitable is that different pupils (with by nature different background experiences) will bring very different interests to bear on any scheme of work, and it is not always straightforward to arrange teaching situations to accommodate all of these. The fact is that these interests exist (i.e. pupils — no matter who they are — will have some view or other on elements of the theme tackled). They have to be brought to the individual and group consciousness, through the sorts of discussions, exercises, preliminary visits out of school, which provide a relaxed setting for pupils to become familiar with their own as well as other pupils' viewpoints.

Additionally, the fact that typical primary school topics are broad in scope is helpful, for they provide within themselves infinite possible avenues of enquiry. Pupils exploring along these avenues must be seen as progressing in strategically worthwhile directions. Topics are not only means to an end, but in their very openness of access they are 'ways in' to more focused study, provided we accept that the focusing will come from a pupil perspective which may well be different from our own. This is partly why class discussions should regularly involve the sort of open hypothesizing Bruner encouraged. In his MACOS humanities work (Man A Course of Study: discussed in Stenhouse, 1983, p. 186), Bruner gives us some of the best examples we have of open-ended curricula which by their nature stimulate a wide diversity of learner perspectives upon curricular questions. For example, when looking at the question 'how did early man learn to speak?', rather than list possible answers Bruner asked his students how they might go about finding out and then helped them to test out some of their own hypotheses. What he is achieving through this procedure is a socializing of pupils into habits of mind which help them to value their own efforts at problem solving as well as teaching them hypothesis-testing itself (a so-called heuristic). And he is guiding them 'courteously', as Stenhouse describes it (1983, p. 186), from their own preconceptions towards those of others.

To pre-empt becoming swamped in detail, the rule here is that of approaching studies along a wide band of possibility to respect the diversity of views found in almost any group of children. Such diversity of approach gives access to something else, rather than being an end in itself. Notably, the extent to which out-of-class experiences are discussed in classrooms (in the manner favoured by constructivists) will depend on the approach pupils actually do take: that is, a teacher moving towards a topic from material which is already familiar, will know that his or her pupils do have opinions to hand. The issue is not one of eliciting experiences for the sake of doing so (one can end up listening endlessly to pupils' anecdotes of holiday adventures, hobbies, new purchases, birthday treats and so forth) as of latching onto perspectives relevant to the new learning. Although this distinction might seem somewhat trivial, it takes us a little way towards understanding some of the changes which occur when anyone comes to grasp new ideas or learn new skills.

3. Teachers should help pupils acquire those general and specific skills which pupils need to access school and classroom knowledge

There are two influences deciding educational success, the skills of teachers and the skills of pupils. For any educational process to work, it is not enough for teachers to be good teachers, pupils must also become good learners. They must know how to

Informal Teaching Methods

listen and take notice of teachers' advice (i.e. benefit from skilled teaching), they must recognize when to ask questions where they do not fully understand what is required of them, they must gradually develop the very sophisticated skills required for cooperating with others (who may not always be equally socially skilled), they must have the esteem and confidence to be able to work independently without distracting others, they must learn how to speculate and hypothesize, to precis and summarize, as well as how to record and report their achievements in a variety of ways (the list is not comprehensive!).

These sorts of general classroom skills are not usually to be trained or instructed, they are ultimately part and parcel of learner-centred work, in that learners who are engaged with school curricula will, as part of that engagement, focus their listening skills (and thereby refine them), be motivated to ask questions which they genuinely wish to be answered, be anxious to share their views with others and so on. But insofar as teachers are organizing child-centred work, they will monitor the development of such capabilities, signalling their importance to pupils through illustration and discussion. It isn't that teachers should never teach core learning skills. A balance has to be struck between structured activities, where these skills appear slow in developing, and the mainstream child-centred work which should foster them as a matter of course.

The reason why teachers should not *as a main policy* teach learning or study skills in isolation from the subject matter to be learned is that to do so is to risk separating means from ends in a way that makes it less rather than more likely that the ends themselves are achieved. Making means into ends is to mix up one's values (as argued earlier) and may give confusing value-signals to pupils. A good example comes with the advice (not infrequently heard) that teachers should raise pupils' self-esteem. This advice might be thought good advice, since high pupil self-esteem is found to accompany effective teaching (see Sammons et al., 1997) and one might suppose that raising pupil self-esteem is a strategy guaranteed to improve teaching outcomes. Yet if pupils' self-esteem does improve in the absence of commensurate learning, teachers are saying that it is quite admissible to 'feel good', even in situations which do not merit our feeling good. This is, in short, to breed either complacency or distorted values. Presumably, we would not wish pupils who engage in racist taunting, bullying or undisciplined behaviour to have raised self-esteem. Levels of self-esteem should vary with personally recognized achievement, otherwise how do we know that we have achieved anything? Self-acceptance is a different matter: we must all feel at ease with ourselves. What Rogers (1983) called 'unconditional positive self regard' is probably a prerequisite of consistently achieved learning, but this does not presuppose any artificially set standard of self-liking.

Except with those cases where children with clinically low levels of self-esteem need extra help, what teachers are striving for is to raise pupil self-esteem as part of raising standards of achievement. The equivalent point was made earlier about the teaching of oracy, literacy and numeracy skills, and it returns us to first principles. If learners are to be agents for their own learning, they must not lose sight of the connections between schoolwork and the ends for which the work is

115

organized. Learning to read, write, spell or whatever should not become 'school-focused' activities, undertaken only because they happen to be organized within a timetable. It is obviously vital that pupils, as good learners, do become proficient at literacy, numeracy and oracy, and so on, and exercises in numeracy and literacy might be useful adjuncts to a main methodology. It is also vital that pupils grow in confidence and self-esteem. But pupils' skills, attitudes and developing values are there to be fostered within the culture of a classroom. We should be wary of trying to 'instil' them in isolation from other activities, no matter how much we might believe we can succeed in doing so.

As well as the general study skills which pupils need to acquire as part of their learning, there are context-specific skills which have to be directly taught since these mediate all pupil activity and there is little danger that the purpose of gaining such skills will be misunderstood. Briefly, pupils coming to manage their own work will better do so given a full understanding of their own classroom and school. It is unnecessary for teachers to wait for pupils to 'pick up' such knowledge (for this can take longer than one might think): it should be common practice for teachers to teach pupils to use their classroom technology, to locate themselves comfortably within a school, to know all who work in it, to be able to avail themselves of the right sort of help from the right person, and to know their own school's customs and rituals. As an initial step in their 'transformation' of culture, pupils should become familiar with that boasted by their school. What might need adding is that this familiarization process is not at all the same as what is sometimes meant by the term 'socialization' (i.e. the largely unconscious business of assimilating cultural meanings): the very process of consciously teaching pupils about their schools ought to pre-empt (as far as one can ever pre-empt) too much assimilation of hidden teaching, covert values or indoctrinated habits.

4. Teachers should be pragmatic in a creative, experimental sense to ensure pupil involvement in curricula

Peter Woods (e.g. 1995) is, perhaps, the writer whose ideas most come to mind when one is considering the creativity of teachers. And his realization that creative teachers are those who unlock the potentialities for learners to learn independently is pertinent for this set of proposals. A pragmatically creative teacher will be one who knows his or her pupils, recognizes exactly the accommodations that need to be made to meet their problems and difficulties with realistic solutions, will be endlessly resourceful in dealing with these and not afraid to experiment in ways geared to trusting pupils to take responsibility and make decisions for themselves. There aren't any 'no-go' areas in teaching, apart from those which are seen as immoral or known to be ineffective.

It would be mildly counter-productive to exemplify teacher creativity, for it is in the nature of the beast for it not to be readily captured, even for sake of illustration (though see Woods, 1995). All that might be said is that creative, pragmatic teaching is not itself exempt from the general guidelines of ensuring that learners access curricula for themselves. Teachers might be creative in ways which would close doors for pupils — even teachers skilled at social interaction can set standards which are too high or boringly low, or believe that their own self-recognized skills at communication make certain the communications are grasped in ways intended. Creative teaching has to be that which facilitates pupil learning: there is no other legitimate purpose for it.

The cultural transformation of individuals

5. *New knowledge should be introduced by teachers in a wide variety of ways*

In Resnick et al.'s (1992) action research programme, new knowledge was introduced quickly and in a way encouraging 'real' mathematical discussions and debates. It was introduced into a thoroughly prepared context where pupils were already familiar with the issues under discussion. The point is that pupils in Resnick et al.'s research were able to 'fill out' newly met terms with familar thoughts, judgments and perceptions. But teachers have, still, to beware of introducing knowledge along a narrow spectrum such as to bypass student viewpoints. The notion to which we have to keep returning is that of the matching of pupil perspectives to publicly valued knowledge, and this matching entails twin accommodations — the channelling of pupil ideas towards valued ends, and the presentation of what has to be learned in ways meaningful to pupils.

In principle, new knowledge has to be presented in as wide a variety of ways as possible. The rule is not that learners should only meet knowledge in familiar ways, but that there should be many 'channels of access' built into the content presented in a classroom. Media technology (films, tapes, computers, television, books of course) are designed to present material in novel forms, and one of these forms might, just, stimulate a learner's cognitions to positive action. Primary, firsthand experience is a skeleton key to practically any sort of study, for it is a base encounter with experiences academic studies usually attempt to explain.

6. *Discussions and learning activities should be structured so as to encourage a dialectical interchange between old and new knowledge*

The pattern of teaching, activities and discussions in primary school classrooms will regularly move from known to unknown, from familiar knowledge to new ideas and back. To repeat the core principle yet again: pupils will take soundings from where they are, cognitively, to where they need to be — then they will look back at their prior understandings to modify these. Cognitive change is, invariably, the modification of the world from a self-realized perspective, and the modification of a previously believed position from a newly grasped one (co-construction). Classroom discussions, especially, should reflect this sort of dialectical interchange, with teachers almost religiously ensuring a regular revisiting of what pupils already know to reinterpret these in the light of a new finding. By this means teachers can fairly quickly during a programme of study engage pupils with 'real' academic debates and issues. There is nothing academically soft-centred or low level about progressivist methodologies: their very rationale impels them to work to guarantee student access to whatever debates and issues are topical or socially relevant. Where they score is in their promise that classroom learning will be of high quality. Where they are problematic is that, in the very diversity of curricula teachers are forced to implement, pupils may appear to make slower progress (regarding common educational aims) than they might make otherwise.

Staying with this theme, it will always be tempting for teachers to surge ahead with new topics once the first stages of learner familiarization with materials is past. But they should resist that temptation. Pupil perspectives are not singular, but consist of multiple channels of access to material, and learning is as much a process of self-discovery as of assimilating ideas in a once-and-for-all manner: so it is vital enough that pupils do have the opportunities consistently to rethink their own views, opinions, attitudes from the standpoint of what is being learned, even where this might seem tedious.

Another way of putting this is to say that the axis of interchange between old and new is the democratic nature of progressive primary school classrooms. It is by questioning their own efforts from viewpoints of others that pupils confront the weaknesses in their own thinking. Piaget knew this some time ago (1932), and one of the origins of his valuing of peer interaction for moral development was his belief in the democratic structure of reflective thought — the idea that we see the errors of our own positions by listening to others. This dimension of the individual–social dialogue is also exemplified by Osborne's (1997) unmasking of the tensions which exist between individual efforts and group comment, showing that these are, on the whole, not only benign but conducive of pupils raising rather than lowering their sights for achievement.

Such writings tell us much about the value of a democratic form of classroom organization. Both individual effort and public evaluations are backbones for change (something has to be changed, and there has to be an agency for change). A slow modification of view happens when divergent opinions can be freely stated and power distributions are fairly regulated. In such circumstances, change happens at its own pace. When teachers too readily 'take charge', they can leave pupils too long with their existing biases, or seek to move too quickly to new ground. Always, the balance of interchange between the two sorts of perspective lodged in the idea of 'co-construction' has to be preserved, and one guarantor of this preservation is a truly democratic, rule-governed system.

7. Teachers will 'scaffold' children's learning in a number of ways bridging between individuals and knowledge to be gained

There are a number of ways teachers can 'scaffold' pupil knowledge in the way popularized in the educational literature (e.g. Bliss et al., 1996), though these can be classified as of two types. They can gradually refine pupils' understanding, supporting them at each stage of improvement with encouragement, help and advice (essentially the nature of scaffolding) in ways pupils themselves direct; and they can lead pupils on in ways that are mainly teacher-designated. To opt only for the former risks never reaching a long-term cultural destination; to opt only for the latter risks 'losing' pupils *en route*. Practically speaking, this dual reformulation of the 'scaffolding' concept is not hard and fast but is meant to clarify what the teacher's role actually is in the gradual monitoring of progress to be sure that it occurs. The two types of scaffolding tend to surface for teachers in their own organization: they notice when pupils struggle to express their own ideas, and they know when pupils are finding some new task hazardous. Correspondingly, if children are finding it hard to realize ideas they have themselves initiated, it is likely that they will need a new language to help them. If children are finding new material or form of discourse difficult, it is likely that they will need to fall back on already secure ideas for support.

Looking back at this, a critic might wonder why one can or would wish to divide a pedagogic strategy, usually regarded as already highly structured, in the way argued. One might, for example, suppose that a 'scaffolding' technique is always one which moves back and forth from known to unknown, and indeed it is. But, as Bliss et al. (1996) emphasize, it is never easy for teachers to know what children are thinking in order to support it skilfully. The 'scaffolding' concept is educationally attractive in crystallizing the sensitive, supportive relationship between teachers and pupils, but it is hard to accomplish as a practical technique. And while teacher support inches slowly towards a consciously known goal, it is always possible that where teachers predominantly head towards their own goals, children's commitments will flag. The 'child-centredness' of the process is maintained when progress towards teacher-designated ends happens within a context where pupils are already, emotionally and intellectually, prepared to work towards them.

8. Exercises in knowledge transfer and flexible application should be built into progressivist curricula in a learner-centred manner

Listing principles discretely often misleads, because in their application they will often overlap. This is very obvious with the eighth principle which is found to figure anyway in the democratic, 'dialectical' discussions and hypothesis testing mentioned previously and in the normal course of anyone teaching new material. Yet if there is a matter of principle involved, this has to be stated separately, and we know from the work of researchers (Adey and Shayer, 1996; Désforges, 1997; Resnick, 1985; Voss, 1987) that the best tests for conceptualization are probably whether or not new learning can be applied and transferred between situations. A 'learner-centred' approach to this can be devised in many ways. If, for instance, we assume that learners are achieving new knowledge (principles 5 to 7 above), one test of whether they are properly assimilating it is to require of them that they apply it to aspects of life which they themselves choose.

It might seem sensible for, say, a teacher to exemplify a scientific rule with its most characteristic application (concerning, say, gravity or the behaviour of steam or electricity), but if pupils really grasp a rule they will show that through their own illustrations. Following Bruner (1972), teachers might give this assignment to pupils as something to discuss with friends and parents, or to follow up in reading or through watching a particular television programme, or by means of recommended computer software — the issue is that of teachers ensuring as much as is humanly possible that new knowledge attains that luminosity which it must have if it is to be grasped at the most profound level. It would be wildly ambitious for a teacher to imagine that all teaching could end in such a way, but curricula systems have to be designed which, at least, make such a conclusion possible.

Another option is to follow Adey and Shayer's (1994) method of 'scaffolding' students' thinking until they glimpse whatever principles underlie the knowledge being acquired. To become aware of the underlying principle is to gain the sort of metacognitive overview which a properly understood idea gives us. From Adey and Shayer's position, remembering that they were teaching young adolescents, the formulae of science are, by their nature, metacognitive, in that they are the scientific means by which we are able to make sense of happenings in many different contexts. With younger children, principles are likely to be practical and concrete and therefore less flexible in application, but precursors of formal operations are probably the realizations by young learners of what is significant about these achievements for the events of their own lives.

In conclusion, and as an addendum to the eight indicative principles listed, they have been categorized in order to reflect as closely as possible principles of analysis. In practice, overlap and integration between procedures will be commonplace. But in all that teachers do, they should know the difference between an activity where pupils' *existing* skills, capabilities and qualities are being accommodated to the task, and where *new* tasks are being accommodated to an existing perspective — even where they are bridging back and forth between the two. The reason for elaborating this point repeatedly is that it isn't so much that the child-oriented and teacher-oriented tasks are always in practice distinguishable, but that teachers must themselves know what the nature of their task is. And, certainly, as defined, it is to ensure that a publicly defined culture is properly contextualized within a pupil culture. It is by no means the case that public education policy over the past decade or so has stimulated teachers to apply principles such as those listed.

Chapter 9

Choice

Liberating learners

Progressivism's public image has pupils 'choosing' how and when to work at classroom tasks. Unless qualified, this bare admission condemns child-centred teachers as culpable of professional negligence. Partly on such grounds, Kenneth Clarke sponsored the 'three wise men' report, ridiculing the 'bizarre notion that young children should choose what they do' (1991, para. 29). Academics (e.g. Clarke, 1988) question the belief that school pupils who have yet to develop rationality can be expected rationally to decide about their own learning. Of course, though giving pupils responsibilities for which they are not ready can only be regrettable, the dangers of expecting them to take charge of situations they have neither the authority nor the understanding to deal with has to be relative to two factors — the actual decisions to be taken, and the developed capabilities of the pupils concerned. To 'liberate' learners might mean no more than to teach those skills and attitudes which independently minded pupils require to act in personally and socially responsible ways. Such an approach would suggest not the abrogation of responsibilities by teachers (which both Clarkes seem to fear) but an enhanced role, whereby pupils are taught a form of decision making appropriate for curricular and classroom contexts.

We have, again, to separate general issues requiring clarification from the strategies teachers in fact use. For one thing, there will always be disagreement about what pupils can decide for themselves. Teachers in experimental schools in the past, such as Dartington Hall at one point in its history (Punch, 1977), Summerhill (Neill, 1945) and some nineteenth-century 'New Schools' (Holmes, 1995) freed pupils in unconventional ways. These have to be judged as individual cases. Modern progressivists are rather more in tune with public expectations and have learned from their early experiences. Dewey (reported Dykhuizen, 1973), like Holt (cited Meighan, 1995), castigated those progressivists who could not distinguish between a responsible freedom and licence. Their strictures did not prevent teachers in the William Tyndale school, closed for its extreme Marxist-libertarian policies, doing much harm to the progressivist cause.

What a revised progressivism has to tell us are the parameters within which any educational process must work to realize the humanitarian ethic at the heart of child-centredness. We have to marry our idealism to what is practically possible. But this is not as difficult a task as might at first be thought. In the first place, if teachers are to organize their classrooms with real pretensions towards their being democratic, this assumes some devolution of classroom power. What we require, next, is a better conceptualizing of what it is 'rightful' for pupils to decide on regarding their own futures: what powers *should* they have? As it happens, progress made recently in legal and moral affairs has brought us much closer than we have ever been to establishing that children really are (in terms of their endowed capabilities and the structured nature of their personalities) 'fully formed' individuals, with ultimate rights over their own cognitions.

Pupil rights

When, in 1975, John Holt wrote:

> the Right I ask for the Young is the right that I want to preserve for the rest of us, the right to decide what goes into our minds (p. 184)

his plea was a radical one for any adult to make, and even more unusual for a teacher in its historical period. A similar plea made today would sound neither as strange nor as isolated. Davie (1996), referring to a lecture he gave to the British Psychological Society's education section in 1991 entitled 'Listen to the Child', recalls how his predominantly educational audience was even at this date unused to the idea that children may have the 'right to be heard'. He goes on to reassure us that the situation is speedily improving, as teachers become familiar with debates and developments in the area of children's welfare rights, such as those resulting from the publishing of the 1989 Children's Act.

Davie's case is that educators have little option but to catch up with innovations in other fields catering for children's welfare. It has become standard practice in law courts (Sherwin, 1996; van Bueren, 1996), in areas of social work (Smith, 1996) and in venues concerned with children's mental health (Glaser, 1996) and physical disabilities (Russell, 1996) to judge children's views on their own merits, rather than these being thought inferior in terms of their likely veracity to an adult's. Davie names the 1994 Code of Practice on the Identification and Assessment of Special Educational Needs (DFE, 1994) as the piece of legislation most influential in 'placing the involvement of children in decision making on the educational agenda' (1996, p. 2). He cites as its core principle that:

> Children have a right to be heard. They should be encouraged to participate in decision making about provision to meet their special educational needs.

Davie's efforts to persuade us to heed children's views reinforce the main thrust of the United Nations Convention on the Rights of the Child, which is unequivocal in its demand for the empowerment of children in educational decison-making. Osler's (1994) discussion of the UN convention finds a number of its principles consistently broken by teachers because they are straitjacketed by legislation. This is true, most, of article 12:

Article 12: the child's opinion
The child has the right to express his or her opinion freely and to have that opinion taken into account in any matter of procedure affecting the child.

Current legislation related to the National Curriculum does not encourage pupil decision making, or pupils' participation in the governance of schools or curricular implementation. Participation rights are, according to Osler, those most deeply embedded in the convention, and she tells us that:

> the aims of an education compatible with the principles of the Convention must be to empower the child by providing opportunities to practice and develop ... skills of participation. This ... may involve the individual teacher in a complete reassessment of her or his role. (p. 147)

It may seem preposterous to say that a standard curriculum is a barrier to the fulfilment of children's rights, for the National Curriculum is an 'entitlement' curriculum. By the fact that it is a nationally distributed set of orders binding on teacher behaviour, it establishes all children's rights to an equivalent education. However, remembering that curricula access cannot be managed by prescription alone but has to be achieved via students' own purposes, the weight of enforcement of a National Curriculum will inevitably prevent access for some pupils. It is not accidental that a gradually awakening national consciousness of pupil rights (of expression and participation) coincides with our emerging awareness of the practical need for such an expression and participation if pupils are to be educated at all.

Advances in the establishing of children's rights and constraining the way 'care' professionals treat children's involvement in their own education and general welfare are not straws in the wind but represent an internationally based trend. We can be sure, in general, that this is so because, as just argued, these changes forcefully return us to our heightened awareness of children's role in their own learning, as well as pushing towards a fairer stance for a group rarely acknowledged as having a status independent of the adults around them (Hendrick, 1992). John (1996) talks of her work with children as research with 'the silenced'. Sherwin (1996) homes in on the issue by identifying what he calls the 'child-centred' principle applied by law courts when admitting how a child below the age of 16 should be able to give valid consent (or deny consent) to various treatments (such as medical treatments) 'if the child understands the nature of the advice being given and has sufficient maturity to understand what is involved' (p. 23). What legal rulings founded on this precept acknowledge is that chronological age is no longer the sticking point in validating children's opinions; such rulings have to be grounded in the child's actual competence *vis-à-vis* the decisions being taken.

If we accede to the above moral and legal arguments, combining these with the lessons taught to us by developmental psychology, we are compelled to question any attempts to deprive children of their rights of involvement in matters concerning them, even when we might believe the reasons for this deprivation are sensible enough. Children are, arguably, the single group most disenfranchised by the implementation of the English/Welsh National Curriculum, during a period when they have lost their rights of free movement on the streets as well as in classrooms (Hillman, 1997). It is parents, not children, who are regarded as a school's natural 'clients' (Wyness, 1996). Whereas in the post-Plowden era teachers could at least give pupils some choice in what (as well as how) they learned, this possibility has all but vanished following the imposition of a standardized curriculum.

Teachers, whose work as educators must be integrated with that of other 'care' professionals, have to listen to advocates for children having some say in their own affairs. In current educational practice, anyone wishing to influence a child's future has to do so through compliance, not coercion: pupils' interests are not an irritating irrelevance. And although learners cannot always know what is 'in their interests', teachers are obliged to lift their pupils to levels of maturity which will allow them to make just that judgment. Yet because the principle of pupil involvement in decision making is a qualified one — that is, we have always to relate the decisions to be taken to the context concerned — it is important to know where we are with it in terms of the practicalities implied by child-centred procedures. Progressivism's dedication to promoting as well as recognizing children's rights within classrooms puts it at the cutting edge of those movements watching out for all human rights as these are expresssed in education. Yet the extent to which this stays true must depend on the potential effectiveness of the child-centred policies themselves.

Pupil autonomy

The 'liberationist' dimension of progressivism has three parts to it which are integral — each assumes the others. Firstly, personal autonomy is something all child-centred teachers value as an extension of their 'process' aims. Secondly, nurturing pupil independence by devising curricula which overtly foster it is a means to that end. Thirdly, creating opportunities for pupils to engage in responsible curricular decision making is a stage towards autonomy following from the other two. The teacher's role in each part may not always be straightforward: there will be a slow 'scaffolding' of pupil freedoms, and these will never be absolute for reasons which were earlier mentioned and which all welfare-professionals recognize — that children's intellectual progress is specific to the rules of the culture context in which it is being fostered. Put another way, the freedoms of pupils, as with adults, are intimately bound up with their understanding of the environments in which they live. And it is a teacher's job to calculate how far pupil's understanding merits the exercise of autonomous choice and how far such choices have to be limited.

This cautionary point strengthens what is already a commonplace phase in any education for independence and is part of the ordering of a democratic organization — the negotiated settlement. Such negotiations are at times onerous, but are warranted because blocks met by the learner are balanced against curricular justifications offered by the teacher. Rowlands' negotiated curricula (1987) and Fisher's negotiated classroom (1996), like the progressivist 'integrated day', suppose that teachers and pupils compromise on what should be learned and how learning should proceed. Not all disagreements are easily resolved, and there are ethical and practical matters which intercede: Galton (1989b), perceptively, draws our attention to some of these. But that is no bad thing. Anyone who has studied curricular theory knows that underlying questions about aims and method are debated by philosophers and social scientists alike. No one has ever been certain about what should be learned or what are the best pedagogies. As part of the day-to-day business of planning activities, these issues have somehow to be resolved by teachers, and those who accept a democratic classroom framework, truly negotiating curricula with pupils, meet such issues head on; they do not shirk them by adopting a legal, authoritarian stance.

If we search for empirical justification, we have, unfortunately, little research evidence revealing the effect upon learning outcomes of teachers following this policy in a wholly dedicated manner, possibly because teachers preoccupied with a burdensome curriculum have less and less time to spend attending to their pupils' views. But what evidence we do have is suggestive in pointing to the sorts of benefits we would, in theory, expect. Jeffrey and Woods' explorations of creative teaching (1997), which they substantially define in terms of teachers' abilities to liberate pupils as contributors to their own learning rather treating them simply as clients, find that it improves pupils' 'metacognitive' awareness of their own attitudes and skills. As they put it, innovative teaching leads to innovative learning, where pupils are more likely to learn with thoroughness and make what they learn their own. In a very different research project, focusing on socio-behavioural adjustment, Stacey (forthcoming) tried to teach upper primary age children the skills needed to mediate their own disputes in an attempt to reduce the frequency of bullying incidents in her target schools. When she analysed her test–retest data, she discovered that what made the difference in reducing bullying was not just the fact that pupils were taught socio-behavioural skills (this teaching alone had little obvious effect upon pupils' peer relationships) but depended on their being given actual responsibility for mediating peer quarrels and arguments. Where children were trusted to sort out their disputes, they did so — more frequently and effectively than their teachers previously had. From a progressivist viewpoint, this sort of finding underlines the belief that skilled pedagogy in itself does not lead to successful learning: we have in addition to enhance the role of learners.

Paying closer attention to pupils' voices can reap other sorts of rewards. Davie (1996) refers to research showing how even experienced headteachers can be 'transformed' (i.e. they acquire a professionally relevant knowledge they hadn't dreamed existed) when they are obliged to listen closely to the voices of the children in their charge. In such circumstances, pupils and teachers become more in tune with each other and teachers are more likely to facilitate the cultural transformation which education entails. In more practical terms, benefits to teachers of economy and efficiency are spin-offs from devolving responsibilities to pupils, though at first sight 'child-centredness' might not appear an efficient form of curricular organization. We have to be sure that it is, and a little thought soon clarifies that it would be difficult to think up a more economic mode of teaching than that which exploits the full talents and energies of learners.

A research outcome much discussed during the early 1990s is that reported by Mortimore et al. (1988) who showed how diverse classroom activities are more difficult to manage than fewer or single-subject activities. How far teachers limit their objectives provides some index of the extent to which they can achieve them. This is another instance of common sense being confirmed by research: teachers need to set for themselves attainable goals. They should focus rather than dilute their attentions insofar as they can. Since diversity is a feature of progressivist classrooms, Mortimore et al.'s criticism was widely seen as a criticism of child-centred teaching: Galton (1995) cited it for this purpose, as did Alexander et al. in their response to government on primary school curricular organization (1992). A classroom where teachers organize many topics presents more managerial challenges than one where they organize few. Yet, as it stands, the idea that diverse curricula are harder to manage than a single curriculum compares two 'formal' modes of curricular organization; it does not do adequate justice to progressivist curricular policies which generate diversity through pupil involvement.

In other words, it is because learning is to a degree self-managed and topics are paced to suit individuals and groups that diversity in child-centred settings arises. Mortimore et al.'s discovery that many curricula are harder to manage than fewer curricula is bound to be true (it could hardly be otherwise) — unless there is more than one 'manager' in a classroom, then the mathematics affecting the situation alter. No classroom approximates to an ideal type, but a teacher who organizes pupil management through joint negotiation is doing so with one eye on personal savings. He or she knows the considerable amount of time self-direction can 'free up', assuming negotiated settlements are genuine and not a cover for indirect teacher control (Warham, 1993). Progressivist, self-managed (through jointly negotiated) curricula provide perhaps the best option teachers have of organizing their teaching in ways allowing them to make optimum use of their own time and energy.

Returning to the business of pupil autonomy, the attempt to balance pupils' individual and personal tendencies against wider public responsibilities through the vehicle of teacher–pupil negotiation should not hide the deeper question of how far pupils (even with a negotiated framework) can and should be allowed to control their own educational destinies. To establish children's rights of participation and expression is one thing; to say that teachers should act according to the will of their pupils rather than applying their own professional judgment is quite another. Although teachers have a professional responsibility for ensuring that pupils don't negotiate themselves into a corner so to speak, working against their own interests, this safeguard does not quite say enough about either the ability of children to articulate what is in their interests or the practical difficulties of teachers who are convinced that pupil autonomy should be nourished.

Progressivists are unreserved in their beliefs about pupils' naturally endowed capabilities, the associated rights and the essential roles learners therefore have to fulfil within their own education. All progressivist eggs fall into these baskets at some time or other. What we must also judge are the limitations teachers should ascribe to these roles on professional grounds. That is: the question of how far pupil autonomy can be allowed free reign within schools and classrooms, albeit within carefully negotiated situations, is one which hangs fire often enough during ideological debates. Nothing written here so far limits pupil decision making beyond stating the general principle that educational change, like developmental change, is and has to be 'co-constructed': it is a product of a truly democratic teacher–pupil enterprise, not of a venture where one partner's wishes invariably dominate those of the other. And the part played by education in developing pupils' autonomous decision making has only been generally stated. How far such decision making can ever be embraced within a teacher strategy is for child-centredness the 64 thousand dollar question. To put the question straight: how far can we ever *trust* pupil decisions regarding their own welfare, regardless of the 'independent learning' skills we may be trying to foster? This has been left as a matter of pragmatic judgment, not one answered from principle, and how it is answered will make all the difference as to whether a classroom is really child-centred or, simply, tokenistically so. One of the easiest traps for teachers to fall into is that noted by Warham (1993) of seeming to give pupil views credence during curricular negotiations while, actually, covertly closing off all options but the one a teacher wishes to be chosen.

As a way of summarizing, anew, material previously aired about pupil involvement and participation and of starting to conclude arguments prior to a wider summing up, a model of pupil autonomy will be sketched to attempt some degree of precision regarding the question just asked. A rough definition of personal autonomy is that accepted by philosophers of education (Dearden, 1972b; Quinn, 1984) which sees autonomous people as able to determine their own lives through exerting their own capabilities and exploiting their own resources in the face of prevailing circumstances. The Aristotelian definition of autonomy as 'self-sufficiency' (May, 1994) is contained in this definition. Autonomous school pupils would be those able to fulfil their own interests from inside those social and educational circumstances which they routinely experience, and it might seem intuitively true that most have to develop skills and attitudes over a lengthy period.

What is proposed is that although teachers have to educate for autonomy, as defined developmentally, all pupils have a 'latent' autonomy by virtue of their innately given competence for making decisions on their own behalf. They are 'whole persons', as progressivist teachers like to say. The extent to which their judgments and decisions can be trusted as likely to further their own interests is no more and no less than the extent to which any human being's judgments and decisions are to be trusted once we partial out the circumstances relating to developmental change. Following from this, it will be shown that teachers — even working within standard curricula — can and should give credence to pupils' views providing teachers keep within the boundaries of their own and their pupils' contextually defined skills. So there are two connected issues: the nature of children's innate competence and the nature of the context-specific practices which liberate it. Each issue will be considered.

New Progressivism

Innate competence and its contextual expression

Newborns are in a transformational relationship with a world in which they must learn to live. They do not, because they cannot, somehow wait for time to pass before beginning to cope with this world, and psychologists' experiments with newborn babies shows that they are expert problem solvers. Newborn infants taught to turn on a light by head-turning will do so purposively (Bower, 1971); nurselings taught to focus a picture on a ceiling by sucking on 'comforters' will occupy themselves pleasurably by controlling their sucking in a similar instrumental fashion (Bruner, 1968). Babies acquire the means to their personal ends, but they do not have to acquire problem-solving skills in general. Contemporary models of neonates see them as 'active, constructive and self-modifying' (Meadows, 1993, p. 233): it is these models (reviewed Meadows, 1993; Cousins, 1996; Siegler, 1991) which prime us for 'constructivist' assumptions that learners are always voluntary agents for their own learning (Von Glaserfield, 1995).

'The competent infant' (Siegler, 1991, p. 5) is a contemporary idea. As Siegler outlines it:

> ... infants have much wider range of perceptual and conceptual understandings than had previously been suspected. These capacities allow infants to perceive the world quite clearly and to classify their experiences along many of the same dimensions that older children and adults use. (p. 5)

When Thelen et al. (1993) observe infant reaching behaviour, they judge that prevalant theories about how babies achieve this fall before the very ubiquity of human intelligence: 'infants assemble reaching skill in a dynamic context-specific fashion, using whatever components they individually [have] available for the task' (p. 1093). Human intelligence is, from the start, ubiquitous in application and malleable.

Of course, babies do not normally use their head-turning to switch on lights or their sucking to focus a picture on a screen. What these projects suggest is that how human beings deploy their problem-solving skill is limited more by expectation than by innate mechanisms. Babies, like the rest of us, conform to the expectations of others — up to a point. And the final proviso is significant. Otherwise, we could become wildly overambitious regarding our young children's capabilities. Knowledge and skills have a structure which precludes an infant Einstein developing relativity theory and babies winning Olympic medals. If cognitive competence is a condition of being human that does not mean it will express itself in any situation. There is a rather naive belief in innate capability prevalent in the developmental literature, according to Campbell and Olson (1990), which finds infants able to develop practically any sort of skill, overlooking the degrees of difficulty existing between infant and adult categories of problem. One nonetheless supposes that all human beings at all stages can achieve more than we would normally expect. What must rule our ambitions for our children is what we believe to be their appropriate lifestyles, given our privileged position as adults able (to an extent) to anticipate future lives. 'What sort of lives do we want for our children?' is a slightly better question to ask than 'what are the outside limits of capability we might think they can reach?', though the reason we have to ask the first question is implied in the possibility of asking the second.

The issue of whether the idea of 'infant autonomy' is really just a gloss on 'infant competence' introduces other questions. We tend to think that people become autonomous through achieving mastery over circumstances. So for Hargreaves (1997), children have to learn both about their own and other cultures if they are to be regarded as autonomous persons within their social environments. Yet Cousins (1996) discusses ways in which even babies are 'empowered' to behave autonomously in a nurturing home. If we accept that it is inconceivable that anyone should attain *absolute* autonomy — i.e. be wholly self-sufficient in any setting — then we are left with the earlier realization that we really do have to talk about degrees of autonomy, assessed according to the relationship between an individual's personal resources and specified situations. What matters is always a combination of developed abilities *viz-à-viz* a set of problems to be dealt with. And all human beings, regardless of age, can potentially acquire the capabilities needed to meet context-specific tasks, though they will acquire them at different rates and to different levels of achievement. In other words, it would seem quite sensible to talk about individual autonomy as a condition of being human, and that this condition can be expressed to a degree, or constrained, or concealed, but not destroyed, by circumstance — unlesss our humanness is somehow taken from us.

So two critical variables in the expression of personal autonomy are context and development — the latter being a way of recognizing the way contextual factors change as children grow older. There is no built-in directionality for human intellectual progress: cognitive development, as Adey and Shayer (1994) say, is directionally blind. The fact that newborns face a physically and socially ordered world which tests them intellectually, leading invariably to some form of internally structured phasing of developments, doesn't alter base theory, and it does bring into view value-issues arising pretty much as soon as we are born. Although no one can behave in ways for which their experiences have not prepared them, what is left open are the sorts of contextual experiences we believe are suited to any age group (even the youngest) and the purposes we would tie in with them — accepting the broad parameters set by common sense. Babies normally have purposes concerned with sensory pleasures: one cannot easily imagine them curious about the function of objects in the way toddlers are, and not at all acquiring the drive and wherewithall to replicate complex adult achievements. Babies are skilled manipulators of their own social and physical environments, bent on survival and on making first contacts with the sensory and social features of their worlds.

Transferring this judgment to a school setting: pupils will learn to judge what is in their interest regarding the situations they know well. Children familiar with homes and classrooms will ascertain how happy or sad, comfortable or uncomfortable they are within these; they will also perfectly well assess the social and physical circumstances which directly affect them and will follow these with commitments to individual ventures tailored to their own growing self-knowledge. It is easier to underestimate than overestimate the rational basis of children's decision making. Holt rightly chides us with his observation that 'schools are places where children learn to be stupid' (1994, p. 9). Unless we trust children to have minds of their own, they will develop the minds we think they have.

Even very young children are usually able to manage self-reflections fairly accurately (Burden, 1996) and can make very good sense of their social experiences — even those known by others to be racist in origin (Connolly, 1997). Infants reason about social class issues in ways which, in the absence of research like that of Short (1991), we might not think possible. Providing they are treated as responsible citizens, children can be delegated to international conferences and take part in political debate (Eskeland, 1996). As soon as we listen to what they tell us, we find, as Davie (1996) says we will, that children grasp much more about their own worlds than we know through observation. The psychological base of human autonomy — an innately endowed cognitive competence — should not be in doubt. And if the settings we organize for children are appropriate, the experiences entailed by those settings presume judgmental skills for those whose lives come to depend on them. In the social, political and intellectual circumstances of schools, pupils will comprehend just about as much of those circumstances as we allow.

What children cannot know about is a wider future — vocationally, professionally and personally. But it is hard for adults to engage in crystal-ball gazing on behalf of themselves, let alone others. The limits we must set on behalf of primary school children, we must set on behalf of everyone: limits of comprehension are given by our experiences and developmentally acquired capabilities not by our age, though age is an indicator of both experience and development, which is why we take notice of it. To stick fast to the principle itself: although we will never ignore age — because it cues us for the likely mental maturity or immaturity of learners — we must never believe that age will in itself tell us what a learner can or cannot know. To make decisions about actual capacity, we must look directly at what experiences children have had, what purposes and perspectives have developed out of those experiences, and how rationally expressed (not necessarily through verbal expression) judgments made actually are.

Human beings make judgments and decisions about themselves, *in context*. In that sense, we are all agents for the fulfilment of our own purposes, unless these purposes are constrained by others, and unless we impose constraints upon our own freedoms. Age has no bearing on this fact beyond the one stated. What's more, people will usually wish to exercise their independence whatever their age. This is one of the compelling signs of humanness: we all notice when our natural freedoms are being eroded and are likely to become bothered by such erosion. Pollard et al. (1994; also Trigg and Pollard, 1998) find that the National Curriculum's closing down for pupils of the opportunity to exercise curricular choice is not a pleasing situation, even for the youngest. Almost two-thirds of pupils at Key Stage 1 would prefer to have some say in what they study (reducing to around 44 per cent by year 5) — not typically because they believe that work which is self-chosen might in some sense be easier, but because they wish to stay in control of it (Trigg and Pollard, 1998, p. 112).

To accept that contextualized autonomy is a norm for all human beings, and that children as a group no less than adults adhere to this norm, might not lead us to exhort teachers to fufil children's rights (in the sense of making the fulfilment of those rights empirically possible). For we could decide that it is in children's interests not to take part in educational decision making even though, intellectually speaking, they are fitted to do so. Adults might regard it is as 'playing safe' to shelter children from irrevocable decisions, or until the adults are absolutely sure that their children will not by choice close future vocational doors or stray into harmful or in some sense unpromising fields of study. We might think that the role of parents is exactly that of making decisions on behalf of their children in those important matters — such as the educational — on which futures depend. So, while recognizing children's capabilities and accepting that they have, in general, rights of participation, what should the attitude of primary school teachers be to pupil competence?

Teaching for autonomy

It is a teacher's job to give pupils opportunities to develop means for expressing their own individuality which are believed culturally viable and worthwhile. Where teachers accede to the recommendations made at the end of the last chapter, they will help pupils make value-commitments which they will wish to make in order, freely, to 'actualize' their own positions in relationship to the world. Teachers cannot do this without giving pupils 'rights of participation', though such rights do not imply a disempowered role for teachers. What we can check out are the separate realms of decision making which accrue to the adult–child partners within this enterprise.

Teachers only ever *guide* students' value-commitments to particular types of study, forms of understanding and the application of these in one direction or another. Friendly exhortations, benevolent coercions, the judicious use of rewards and the withholding of rewards, the creation of bonds of relationship and so forth are ways of shepherding pupils towards a leap of commitment and responsibility. Whether they make that leap will be determined by pupils' own purposes, and these will have other antecedents than those initiated by schools. Usually, pupils' intentions will harmonize with those of teachers. We formulate our intentions as individuals, but we will be guided by what is believed appropriate within the wider community. What broader, communally decided value systems do is contextualize the individual — labelling these as possible or impossible, worthwhile or not, pleasurably fulfilling or as predicated on much labour and toil for little emotional reward. What they don't do is predetermine individual choice, which, as repeatedly stated, will not only try out novel forms but may well refashion these, and will certainly be uniquely related to them.

As part of an investigation into pupils' views of their own curricula, an interesting picture emerged as to pupils' acceptance of what they learn in school which has a bearing on the argument being made. Relevant data is partially reported in

Wyness and Silcock (1997), but the particular example to be given is not. The lack of public validation of the data should not be regarded as an issue, for the example will be seen to be validated by circumstance — i.e. it would be a fairly inevitable by-product of primary school life in 1996–7. What was found by researchers is that, at the time, there was a small sub-group of primary age pupils who were not at all pleased with the curriculum which was on offer to them, for very understandable reasons (there were others who were displeased for more idiosyncratic and less overtly justifiable reasons). These are pupils who saw in themselves a musical or sporting predisposition, a budding talent for dance or gymnastics, or as boasting creative skills of other sorts. They often looked to a future in some sort of 'performance' venue, and had come to recognize that their school curriculum (i.e. in 1996–7) had built-in priorities different from the ones they would like (i.e. time to devote to arts teaching had become noticeably reduced *vis-à-vis* other subjects over the period of these pupils' school lives).

Now, it is not a matter of how many pupils fit into a category of disenchantment with the National Curriculum, nor really whether they have a case against those enforcing it, but how teachers regard the value commitments such pupils are proferring. Can or should teachers tempt such pupils into other activities, where their schools can arrange more suitable courses and fuller resourcing? They probably can. But of course they should not. It isn't suggested that other activities are removed from pupils' repertoires of study, only that they cannot be somehow inserted into the value-systems of the pupils concerned. And there are no circumstances one can think of where pupils should be strong-armed into accepting one set of values rather than another, for reasons (as argued) connected partly with the developmental nature of processes which allow such commitments, partly with our definitions of values as personally chosen, and partly with what we mean by pupils having rights derived from our beliefs about human rights.

It is well-known for primary school boys to wish to become soccer stars. Parents and teachers who realize that these boys may have little natural talent and practically no prospect of succeeding with a sporting career might seek to guide their charges towards more profitable vocations. They can only seek to guide their children in the light of the children's own commitments. Anecdotally, the author remembers as a primary school teacher watching year-group after year-group of boys who had to live through long spells of being hypnotized by the 'glamour' of soccer before growing into more 'strategic' interests. Such maturation took much longer for some boys than for others, and for a few the obsession paid personal (and occasionally professional) dividends over the longer term. No adult should want to bar even the youngest children from making such commitments, or from behaving in specialized ways in the light of them.

Once we agree that knowledge-contexts are not somehow finalized sets of concepts, skills and values which we either can or would wish to transmit directly to pupils, we will realize that they resemble more maps of territory, where some cities and towns are well known and localized as centres of communications while others remain partially unexplored and there is a lot of unknown terrain vaguely perceived in the distance. Using such a metaphor, and setting our sights only on teaching for autonomy (as this either supports or is a derivative from other kinds of teaching), we can summarize the functions of an educational system, when examined through progressivist eyes, as being of three sorts. It will have a *mapping* function, a facilitating *or assisting* function and a *guiding* function.

Conclusion: educating for autonomy — mapping, assisting, guiding

It is the job of educationists through research and scholarship to map out new cultural territories in a manner making these visible to learners. Teachers may not work at the 'cutting edge' of research (though they sometimes will), but they will work hand in hand with researchers to translate new understandings into programmes which can be taught. It is a teacher's job to assist pupils' journeys through these territories, by ensuring that skills and concepts pupils need to make it are learned and that opportunities arise for pupils to commit themselves to various routes and prepare themselves for their cultural adventures. But it is the pupils who are the explorers, and their routes will be both self-chosen and made according to unique purposes, albeit aided and advised through contact with others. In the clear labelling of landmarks, routes and destinations, the proper preparing of necessary capabilities and skills, teachers guide pupils along their self-chosen pathways to make sure they don't stumble into potentially harmful pits along the way, and to make sure they are heading in worthwhile directions.

School pupils are — in normal circumstances — competent learners. They have inalienable rights. And it is perfectly possible for teachers to fulfil pupils' rights within educational environments generally, though it is not that easily achieved within a standard curriculum, as noticed, for a pre-set curriculum may stop pupils fulfilling their more basic entitlements to control their own destinies in their own ways. But, in the sense that pupils are 'whole persons', we can trust them to understand the constraints under which teachers themselves work, simply by spelling out the nature of whatever curricular dictates operate at any one time. In the end, teachers must trust their pupils as being responsible agents for their own learning, without thinking that this means any loss of rigour in terms of the way they, the teachers, deploy their own scholarly knowledge and pedagogic skills. What is at issue is the extent to which we can acknowledge and enhance the role of learners, not diminish the roles and responsibilities of teachers.

Taking on board arguments meant to show how we can help pupils express their individuality edges us a little way towards exerting pressures on governments to create the right climate of resource and expectation for making that task feasible. After all, the chances of effecting change within a democratic state should arise often enough. At the time of writing (Autumn, 1998), the QCA (Qualifications and Curriculum Authority) is following the SCAA (School Curriculum and Assessment Authority) in finalizing its review of the English/Welsh National Curriculum. Possibly, this review will recommend a curriculum with fewer standard and more optional elements to satisfy the demands from those who know the value of mixing diversity with prescriptions: steps in this direction have already been taken by the present government. Such an outcome will play directly into the hands of child-centred practitioners who should, again, seize an opportunity to enfranchise pupils in helping to manage their own curricula. The great benefit derived from doing so is that pupils will more readily confront what is standardized from the springboard of what they have chosen to study for themselves.

Chapter 10

Modern Progressivism

If Webb and Vulliamy et al.'s (1997) observation that teachers' personal and professional beliefs threaten to break apart under the weight of outside intervention proves prophetic, this will not signal the end of ideological influence on education. It will mean that government-sponsored ideologies will prosper, and since governments (even left-wing ones) are instinctively traditionalist in beliefs, such an outcome could easily reverse the real progress in the democratizing of classrooms which has been discernible in primary education over many years. Such misfortune should not happen, because teachers can look to their own beliefs, not those of governments, to sustain them. And what is characteristic of child-centred beliefs is that their caring, humanitarian ethic is an engine of real power: it inspires teachers of young children with an emotional resource enabling them to continue with work which is, often, arduous and demotivating. In so far as the ideology continues to survive in schools, it will evolve, as it must, in ways which mutually invigorate both 'child-centredness' and the ongoing development of the English/Welsh National Curriculum.

There is no ambiguity involved in allying diverse, self-managed curricula to socially responsible aims and industrial need. On the contrary: it is likely that the most responsible citizens and best workers are those whose ambitions are coupled to cultural ideals through choice. Child-centred commitment to individualized learning is not a commitment to radical politics or some sort of postmodern denial of absolutes. It can guide learners in whatever directions the state decrees, while keeping a weather eye on what pupils' own choices dictate: the art of progressivist teaching is to help learners address one goal from the perspective of the other.

New progressivism embraces old values. Yet its aims are more affected by social, moral and industrial demands than was needed mid-century. Politicians ruthlessly seek to control educational outputs now, and it is unlikely that state interference will quickly disappear. So, it is desirable to reassess progressivist claims for sake of today's accountability. As Richards suggests (cited Galton, 1989a), it was probably lack of accountability which in the past led some forms of progressivism to descend into a laissez-faire free-for-all. Modern progressivists will welcome appraisals of their aims and methods, providing there are no misperceptions of their belief-systems. Teachers should avoid helping critics by falling back upon simplistic polarizations and doctrinaire stubbornness as replacements for reasoned argument. They need to be pragmatically flexible and politically astute in realizing what is essential to their philosophy and cannot be compromised, and what might be left in abeyance until political fashions change.

To remind ourselves of what progressivists should in no circumstance compromise, a final summary of the preceding argument will review main principles and criticisms. When making a cumulative case, it is easy to lose sight of the reasons why one idea was chosen rather than another.

Ideological foundations

New progressivism is founded in developmental, humanistic, democratic and pragmatic ideas: there are empirical, ethical, socio-political and practical grounds for choosing to be a modern, child-centred teacher. Each theoretical pillar is structurally related to the others, rather as the pillars of a temple are planned to harmonize architecturally in order to contain a specialized set of activities. So to concede the relevance to the whole of one kind of support is to predispose oneself to seeing the relevance of the others, whereas to find weaknesses in one makes it likely that weaknesses will be found in all. This happens because new progressivism builds on an association between children and cultures which stretches beyond developmentalism into philosophy and politics, though it receives testimony, at a factual level, from constructivist and neo-Piagetian psychology. From this relationship with psychology is taken a definition of personal autonomy which humanism reinforces on a philosophical level. When asserting children's rights, humanistic writers often acknowledge the concept of proactive individuality promoted by progressivists and constructivists. Establishing their ethical justification gives additional support to progressivist teachers' aims and values.

The complementary culture concept arising from a transformational view of individual learning and development is a dynamic one providing a rationale for that mutually invigorating interaction between individuals and groups we call democratic. Since the role of a teacher is to help pupils become educated through a process of 'co-construction', modern child-centred classrooms have to be democratically organized with children given rights and properly designated roles of responsibility within them. It follows that primary school teaching's pragmatism becomes channelled into the fitting of individual needs to social opportunity, and social need to individual purposes. This interrelationship of parts to whole underwrites the structure of progressivist ideology, as is seen by briefly revisiting each area of study.

Developmentalism

Children transform their cultures and cultures transform individuals: there is a growing consensus among contributors to developmental studies about this. Where there is dispute is in the detailing of mechanisms explaining how the individual/social interaction is managed. Few cultural psychologists banish individuals from any role in their own development, but there is a gulf between those who agree with one theme in Vygotsky's writings, that individualism is a 'subsidiary and derivative' childhood role (cited Wertsch, 1991, and with Smolke, 1993), and neo-Piagetians who believe that individuals construct their minds, accessing culturally valued knowledge and skills through their own agency. Progressivists take the latter view, for the former can lead to a highly structured and formalized type of education thought to imprison rather than liberate individual personality and character.

To throw in one's lot with neo-Piagetians and constructivists is to believe that teacher interventions have to ensure that child development occurs as a cumulative, stage-wise building of capabilities. Because we no longer think that children progress, as a matter of course, toward 'higher-order' skills, we have to become clear-minded about the sorts of educated citizens we want. If we value critical argument and self-regulation, the abilities to apply and synthesize knowledge, the understandings and academic sensitivities we have always prized, we cannot believe that these will develop in some sort of unmediated way. Such a conclusion returns us to the conviction that first-hand experience and stage-related activities are as vital to childhood education as they have ever been. For unless these forms of experience are arranged through intervention, they might not happen at all, impairing the long-term cognitive growth educational curricula (such as the English/Welsh National Curriculum) require.

Constructivist and neo-Piagetian teaching programmes, such as the Adey and Shayer project at London University (1994, 1996) and those discussed or reviewed by Driver (1983), Littledyke and Huxford (1998) and Sutherland (1992), provide evidence for the effectiveness of teachers intervening in children's development. While sanctioning the role of individual experience and personal perspective-taking, they are not mealy-mouthed in challenging pupils with tough academic problems, and guiding them towards public modes of explanation. In Adey and Shayer's case, these public modes are the 'formal operational' principles of science. In contributors to Littledyke and Huxford's discussion of constructivist teaching (1998), they are skills and concepts intrinsic to all primary school curricular subjects, including PE, Art, Music and RE. The twin principles of individual experience and culturally valued knowledge become child-centred when we employ the 'constructivist' maxim that individuals reach cultural goals through their own volitions: goals must be consciously known, reachable and structurally related to the academic subject studied. A learning context will facilitate pupils' willingness and ability to adapt their existing views to new ideas. In curricular terms, there are affective, cognitive and socio-political dimensions to constructivist learning to be catered for (commitment, control and comprehension were suggested as central 'process' characteristics). There are no short-cuts which bypass such a provision.

Humanism

From developmental studies we abstract a concept of individuality which happily blends research findings with humanist philosophy. If children shape their own minds through their own actions, they can be regarded from the start as fully-fledged 'whole' persons, to be accorded full human rights like anyone else. One supposition is not implied by the other: but to recognize that children have a potential for voluntary action which will ultimately give them rationality takes us some way towards admitting into classrooms their personal views of life, and respecting these in schools as elsewhere. Educationally speaking, the humanist directive is to 'teach for autonomy' such that children take full advantage of their natural rights. No one believes that children should be given full control over their own learning, but many these days see the practical as well as ethical advantages flowing from enfranchising learners as early as possible. There is no 'bottom' limit to the recognition of human autonomy, provided we define the qualities of mind composing it within the context where it has to be expressed: no matter how young a pupil is, he or she will have some decision making capability.

To believe that learner perspectives upon curricula should be 'transformational' means designing curricula to be understood, owned and potentially managed by pupils, in negotiation with adults whose wider perspectives allow them to guard against false allegiances and corrupting influence. Whereas we have to give regard to pupils' expanding ambitions, we have also to admit that these may not always be — strategically — in their interests. So teachers 'liberate' pupil capabilities through regulating individual purpose within constraints of social responsibility and a benevolent rule-governed system. Their success in implementing curricula will be detectable through the 'process' criteria indicating quality learning.

Democracy

School communities are places where teachers, as well as pupils, have rightful views, informed by the opinions of politicians, parents, OFSTED inspectors, educational advisers, technical advisers, industrialists looking for a workforce, peers and other professionals and welfare workers, etc. etc. Intrinsic to the conceptualizing of a child–culture relationship as transformational is a culture concept equally dynamic. Cultures are webs of influence to which we attach our own personal contributions; they are treasure-houses of habits and attitudes from which we steal. As Dewey tells us: individuals and societies, children and cultures are complementary not competing agencies within the educational system.

If learners are to make their own ways in the world, they can only do so by reference to the choices of others. Which does not imply that a rough-hewn individual aspiration must, somehow, become smoothed out through social encounters. Sometimes, it is a whole culture which is altered by the ideas of a Freud or a Darwin, a Rousseau or an Einstein. Often enough we have to live with compromises respecting the integrity of opposing views, and leaving, as an accompaniment of an 'open' forum of teaching, a conflict of purposes, unreconciled for the time being but providing some stimulus for further inventions. This is the nature of a pluralist, diversely populated democratic state. Encouraging disputes, fostering peaceful argument and reconciling views without diminishing them are the food and drink of any democracy, including primary school democracies. And to state that the perspectives taken from individual and cultural purpose are both transformational is to state that each will seek to challenge the other by nature, and that this bi-transformation (or co-construction) is not only legitimate but is the only way each one of us can carve out his or her own cultural niche.

Pragmatism

Reconciling the twin demands of individuals and society is seldom a balanced job in the way educational dilemmas have to be resolved. Situations always fluctuate between one pole and another. Teachers may no sooner have sorted out someone's emotional difficulties than they have to rejig a task to make it acceptable to the learner without coming off-track with regard to their objectives. One cannot prescribe for this sort of pragmatically flexible application of skill, except to realize, as Dewey did, that the two poles of attention are not opposed to each other unless we believe that they are. It is possible to give all one's time to designing a perfect curriculum without taking the trouble to match it to individual need, and it is just as possible to become preoccupied with keeping individual learners content without taking cognizance of broader aims. The art of child-centred teaching is to maintain a balanced requirement within those terms of reference (neo-Piagetian or whatever) which separate progressivism from other ideologies.

Ideological roots

An alternative structure for this book would have been to start with a listing of the main criticisms of progressivist ideas alongside their rebuttals, followed by a justification for revising the ideology and a discussion of the revisions themselves. Unfortunately, since many criticisms are integral to the revisions needed, following that plan would have led to much repetition and overlapping material. So, the rationale adopted integrates criticisms as part of a continuing dialogue between criticism and response. To retrieve something of the clarity that the alternative structure would have produced, it is possible, by focusing on writers and texts, to summarize the case for a new progressivism, sort out its newness and the sense in which it is not at all novel, unravel strands of argument and be as fair as possible to critics.

Three bodies of literature have been explored. There are standard commentaries upon progressivism; there are critiques of the contemporary educational scene justifying a search for alternatives; and there is the array of writings from which a progressivist can draw to restore the ideology's credibility. Referring again to each area will be enough to recall any claims being made without a reader having to suffer distractions from the flurry of examples or secondary points which the main discussion contains.

New Progressivism

The critics

There are three standard types of criticism made of progressivist thinking. Firstly, there are the criticisms of those who see ideological theorizing as either unnecessary or biased. Secondly, there are objections stemming from those empirical research conclusions meant to test out progressivist claims. Thirdly, there are the critiques written by those who, while conceding the validity of ideological debate, nonetheless find progressivist beliefs wanting in some way or other.

Firstly, politicians, pragmatists, postmodernists, those philosophers of education and sociologists who stigmatize ideologies as by definition one-sided, warn us against ideological decision making. This is despite the fact that to follow through the pragmatist's arguments and draw a neutral mid-line between ideologies is to assume that whole network of belief called an ideological perspective. Robin Alexander's hostility towards the detrimental effects on education of progressivist rhetoric bows suitably towards a recognition that much achievement in primary schools is owed to child-centred ideals (1992, 1994, 1995). What he is concerned to spell out are the dangers of teachers feeling so pressurized by orthodoxies that they adopt inflexible classroom policies. Such a false polarization and dichotomizing of aims and methods shore up many attacks, given that the flux of 'post'-modern life demands a flexibility of approach, not one bound by doctrines. Philosophers such as Richard Pring (1989a) reach the same conclusion: on strict, logical grounds we cannot value the views and interests of children without seeing what might, very differently, be in their interests. Richard Peters' defining of education as 'initiation into worthwhile forms of life' (1966) sealed the nature of this debate for many, making very precarious any idea claiming that we favour an educational process which only looks at children's views, or the processes signalling their relationships with knowledge, without taking cognizance of what might follow.

Ideologies need not and should not polarize. If they do, it is probable that the teachers concerned do not fully understand their own beliefs and demonstrate in their mediocre teaching or biased discourse not just the problem with ideologies as the problem with any form of behaviour relying on poorly known principles. If we believe teachers should be able to justify what they do, they must come to some understanding of theoretically framed justifications, whether these are ideologically charged or ideologically neutral. When we do engage in ideological study, we discover that progressivism and traditionalism, as the two easiest ways to group differences, split from each other at the level of values, but need not polarize at the level of practice or belief. This difference between a real and false dichotomy has so plagued discussions it is worth trying to fix it within a metaphor.

Progressive and traditional ideals can be thought of as mountain peaks, distanced from each other in the sense that they rise out of different value-orientations. But the routes to these different values are often enough (not always of course) common. The peaks share common foothills. Teachers working in one tradition or another will often slog through these foothills, and their attitudes and practices will not be much different from those of others. But the teachers will be striving towards very different peaks of achievement, and it is in these intentions that we will sense the deeper level of values dividing them from each other.

Moreover, teachers do need the guidance of beliefs, for there are questions bound up with professional educators' practices which cannot be answered factually. Questions of fact and value interweave in educational affairs, and we have to disentangle them in order to answer theoretical questions. But in a teacher's daily work, pragmatic considerations always, somewhere, serve more fundamental values, and to pretend that this is not so is tacitly to adhere to those pragmatic ideologies which can only lead us into a confusion of ends and means, and the likelihood of designing school curricula which try to achieve too much and end up achieving very little.

The same end waits for those postmodernists who wish to discard superordinate ideas because none are thought reliable. We should distinguish texts which do no more than limit the effect of principle through indicating the role of 'grounded' skills and implicit theories (as Schôn, 1983) or the crucial influence of social context (Mackenzie, 1997) and the radical doubting of all universals. The latter takes away from us hierarchies which most education systems suppose: i.e. teachers have gradually to coax children from one immature type of views towards more reliable types. The fact that these are never absolutely proven does not make them unworthy of support relative to the less clearly glimpsed notions of childhood. To misunderstand this role played by academic knowledge which is by nature fallible and provisional leads into self-contradiction.

Ideological bias is well known not only in education but in politics, religion and any academic pursuits which have human conduct as a primary reference. Philosophers, psychologists and sociologists tend, themselves, to be members of 'schools' of thought, applying their disciplines in partisan ways, and one understands those social scientists who wish to free their subject from the snares of political correctness. There is no virtue in prejudging ideas before fully considering them. And this is no less true of progressivist ideas. They can be perfectly workable and worthy of support, while being structured as ideologies.

Secondly, Alexander et al.'s 'discussion document' (1992), sponsored by Kenneth Clarke during the Thatcher administration, was meant to move primary school teachers forward away from their entrenched positions. To achieve this, a host of research findings informed it; many meant to show that progressivist methods didn't work, didn't exist or were flawed in conception. The lengthy trail of such findings winds back to the immediate post-Plowden era when erratically achieved formal skills were blamed for Britain's unsatisfactory trade and industrial performance worldwide. The year 1976 was that of Callaghan's Ruskin speech, and the year Neville Bennett's comparisons of progressivist and traditionalist teaching styles were published in the wake of the William Tyndale affair (Ellis et al., 1976) and 'Black Paper' attacks (Cox and Dyson, 1960, 1971). Some were even questioning whether primary school teachers were really implementing 'Plowden' policies at all (Sharp and Green, 1975), a view which has become accepted wisdom (Galton,

1989a; Simon, 1981b; Mackenzie, 1997; Sugrue, 1997). The Bennett research and the influential ORACLE studies (Galton et al., 1980), trying to draw together teaching styles, pupil behaviour and outcomes in order to test out the efficacy of the former, purported to show that child-centredness — as the researchers defined it — was not producing the quality outcomes it was supposed to produce.

But any unambiguous classification of styles risks missing that very mix of techniques and strategies which work, because they have combined pragmatically to achieve their ends. Bennett (1976) noticed that the most effective teacher met during his research used a mix of methods, implying that she was neither child-centred nor traditionalist in orientation. Yet to mix methodologies says little about ideology. It is not methods but the values justifying them which create child-centredness. This is not to deny that methodologies become grouped under ideological umbrellas — it would be surprising if child-centred teachers sought at all costs to avoid contact with individual learners! But any teacher who seeks solely to work with individuals and small groups is raising these forms of organization themselves to the status of value, not the interests of children as individuals.

Sugrue's case studies of child-centred teachers (1997) showing the communication linkages between beliefs and attitudes, intentions and actions, and the action-research neo-Piagetian projects cited (Adey and Shayer, 1994; Resnick et al., 1992), are programmes designed to penetrate to the ideologically sensitive differences between educational approaches. Experimental and observational research projects are not. It isn't that standard testing of pupils is anathema to progressivist teaching, it is more that high scores on standard tests aren't a constructivist teacher's first goal. If they were, then the teacher wouldn't be constructivist. But they are a subsidiary goal signposting the achievement of a more fundamental target: that is, if progressivist/constructivist methods facilitate qualitative leaps in progress, one spin-off must be a pupil's enhanced ability to cope with formal tests. All teachers teach to the tests which most suit their methods, and the immediate benefits from methods meant to enhance development are not the learning of pre-specified material. This is likely to be a delayed not an immediate outcome.

Anyway, the interpretation of research findings is no hard and fast business: researchers select and interpret from their findings what suits their own purposes. This is not to be cynical, simply to notice the different agendas of educationists who are testing hypotheses belonging to distinct belief systems. Politicians make, similarly, their own selections from research to justify policy aims and political strategies. As a case in point: Taberrer's address to the 1998 ASPE conference, as a DfEE adviser (Taberrer, 1998), celebrated teachers' achievements in various subjects but especially in basic skills in the light of statistics gained through international comparisons. His exercise contrasted sharply with attempts no more than 18 months before to show through cross-national comparison British underachievement in subjects such as mathematics (Reynolds and Farrell, 1996). In absolutist terms, one or other view has to be false. Only, when one looks at the circumstances giving rise to the interpretation made, one sees that even contradictory conclusions live together within broader verities. In this instance, the complexity of lifting educational products from their cultural processes makes both sets of conclusions either doubtful (as sure guides) or useful (as exemplars of the way cultural circumstance and educational process interact).

Texts discrediting the Piagetian infrastructure of progressivist theory fall into two piles. Among British educators embracing a socially mediated approach to teaching, some were led by Vygotskian empiricism to misconstrue Piaget's theorizing as wholly individualistic, not only in conceptual positioning, but in the scope of its explanations, and therefore to be superseded. While, reasonably, declaring the value of linguistic intervention, they have tended to underplay the skills, capabilities and constraints learners bring to school situations. Alexander (1994), Antony (1979), Bennett (1987, 1992), Galton (1989a), Littledyke (1998), Mackenzie (1997), Pollard (1994), Tizard and Hughes (1984), Wells (1986) and Woods (1994), each in his or her own way echoes Halsey and Sylva's (1987) verdict on Plowden progressivism that its death had to follow on the heels of Piaget's dethronement from his dominance within developmental psychology. That dethronement has been postponed. And, year on year, it looks less and less likely to happen. Neo-Vygotksian cultural psychologists (Bruner, 1995; Cole, 1996; Cole and Engestrom, 1995; Cole and Wertsch, 1996; Wertsch, 1979, 1991; Wertsch and Smolke, 1993), who seek to make a solid case for the cultural origins of children's thinking and problem solving, know well enough the resilience of the Piagetian thesis while trying to make inroads into it. The questions is not (and never has been) which of the two psychologists is correct or of whether individual and social action both have a place in educational success. It is a question of which perspective serves our best interests regarding educational policies, and of how, ultimately, both sets of perspectives might be harnessed to facilitate our practices.

Anyone wishing to understand contemporary developmental theory in order to apply it to modern classrooms has to skip back and forth through research discussions, building up a library of typical problems and overlapping conclusions found, for example, in papers by Astington and Olson (1995, alongside the commentary by Bruner, 1995), Cole (1996), Cole and Wertsch (1996), Kitchener (1996), Lawrence and Valsiner (1992), Lucariello (1995, with commentary by Cole and Engeström, 1995), Moll (1994, with commentary by Wertsch, 1994), Smith (1996), Nelson et al. (1998, alongside a commentary by Astington, 1998), Wertsch (1979,1991), Wertsch and Smolke (1993). These papers exemplify much broader debates (most, though not all, found in the journal *Human Development*) that leave open the precise nature of the Piaget/Vygotsky reconciliation which will, surely, one day occur. A hypothesis receiving approval, that the internalizing of culturally derived knowledge happens through children's voluntary actions, albeit within a controlled context (Adey and Shayer 1994, 1996; J. L. Biggs, 1992; Gaskins et al., 1992; Tharp and Gallimore, 1993; Silcock, 1996; Valsiner, 1992, 1996), gives progressivists the new starting point they need, resiting child-centredness within neo-Piagetian theory as an interventionist approach to teaching.

Thirdly, traditionalists (such as O'Hear, 1987) look to the weaknesses of progressivist thinking as inhering in the ideology's very diversity and pluralist pretensions. Black paper writers (Cox and Dyson, 1960, 1971) and neo-right-wing critics (e.g.

Lawlor, 1990; O'Keefe, 1990) similarly fear or feared that the dilution of a traditional culture by attempts to widen access to it threatens established modes of academic achievement, such as the ability to exercise formally acquired skills and memorize well-loved texts. Critics more to the left of the political spectrum (Boyd, 1989; Brehony, 1992; Epstein, 1993; Jones, 1983; Lawton, 1989; Onore and Lubetsky, 1992; Lowe, 1987; Walkerdine, 1994) attack progressivism for the opposite reason: they surmise that its individuality diverts it from socially responsible ends. Again, these are not contradictory criticisms. For the former group regrets that child-centred teachers embrace diversity of outcome and sees this as problematic in itself, while the latter desire in learners a particular attitude towards diversity — i.e. a pre-specified attitude of social responsibility, tolerating differences and recognizing issues of prejudice and discrimination.

Neo-progressivism's developmentalism, redefining individuals and cultures in relationship with each other, while insisting that it is pupils who construct their minds for their own purposes, conceives as part of that construction process a dynamic notion of culture itself. This notion makes possible the articulating of a role for teachers and structured curricula in both educational and developmental schemes. All developmental-stage theories, as all educational systems which relate somewhere to them, are value-driven. So there is no conflict between an education which gives succour to personal ambition while insisting that developments must be guided. This is to acquiesce with the second sort of criticism above, while redrawing the line between progressivism and the traditionalist ideology sponsored by the first. Traditional values, depending on a 'transmission' hypothesis, have their place within a community wishing to maintain a homogeneity of aim, a commonality of lifestyles and a consensus on values, but not, it is suggested, within a society fluctuating in what it takes to be appropriate lifestyles and achievements and highly patterned in terms of values and ideals, as western societies are likely to stay for the foreseeable future.

Critics of the English/Welsh National Curriculum

A desire to return to progressivist theory is awakened by the sight of a failing traditionalist system. The English/Welsh National Curriculum, established in 1988/9, was a top-down superstructure, composed of carefully worded content statements. It was openly traditional in its assumption that teachers would happily 'transmit' or 'deliver' what was written as subject orders. Critics who saw both technical and practical problems with it were not usually progressivists looking to retrieve influence: if they had been, we might have questioned their motives. Usually, they were writers seeing merely that there was something amiss. Empiricist accounts of teachers who could not cope, practically, with an enormously weighty timetable and an overload of accompanying bureaucratic tasks, recording the losses in terms of teacher morale and pupil motivation, were meant to be factual (Campbell, 1993a and b; Campbell and Neil, 1992; Silcock, 1990, 1992, 1995; Silcock and Wyness, 1997, 1998; Pollard et al., 1994; Webb, 1993). These researchers were among the first to perceive that the National Curriculum had severe problems of curricular overload and could not survive long in its initial form.

Worries about the autocratic overtones of the English/Welsh National Curriculum were not confined to empirical researchers. Professional associations within education have from time to time joined forces to seek a more professionally democratic solution to curricular and other educational questions. For example, it is possible to identify some researchers not only by scrutinizing their research agendas but by their allegiance to the Association for the Study of Primary Education, within which all the above empiricists, for example, hold or have held office. ASPE is a professional association of lecturers, researchers, teachers and administrators, with its origins, around 1988, in the fears of academics that educational research and scholarship might suffer within an imposed framework of opinion, given the National Curriculum's bureaucratic centralizing function. ASPE's present chairman, Colin Richards, whose background as an HMI and chief primary adviser at OFSTED sensitizes him to the tendentious flavour of much recent government policy, advocates a second, genuine 'great debate', where all with a stake in education have an empowered voice (1998).

Although critics of government policy over the past decade are by no means all progressivists, they have pressed for changes to the National Curriculum in the light of various reasons for dissatisfaction. In this way, they inexorably edge public opinion back to a position where a request to prove the worth of child-centred curricula can be reinserted into debates. Such an equivalence of aim is less true of critics with ideological ambitions already heavily politicized, such as writers of the 'New Left' or the sociologists and reconstructionists who see education as a means to restructuring society. They have some shared ends with progressivists, but tend not to agree at all about means. The point is that the benificiary of researchers continuing to probe the flaws in a traditionalist curriculum is as likely to be a progressivist as anyone.

Modern progressivists

Progressivism's unfashionable image (much like the unfashionable image in a number of educationists' minds of Piagetian thinking) owes much to every educationist's and politician's desire to improve on past ideas. Only when critiques are shown to be based on misconceptions, misinterpretations, risky speculations or dogma dangerously unsuited to a modern-day society might we move forward to a more balanced assessment and, hopefully, a situation where those preferring child-centred forms of teaching will not be shamelessly harassed or scapegoated. It is sad that most writings about progressivism over the past couple of decades have been critical of it, and the success of critics has been to fragment and divide the British movement. Old academic battles over the viability of process curricula recur rarely, notably in Kelly's books (e.g. 1994). There is a neo-Piagetian attempt to reconcile it with a standard curricular structure (Silcock, 1993, 1994a, 1996) and a philosophical defence of its historical roots in the writings of Rousseau and Dewey (Darling,

1994). Neo-Piagetian and constructivist teaching keep alive progressivist rationales in their methodologies, though constructivists themselves often distance themselves from progressivism as 'belonging to the past' (Littledyke, 1998). Sugrue reinvents the ideology as a postmodern survivor of internecine battles (Sugrue, 1997). As a stable vision underpinning primary school practices, progressive child-centredness is only unequivocally supported by writers within early childhood education (e.g. Blatchford and Blatchford, 1995; David et al., 1992; Fisher, 1995).

Apart from early-childhood theorists, writings which renew the effectiveness of a learner-centred approach are the reported experiments of constructivists (Driver, 1983, 1989; Driver and Bell, 1986 — see Littledyke and Huxford, 1998), neo-Piagetians (Adey and Shayer, 1994; Resnick, 1997; Resnick et al., 1992 — see Sutherland, 1992) and humanistic educators working in a Rogerian manner (Brandes and Ginnes, 1986; Hall and Hall, 1988). Constructivist, neo- or post-Piagetian and humanist programmes do not outwardly serve progressivist values (which have an overtly ethical dimension) but are lodged either in a neo- or post-Piagetian empiricism or in the 'social constructivism' of Vygotsky, or in the self-actualization theory of humanist psychologists. The model of autonomous learning central to progressivist systems is not explicit within these other movements, though it has been argued that it is implicit. All learner-centred work is continuous with the progressivist once the value-basis of the learner-centredness is fully explained and political reverberations captured.

The reason why it might be advantageous to start seeing these diverse groupings as contributing to a new progressivist manifesto is not because there is anything wrong with people investigating within limited empirical frameworks, but because educational policies tend to ignore those whose aspirations are, by nature, academically parochial. Teaching is a conservative business given its practical preoccupations. Sutherland (1992) finds, on visiting schools, 'no awareness whatsoever of constructivist ideas' (p. 81). Galton periodically wonders why innovatory schemes in education flop fairly disastrously (Galton and Williamson, 1992). Teachers on INSET courses may find ORACLE enlightening, but they take little heed of its research conclusions in classrooms. Yet many teachers remain child-centred, despite media batterings and political censure. It could be that academics' and politicians' belief that, in order to raise standards, teacher attitudes must change is actually wrong. If we trusted teachers to improve through refining their own skills in the confidence that their professional ideologies were soundly based, educational standards might rise more quickly than through a 'top-down' attempt to wrench improvements out of a profession through unwelcomed reforms.

Primary school teachers whose values have survived the past decades and are unabashed in advertising their ideas about the 'whole child', integrated topic-based teaching and 'informal approaches' are already new progressivists. Their child-centred commitment may not be as it was because standardized curricula are not always immediately attractive to learners and they have had to look for newer ways of applying their beliefs. But these newer ways are in no short supply. We know, now, how to stimulate developmental progress through enhanced problem solving (Adey and Shayer, 1994; Resnick et al., 1992), how to teach skills of mindful knowledge-application (Adey and Shayer, 1994, 1996; Désforges, 1993, 1997), and how to help pupils assess and evaluate their own learning (Emery, 1996), mediate their own disputes (Silcock and Stacey, 1997) and build truly democratic negotiation strategies (Galton, 1989b; Osborne, 1997; Sixsmith and Simco, 1997; Worrall and Ingram, 1993). We are more certain than we have ever been that children, like any other human being, have inalienable rights of involvement and participation (Davie et al., 1996; John, 1996; Osler, 1994).

It should be more not less possible for modern primary school teachers to reach the quite sophisticated ends at which progressivists aim, providing we do not underestimate the time needed to do so. What modern teachers might insist on is that any assessments made of their methods must be more sensitive to cognitive gains than popular 'pencil and paper' tasks which always understate comprehension in favour of accuracy of reproduction and rote capacity. If we want rational, autonomous learners who will pursue learning through life for the sake of public welfare as much as for their own satisfaction, it isn't good enough to use tests which measure very limited skills. If we want high standards in education, we have to devise ways of assessing a quality process.

The benefits which should follow from liberating the professional energies of teachers so that they, in turn, can liberate the drive towards learning springing out of every child's native endowment ought to be self-evident. What is new about neo-progressivism are its adjusted theoretical reformulations to bring it within the value-orbit of a modern industrial society, hungry for growth, social peace and multicultural richness. It is old in its platform of beliefs that individual teachers and pupils will perform their roles most effectively when freed from unwanted bureaucratic interference. There are enormous powers of achievement hidden within even the youngest human beings. Modern progressivist theory reminds us of this without diminishing the role of teachers, analysing their cultural backdrop as a more dynamic and kaleidoscopic tapestry than is often supposed. It is the dualism of responsibilities distributed between teacher and taught, and the friction sparked by these, hinting at the disputatious nature of free bargaining within all democratic states, which distinguishes the new ideology and makes its embodiment in future classroom practices an exciting prospect.

References

ABIKO, T. (1998) 'A critical analysis of the school curriculum in contemporary Japan', *Education 3–13*, **26**, 2, pp. 17–25.
ADEY, P. and SHAYER, M. (1994) *Really Raising Standards*, London: Routledge.
ADEY, P. and SHAYER, M. (1996) 'An exploration of long-term far-transfer effects following an extended intervention program in the high school science curriculum', in Smith, L. (Ed.) *Critical Readings in Piaget*, London: Routledge.
AITKEN, M., BENNETT, S. N. and HESKETH, J. (1981) 'Teaching styles and pupil progress: a reanalysis', *British Journal of Educational Psychology*, **51**, 2, pp. 170–86.
ALEXANDER, R. J. (1992) *Policy and Practice in Primary Education*, London: Routledge.
ALEXANDER, R. J. (1993) *What Primary Curriculum? Dearing and Beyond*, Address to the Sixth National Conference of the Association for the Study of Primary Education, York.
ALEXANDER, R. J. (1994) *Innocence and Experience: Reconstructing Primary Education*, Stoke-on-Trent: ASPE/Trentham Books.
ALEXANDER, R. J. (1995) *Versions of Primary Education*, London: Routledge.
ALEXANDER, R. J. (1996) *Other Primary Schools and Ours: Hazards of International Comparison*, Centre for Research in Elementary and Primary Education: University of Warwick.
ALEXANDER, R. J. (1998) 'Basics, cores and choices, towards a new primary curriculum', *Education 3–13*, **26**, 1, pp. 60–9.
ALEXANDER, R. J., ROSE, J. and WOODHEAD, C. (1992) *Curriculum Organisation and Classroom Practice in Primary Schools: A Discussion Paper*, London: DES.
ANTONY, W. S. (1979) 'Progressive learning theories: the evidence', in BERNBAUM, G. (Ed.) *Schooling in Decline*, London: Macmillan.
APPLE, M. W. (1990) *Ideology and the Curriculum*, 2nd edn, New York: Routledge.
ASTINGTON, J. W. (1998) 'Commentary: theory of mind, Humpty Dumpty, and the ice box', *Human Development*, **84**, 41, pp. 30–9.
ASTINGTON, J. W. and OLSON, D. R. (1995) 'The cognitive revolution in children's understanding of mind', *Human Development*, **38**, pp. 179–89.
AVIRAM, A. (1993) 'Personal autonomy and the flexible school', *International Review of Education*, **39**, 5, pp. 419–33.
BADLEY, G. (1993) 'The quality debate in higher education', *British Journal of In-Service Education*, **19**, 3, pp. 23–8.
BALL, S. J. (1993) 'Education, Majorism and "the Curriculum of the Dead"', *Curriculum Studies*, **1**, 2, pp. 195–214.
BATTESON, C. (1997) 'A review of politics of education at the moment of 1976', *British Journal of Educational Studies*, **45**, 4, pp. 363–77.
BENNETT, S. N. (1976) *Teaching Styles and Pupil Progress*, London: Open Books.
BENNETT, S. N. (1987) 'Changing perspectives on teaching and learning processes in the post-Plowden era', *Oxford Review of Education*, **13**, 1, pp. 67–79.

References

BENNETT, S. N. (1992) *Managing Learning in the Primary Classroom*, Stoke-on-Trent: ASPE/Trentham Books.
BERLAK, A. and BERLAK, H. (1981) *The Dilemmas of Schooling*, London: Routledge.
BERLIN, I. (1969) *Four Essays on Liberty*, Oxford: Oxford University Press.
BIBER, B. (1972) 'The "whole child", individuality and values in education', in SQUIRE, J. R. (Ed.) *A New Look at Progressive Education*, Washington, DC: Association for Supervision and Curriculum Development.
BIDELL, T. R. and FISCHER, K. W. (1992) 'Cognitive development in educational contexts', in DEMITRIOU, A., SHAYER, M. and EFKLIDES A. E. (Eds) *Neo-Piagetian Theories of Cognitive Development: Implications and Applications for Education*, London: Routledge.
BIGGS, J. B. (1992a) 'Modes of learning, forms of knowing and ways of schooling', in DEMITRIOU, A., SHAYER, M. and EFKLIDES, A. E. (Eds) *Neo-Piagetian Theories of Cognitive Development: Implications and Applications for Education*, London: Routledge.
BIGGS, J. B. (1992b) 'Returning to school: review and discussion', in DEMITRIOU A., SHAYER, M. and EFKLIDES, A. M. (Eds) *Neo-Piagetian Theories of Cognitive Development: Implications and Applications for Education*, London: Routledge.
BIGGS, J. L. (1992) 'Mazes of meaning: how a child and a culture create each other', *New Directions in Child Development*, **58**, pp. 25–49.
BILLIG, M., CONDOR, S., EDWARDS, D., GANE, M., MIDDLETON, D. and RADLEY, A. (1988) *Ideological Dilemmas*, London: Sage Publications.
BLACKHAM, H. J. (1976) *Humanism*, Brighton: Harvester Press.
BLATCHFORD, I. S. and BLATCHFORD, J. (Eds) (1995) *Educating the Whole Child*, Buckingham: Open University Press.
BLENKIN, G. M. and KELLY, A. V. (1981) *The Primary Curriculum*, London: Harper and Row.
BLENKIN, G. M. and KELLY, A. V. (1994) 'The death of infancy', *Education 3–13*, **22**, 3, pp. 3–9.
BLENKIN, G. M. and KELLY, A. V. (1996) *Early Childhood Education and a Developmental Curriculum*, 2nd edn, London: Paul Chapman.
BLENKIN, G. M., EDWARDS, G. and KELLY, A. V. (1992) *Change and the Curriculum*, London: Paul Chapman.
BLISS, J., ASKEW, M. and MACRAE, S. (1996) 'Effective teaching and learning: scaffolding revisited', *Oxford Review of Education*, **22**, 1, pp. 37–61.
BLYTH, A. (1984) *Development, Experience and Curriculum in Primary Education*, London: Croom Helm.
BOARD OF EDUCATION (1931) *Report of the Consultative Committee on the Primary School* (Hadow Report), London: HMSO.
BOWER, T. G. R. (1971) *Development in Infancy*, San Franciso: Freeman.
BOYD, J. (1989) *Quality Issues in Primary Schools*, London: Chapman.
BRADY, L. (1997) 'Assessing curriculum outcomes in Australian schools', *Educational Review*, **49**, 1.
BRANDES, D. and GINNES, P. (1986) *A Guide to Student-Centred Learning*, Oxford: Blackwell.
BREHONY, K. J. (1992) 'What's left of progressive primary education?', in RATTANSI, A. and REEDER, D. (Eds) *Rethinking Radical Education: Essays in Honour of Brian Simon*, London: Lawrence and Wishart.
BREHONY, K. J. (1997) 'An "undeniable" and disastrous influence? Dewey and English education', *Oxford Review of Education*, **23**, 4, pp. 427–45.
BRIMBLECOMBE, N., ORMSTON, M. and SHAW, M. (1996) 'Gender differences in teacher response to school inspection', *Educational Studies*, **22**, 1, pp. 27–39.
BRUNDRETT, M. (1997) 'Who should teach teachers?', *Education Today*, **4**, 7, pp. 42–9.

References

BRUNER, J. S. (1968) *Processes of Cognitive Growth: Infancy*, Worcester, MA: Clarke University Press, with Barnes Publications.
BRUNER, J. S. (1972) *The Relevance of Education*, Harmondsworth: Penguin.
BRUNER, J. S. (1995) 'Commentary', *Human Development*, **38**, pp. 203–13.
BRUNER, J. S. (1997) 'Celebrating divergence: Piaget and Vygotsky', *Human Development*, **40**, pp. 63–73.
BRUNER, J. S. and HASTE, H. (1987) *Making Sense: The Child's Construction of the World*, London: Methuen.
BURDEN, B. (1996) 'Pupils' perceptions of themselves as thinkers, learners and problem-solvers: some preliminary results from the Myself-as-a-Learner Scale (MALS)', *Educational and Child Psychology*, **13**, 3.
BURTONWOOD, N. (1996) 'Culture, identity and the curriculum', *Educational Review*, **48**, 3, pp. 227–35.
CALDWELL, B. S. and SPINKS, J. M. (1988) *The Self-Managing School*, Lewes, East Sussex: Falmer Press.
CAMPBELL, R. J. (1993a) 'A dream at conception: a nightmare at delivery', in CAMPBELL, R. J. (Ed.) *Breadth and Balance in the Primary School Curriculum*, Bristol: Falmer Press.
CAMPBELL, R. J. (1993b) 'The broad and balanced curriculum in primary schools: some limitations of reform', *Curriculum Journal*, **4**, 2, pp. 215–29.
CAMPBELL, R. J. and NEILL, S. R. St. J. (1992) *Teacher-time and Curricular Manageability*, London: AMMA.
CAMPBELL, R. and OLSON, D. (1990) 'Children's thinking', in GRIEVE, R. and HUGHES, M. (Eds) *Understanding Children*, Oxford: Blackwell.
CARDELLE-ELEWAR, M. (1992) 'Effects of teaching metacognitive skills to students with low mathematical ability', *Teachers and Teacher Education*, **8**, 2, pp. 109–21.
CARR, D. (1988) 'Knowledge and the curriculum: four dogmas of child-centred education', *Journal of Philosophy of Education*, **22**, 2, pp. 1151–62.
CARR, W. and KEMMIS, S. (1986) *Becoming Critical: Education, Knowledge and Action Research*, London: Falmer Press.
CENTRAL ADVISORY COUNCIL REPORT (1967) *Children and their Primary Schools* (Plowden Report), London: HMSO.
CERYCH, L. (1997) 'Educational reforms in Central and East Europe: processes and outcomes', *European Journal of Education*, **32**, 1, pp. 75–96.
CHITTY, C. (1989) *Towards a New Education System: The Victory of the Far Right?*, London: Falmer Press.
CHITTY, C. (1996) 'Ruskin's legacy', *Times Educational Supplement*, 18 October, p. 15.
CLARKE, C. (1988) 'Child-centred education and the "growth" metaphysic', *Journal of the Philosophy of Education*, **22**, 1, pp. 75–88.
CLARKE, K. (1991) *Primary Education — A Statement by the Secretary of State for Education and Science*, London: DES.
COLE, M. (1996) *Culture in Mind*, Cambridge, MA: Harvard University Press.
COLE, M. and ENGESTRÖM, Y. (1995) 'Commentary', *Human Development*, **38**, pp. 19–24.
COLE, M. and HILL, D. (1995) 'Games of despair and rhetorics of resistance: postmodernism, education and reaction', *British Journal of Sociology*, **16**, 2, pp. 165–82.
COLE, M. and HILL, D. (1996) 'Postmodernism, education and contemporary capitalism: a materialist critique', in VALENTE, M. O., BARRIOS, A., GASPAR, A. and TEODORO, V. D. (Eds) *Teacher Training and Values Education*, Lisbon: Departamento de Educacão da Faculdade de Ciencias Universidade de Lisboa in association with the Association for Teacher Education in Europe.

References

Cole, M., Hill, D. and Rikowski, G. (1997) 'Between postmodernism and nowhere: the predicament of the postmodernist', *British Journal of Educational Studies*, **45**, 2, pp. 187–200.

Cole, M. and Wertsch, J. V. (1996) 'Beyond the individual and social antinomy in discussions of Piaget and Vygotsky', *Human Development*, **39**, pp. 250–6.

Connolly, P. (1997) 'In search of authenticity: researching young children's perspectives', in Pollard, A., Thiessen, D. and Filer, A. (Eds) *Children and their Curriculum*, London: Falmer Press.

Cooper, H. (1993) 'Removing the scaffolding: a case study investigating how whole-class teaching can lead to effective peer group discussion without the teacher', *Curriculum Journal*, **4**, 3, pp. 385–401.

Cornbleth, C. (1995) 'Curriculum knowledge: controlling the "great speckled bird" ', *Educational Review*, **47**, 2, pp. 157–64.

Cousins, J. (1996) 'Empowerment and autonomy from babyhood. The perspective of "early years" research', in John, M. (Ed.) *Children in Charge: The Child's Right to a Fair Hearing*, London: Jessica Kingsley.

Cox, C. B. and Dyson, A. E. (1960) *Fight for Education: A Black Paper*, London: Critical Quarterly Society.

Cox, C. B. and Dyson, A. E. (Eds) (1971) *The Black Papers*, London: Davis-Poynter.

Cox, T. (1996) 'Teachers' views on the National Curriculum', in Cox, T. (Ed.) *The National Curriculum and the Early Years*, London: Falmer Press.

Cremin, L. A. (1961) *The Transformation of the School*, New York: Basic Books.

Darling, J. (1994) *Child-Centred Education and its Critics*, London: Routledge and Kegan Paul.

David, T., Curtis, A. and Siraj-Blatchford, I. (1992) *Effective Teaching in the Early Years: Fostering Children's Learning in Nurseries and in Infant Classes*, Stoke-on-Trent: Trentham Books.

Davie, R. (1996) 'Partnership with children: the advancing trend', in Davie, R., Upton, G. and Varma, V. (Eds) *The Voice of the Child*, London: Falmer Press.

Davies, I. (1969) 'Education and social science', *New Society*, 8 May.

Davies, T. (1997) *Humanism*, London: Routledge.

Dearden, R. F. (1972a) 'Education as a process of growth', in Dearden, R. F., Hirst, P. H. and Peters, R. S. (Eds) *Education and the Development of Reason*, London: Routledge and Kegan Paul.

Dearden, R. F. (1972b) 'Autonomy and education', in Dearden, R. F., Hirst, P. H. and Peters, R. S. (Eds) *Education and the Development of Reason*, London: Routledge and Kegan Paul, pp. 451–2.

Deci, E. L. and Ryan, J. M. (1994) 'Promoting self-determined education', *Scandinavian Journal of Educational Research*, **38**, 1, pp. 3–14.

Department for Education (1994) *Code of Practice on the Identification and Assessment of Special Educational Needs*, London: DFE.

Désforges, C. (1993) 'Children's learning: has it improved?', *Education 3–13*, **21**, 3, pp. 3–10.

Désforges, C. (1997) *Childrens' Application of Knowledge*, paper delivered to the Ninth ASPE (Association for the Study of Primary Education) Conference, Dartington Hall, Devon.

Dewey, J. (1900) *The Child and Society*, Chicago: University of Chicago Press.

Dewey, J. (1902) *The Child and the Curriculum*, Chicago: University of Chicago Press.

References

DEWEY, J. (1916) *Democracy and Education*, New York: Macmillian.
DEWEY, J. (1976) *The School and Society*, Carbondale, IL: Arcturus Books (a facsimile of the first edition published in 1899).
DRIVER, R. (1983) *Pupil as Scientist?*, Milton Keynes: Open University Press.
DRIVER, R. (1989) 'Students' conceptions and the learning of science', *International Journal of Science Education*, **11**, special issue, pp. 481–90.
DRIVER, R. and BELL, B. (1986) 'Students' thinking and the learning of science: a constructivist view', *School Science Review*, **67**, pp. 443–56.
DUFFY, T. M. and JONASSEN, D. H. (1992) *Constructivism and the Technology of Instruction. A Conversation*, Hillsdale, NJ: Lawrence Erlbaum Associates.
DYKHUIZEN, G. (1973) *The Life and Mind of John Dewey*, Southern Illinois: Southern Illinois University Press.
ELIOT, T. S. (1948) *Notes Towards the Definition of Culture*, London: Faber.
ELLIOTT, J., STEWART-SMITH, Y. and HILDRETH, A. (1997) *Attitudes to Education — A Three Nation Comparison*, paper delivered to the BERA (British Educational Research Association) Conference, University of York.
ELLIS, T., MCWHIRTER, J., MCCOLGAN, D. and HADDOW, B. (1976) *William Tyndale: The Teachers' Story*, London: Writers and Readers Publishers Co-operative.
EMERY, H. (1996) 'Children evaluating and assessing their progress in learning', in WEBB, R. (Ed.) *Primary Practice: Taking a Leadership Role*, Bristol: Falmer Press.
EPSTEIN, D. (1993) *Changing Classroom Cultures: Anti-racism, Politics and Schools*, Stoke-on-Trent: Trentham Books.
ESKELAND, K. (1996) 'Voice of the children: Speaking truth to power', in JOHN, M. (Ed.) *Children in Charge: The Child's Right to a Fair Hearing*, London: Jessica Kingsley.
FANG, Z. (1996) 'A review of research on teacher beliefs and practices', *Educational Research*, **38**, 1, pp. 47–65.
FISHER, J. (1996) *Starting from the Child?*, Buckingham: Open University Press.
FITZ, J. and LEE, J. (1995) 'Where angels fear...', in OUSTON, J., EARLEY, P. and FIDLER, B. (Eds) *OFSTED Inspections: the Early Experiences*, London: David Fulton.
FODOR, J. A. (1976) *The Language of Thought*, Birmingham: Harvester Press.
FRANCIS, L. J. and GRINDLE, Z. (1998) 'Whatever happened to progressive education? A comparison of primary school teachers' attitudes in 1982 and 1996', *Educational Studies*, **24**, 3, pp. 269–79.
FRENCH, L. and SONG, M. J. (1998) 'Developmentally appropriate teacher-directed approaches: images from Korean kindergartens', *Journal of Curriculum Studies*, **30**, 4, pp. 409–30.
GABELLA, M. S. (1996) 'Postmodern? Perhaps: but historical? A reply to Barbara Norman', *Journal of Curriculum Studies*, **28**, 6, pp. 725–30.
GALTON, M. (1987) 'Change and continuity in the primary schools: the research evidence', *Oxford Review of Education*, **13**, 1, pp. 81–94.
GALTON, M. (1989a) *Teaching in the Primary School*, London: Fulton.
GALTON, M. (1989b) 'Negotiating learning, negotiating control', in BOURNE, J. (Ed.) *Thinking through Primary Practice*, London: Routledge Open University Press.
GALTON, M. (1995) 'Do you really want to cope with thirty lively children and become an effective primary teacher?', in MOYLES, J. (Ed.) *Beginning Teaching: Beginning Learning*, Milton Keynes: Open University Press.
GALTON, M. (1998a) 'What do tests measure?', *Education 3–13*, **26**, 2, pp. 50–9.
GALTON, M. (1998b) 'Back to consulting the ORACLE', *Times Educational Supplement, Briefing: Research Focus*, 3 July, p. 24.

References

GALTON, M. and WILLIAMSON, J. (1992) *Group Work in the Primary Classroom*, London: Routledge.

GALTON, M., SIMON, B. and CROLL, P. (1980) *Inside the Primary School Classroom*, London: Routledge and Kegan Paul.

GASKINS, S., MILLER, P. J. and CORSARO, W. A. (1992) 'Theoretical and methodological perspectives in the interpretive study of children', *Interpretive Approaches to Children's Socialisation*, **58**, Winter.

GAULD, A. and SHOTTER, J. (1977) *Human Action and Its Psychological Investigation*, London: Routledge and Kegan Paul.

GEERTZ, C. (1964) 'Ideology as a cultural system', in APTER, D. (Ed.) *Ideology and Discontent*, New York: Free Press.

GIPPS, C. and TUNSTALL, P. (1997) *Effort, Ability and the Teacher: Young Children's Explanations for Success and Failure*, paper presented to the 1997 BERA (British Educational Research Association) Conference, University of York.

GLASER, D. (1996) 'The voice of the child in mental health practice', in DAVIE, R., UPTON, G. and VARMA, V. (Eds) *The Voice of the Child*, London: Falmer Press.

GREENBERG, D. E. (1996) 'The object permanence fallacy', *Human Development*, **39**, pp. 117–31.

GRIFFITHS, M. and TANN, S. (1992) 'Using reflective practice to link personal and public theories', *Journal of Education for Teaching*, **18**, 1, pp. 69–84.

GRIMSLEY, R. (1973) *The Philosophy of Rousseau*, Oxford: Oxford University Press.

HAKKINEN, K. (1997) *A Case Study of Makilampi School*, paper delivered to the BERA (British Educational Research Association) Conference, University of York.

HALL, E. and HALL, C. (1988) *Human Relations in Education*, London: Routledge.

HALSEY, A. H. and SYLVA, K. (1987) 'Plowden: history and prospect', *Oxford Review of Education*, **13**, 1, pp. 3–22.

HAND, B. and TREAGUST, D. F. (1994) 'Teachers' thoughts about changing to constructivist teaching/learning approaches within junior secondary science classrooms', *Journal of Education for Teaching*, **20**, 1, pp. 97–112.

HARBER, C. (1997) 'International developments and the rise of education for democracy', *Compare*, **27**, 2, pp. 178–91.

HARGREAVES, D. H. (1997) 'School choice and the development of autonomy: a reply to Brighouse', *Oxford Review of Education*, **23**, 4, pp. 511–15.

HAROUTUNIAN, S. (1983) *Equilibrium in the Balance*, New York: Springer.

HARRÉ, R., CLARKE, D. and DE CARLO, N. (1985) *Motives and Mechanisms*, London: Methuen.

HENDRICK, H. (1992) 'Children and childhood', *ReFRESH*, **15**, Autumn.

HIGGINS, M. (1997) 'Whole class teaching', *National Association for the Teaching of Drama Broadsheet*, **13**, 2, pp. 28–34.

HILLMAN, M. (1997) 'Protection racket', *Times Educational Supplement*, 20 June, p. 21.

HODGE, M. (1998) 'A pragmatic ideology', *Times Educational Supplement, Platform*, 12 June, p. 15.

HOLMES, B. (1995) 'The origin and development of progressive education in England', in ROHRS, H. and LENHART, V. (Eds) *Progressive Education Across the Continents*, Frankfurt am Main: Peter Lang.

HOLT, J. (1975) *Escape from Childhood*, Harmondsworth: Penguin Books.

HOLT, J. (1994) 'How children learn . . . and fail', in POLLARD, A. and BOURNE, J. (Eds) *Thinking and Learning in the Primary School*, London: Routledge Open University Press.

References

JARVIS, P. (1995) *Adult and Continuing Education: Theory and Practice*, 2nd edn, London: Routledge.

JEFFREY, B. and WOODS, P. (1997) 'The relevance of creative teaching, pupil's views', in POLLARD, A., THIESSEN, D. and FILER, A. (Eds) *Children and their Curriculum*, London: Falmer Press.

JOHN, M. (1996) 'Voicing: Research and practice with the "silenced"', in JOHN, M. (Ed.) *Children in Charge: The Child's Right to a Fair Hearing*, London: Jessica Kingsley.

JONES, K. (1983) *Beyond Progressive Education*, London: Methuen.

KANT, I. (1781) *A Critique of Pure Reason*, English trans. MIEKLEJOHN, J. J. (1934), London: Dent.

KARMILOFF-SMITH, A. (1992) *Beyond Modularity*, Cambridge, MA: MIT Press.

KAINAN, A. and SHKOLNIK, D. (1994) 'Identifying and developing a school belief system', *Curriculum and Teaching*, 9, 1, pp. 3–13.

KEINY, S. (1994) 'Constructivism and teachers' professional development', *Teaching and Teacher Education*, 10, 2, pp. 157–67.

KELLNER, P. (1998) 'Our mutual friends', *Times Educational Supplement*, 19 June, p. 15.

KELLY, A. V. (1980) 'Ideological constraints on curriculum planning', in KELLY, A. V. (Ed.) *Curriculum Context*, London: Harper and Row.

KELLY, A. V. (1986) *Knowledge and Curriculum Planning*, London: Harper and Row.

KELLY, A. V. (1989) *The Curriculum: Theory and Practice*, 3rd edn, London: Paul Chapman.

KELLY, A. V. (1994) *The National Curriculum: A Critical Review*, London: Paul Chapman.

KENNY, J. (1998) 'Listen to the children: an interview with Seymour Papert', *Times Educational Supplement, ONLINE*, 18 September, pp. 26–7.

KITCHENER, R. F. (1996) 'The nature of the social for Piaget and Vygotsky', *Human Development*, 39, pp. 243–9.

LARRAIN, J. (1979) *The Concept of Ideology*, London: Hutchinson.

LAWLOR, S. (1990) *Teachers Mistaught*, London: Centre for Policy Studies.

LAWRENCE, J. A. and VALSINER, J. (1993) 'Conceptual roots of internalisation: from transmission to transformation', *Human Development*, 36, pp. 150–67.

LAWTON, D. (1973) *Social Change, Educational Theory and Curriculum Planning*, London: Hodder and Stoughton.

LAWTON, D. (1989) *Education, Culture and the National Curriculum*, London: Hodder and Stoughton.

LAWTON, D. (1992) *Education and Politics in the 1990s: Conflict or Consensus?* London: Falmer Press.

LAWTON, D. (1996) *Beyond the National Curriculum*, London: Hodder and Stoughton.

LEE, J. and CROLL, P. (1995) 'Streaming and subject specialism at Key Stage 2: a survey in two local authorities', *Educational Studies*, 21, 2, pp. 155–65.

LEE, J. and FITZ, J. (1997) 'HMI and OFSTED: evolution or revolution in school inspections?', *British Journal of Educational Studies*, 45, 1, pp. 39–52.

LITTLEDYKE, M. (1998) 'Teaching for constructive learning', in LITTLEDYKE, M. and HUXFORD, L. (Eds) *Teaching the Primary Curriculum for Constructive Learning*, London: David Fulton.

LITTLEDYKE, M. and HUXFORD, L. (Eds) (1998) *Teaching the Primary Curriculum for Constructivist Learning*, London: David Fulton.

LIVERTA-SEMPIO, O. and MARCHETTI, A. (1997) 'Cognitive development and theories of mind: towards a contextual approach', *European Journal of Psychology of Education*, XII, 1, pp. 3–21.

References

LOWE, R. (Ed.) (1987) *The Changing Primary School*, London: Falmer Press.
LUBAN, L. (1989) 'Neoprogressive visions and organizational realities', *Harvard Educational Review*, **59**, pp. 217–22.
LUCARIELLO, J. (1995) 'Mind, culture, person: elements in a cultural psychology', *Human Development*, **38**, pp. 2–8.
LUKES, S. (1973) *Individualism*, Oxford: Blackwell.
MACDONALD, J. B. (1972) 'Introduction', in SQUIRE, J. R. (Ed.) *A New Look at Progressive Education*, Washington, DC: Association for Supervision and Curriculum Development.
MACKENZIE, R. (Ed.) (1997) 'A cultural perspective on creative primary teaching and the arts in the 1990s', in HOLT, D. (Ed.) *Primary Arts Education: Contemporary Issues*, Bristol: Falmer Press.
MACLEAN, M. (1993) 'The politics of curriculum in European perspective', *Educational Review*, **45**, 2.
MACLURE, S. (1998) 'Through the revolution and out the other side', *Oxford Review of Education*, **24**, 1, pp. 5–24.
MAJOR, J. (1991) *Address to the Conservative Party Annual Conference*, Blackpool.
MANNHEIM, K. (1936) *Ideology and Utopia*, London: Routledge and Kegan Paul.
MAY, T. (1994) 'The concept of autonomy', *American Philosophical Quarterly*, **31**, 2, pp. 133–44.
MCINTYRE, D. (1992) 'Theory, theorising and reflection', in CALDERHEAD, J. and GATES, J. (Eds) *Conceptualizing Reflection in Teacher Education*, London: Falmer Press.
MEADOWS, S. (1993) *The Child as Thinker*, London: Routledge.
MEIGHAN, R. (1981) *A Sociology of Educating*, Eastbourne: Holt, Rinehart and Winston.
MEIGHAN, R. (1995) *John Holt: Personalised Education and the Reconstruction of Schooling*, Nottingham: Educational Heretics Press.
MENTER, I., MUSCHAMP, Y., NICHOLLS, P., OZGA, J., with POLLARD, A. (1997) *Work and Identity in the Primary School: A Post-Fordist Analysis*, Milton Keynes: Open University Press.
MOLL, I. (1994) 'Reclaiming the natural line in Vygotsky's theory of cognitive development', *Human Development*, **37**, pp. 333–42.
MORRIS, P. (1998) 'Comparative education and educational reform: beware of prophets returning from the Far East', *Education 3–13*, **26**, 2, pp. 3–8.
MORRISON, K. and RIDLEY, K. (1989) 'Ideological contexts for curriculum planning', in PREEDY, M. (Ed.) *Approaches to Curriculum Management*, Milton Keynes: Open University Press.
MORTIMORE, P., SAMMONS, P., STOLL, L., LEWIS, D. and ECOB, R. (1988) *School Matters: The Junior Years*, London: Open Books.
MOUNCE, H. O. (1997) *The Two Pragmatisms*, London: Routledge.
MURPHY, C. and LIU, M. (1998) 'Choices must be made: the case of education in Taiwan', *Education 3–13*, **26**, 2, pp. 9–16.
NEIL., A. S. (1945) *Hearts not Heads in the School*, London: Herbert Jencks Ltd.
NELSON, K., PLEA, D. and HENSELER, S. (1998) 'Children's theory of mind: an experiential interpretation', *Human Development*, **41**, pp. 7–29.
NORTHAM, J. (1996) 'An analysis of school inspection reports', in OUSTON, J., EARLEY, P. and FIDLER, B. (Eds) *OFSTED Inspections: The Early Experiences*, London: David Fulton.
OFSTED (1995a) *Guidance on the Inspection of Nursery and Primary Schools*, London: HMSO.
OFSTED (1995b) *Governing Bodies and Effective Schools*, London: DfE.

References

OFSTED (1996) *The Annual Report of Her Majesty's Chief Inspector of Schools*, London: HMSO.
O'HEAR, A. (1987) 'The importance of traditional learning', *British Journal of Educational Studies*, 35, pp. 102–14.
O'HEAR, A. (1988) *Who Teaches the Teachers?*, London: Social Affairs Unit.
O'HEAR, A. (1991) *Father of Child-centredness: John Dewey and the Ideology of Modern Education*, London: Centre for Policy Studies.
O'KEEFE, D. J. (1990) *The Wayward Élite*, London: Social Affairs Unit.
ONORE, C. and LUBETSKY, B. (Eds) (1992) 'Why we learn is what and how we learn: curriculum as possibility', in BOOMER, G. et al. (Eds) *Negotiating the Curriculum*, London: Falmer Press.
OSBORNE, M. D. (1997) 'Balancing individual and the group: a dilemma for the constructivist teacher', *Journal of Curriculum Studies*, 29, 2, pp. 183–96.
OSLER, A. (1994) 'The UN Convention on the Rights of the Child: some implications for teacher education', *Educational Review*, 46, 2.
PANEL, C. (1997) 'National cultural values and their role in learning: a comparative ethnographic study of state primary schooling in England and France', *Comparative Education*, 33, 3, pp. 249–373.
PAPERT, S. (1980) *Mindstorms: Children, Computers and Powerful Ideas*, Brighton: Harvester Press.
PATTERSON, C. H. (1973) *Humanistic Education*, Englewood Cliffs, NJ: Prentice Hall.
PETERS, R. S. (1966) *Ethics and Education*, London: Allen and Unwin.
PETERS, R. S. (Ed.) (1969) *Perspectives on Plowden*, London: Routledge and Kegan Paul.
PETERS, R. and HIRST, P. (1970) *The Logic of Education*, London: Routledge and Kegan Paul.
PIAGET, J. (1932) *The Moral Judgment of the Child*, London: Routledge and Kegan Paul.
PIAGET, J. (1954) *The Construction of Reality in the Child*, New York: Basic Books.
PIAGET, J. (1970) *Main Trends in Psychology*, New York: Harper and Row.
PIAGET, J. (1971) *Biology and Knowledge*, Edinburgh: University of Edinburgh Press.
PIAGET, J. (1978) *Success and Understanding*, London: Routledge and Kegan Paul.
PIAGET, J. and INHELDER, B. (1969) *The Psychology of the Child*, New York: Basic Books.
LADY PLOWDEN (1991) 'Three wise men in the same boat', *Times Educational Supplement*, 13 December, p. 17.
POLLARD, A. (1990) *Learning in Primary Schools*, London: Cassell.
POLLARD, A. (1994) 'Towards a sociology of learning in primary schools', in POLLARD, A. and BOURNE, J. (Eds) *Thinking and Learning in the Primary School*, London: Routledge Open University Press.
POLLARD, A. (1997) *Reflective Teaching in the Primary School*, 3rd edn, London: Cassell.
POLLARD, A. and BROADFOOT, P. (1997) *Recent Reforms in Education: A Research-Based Perspective*, paper delivered to the Nineth ASPE (Association for the Study of Primary Education) Annual Conference, Dartington Hall, Devon.
POLLARD, A., BROADFOOT, P., CROLL, P., OSBORN M. and ABBOTT, D. (1994) *Changing English Primary Schools: The Impact of the Education Reform Act at Key Stage 1*, London: Cassell.
POPPER, K. R. (1966) *The Open Society and Its Enemies*, 5th edn, vol. 2, London: Routledge.
POPPER, K. R. (1979) *Objective Knowledge: An Evolutionary Approach*, Oxford: Oxford University Press.
POPPER, K. R. (1994) *The Myth of the Framework*, author's note (NOTTURNO, M. A., Ed.), London: Routledge.

References

POPPER, K. R. and ECCLES, J. C. (1977) *The Self and Its Brain*, Berlin: Springer International.
PRAIN, V. (1997) 'Textualising your self: some current challenges', *Journal of Curriculum Studies*, **29**, 1, pp. 71–85.
PRINCE OF WALES (1997) *Interview with David Frost*, BBC.
PRING, R. (1989a) 'Subject-centred vs child-centred education — a false dualism', *Journal of Applied Philosophy*, **6**, pp. 181–94.
PRING, R. (1989b) *The New Curriculum*, London: Cassell.
PRING, R. (1997) 'The community of educated people', *European Education*, **29**, 1, pp. 54–73.
PUNCH, M. (1977) *Progressive Retreat: A Sociological Survey of Dartington Hall School and Some of Its Former Pupils*, Cambridge: Cambridge University Press.
QUINN, V. (1984) 'To develop autonomy: a critique of R. F. Dearden and two proposals', *Journal of Philosophy of Education*, **18**, 2, pp. 265–70.
RANAWEERA, A. M. (1989) *Non-Conventional Approaches to Education at the Primary Level*, Hamburg: UNESCO Institute for Education.
REBER, A. S. (1993) *Tacit Knowledge: An Essay on the Cognitive Unconscious*, Oxford: OUP/Clarendon Press.
REED, E. S. (1997) 'Why perceiving produces ontological knowledge: essay review of *Words, Thoughts and Theories*, by A. Gopnik and A. Meltzoff', *Human Development*, **40**, pp. 245–53.
RESNICK, L. B. (1977) 'A developmental theory of number understanding', in GINSBERG, H. P. (Ed.) *Children's Arithmetic: How They Learn It and How You Teach It*, Austin, TX: PRO.ED.
RESNICK, L. B. (1985) *Education and Learning to Think*, Pittsburgh, PA: Learning, Research and Development Centre, University of Pittsburgh.
RESNICK, L. B., BILL, V. and LESGOLD, S. (1992) 'Developing thinking abilities in arithmetic class', in DEMITRIOU, A., SHAYER, M. and EFKLIDES, A. E. (Eds) *Neo-Piagetian Theories of Cognitive Development: Implications and Applications for Education*, London: Routledge.
REYNOLDS, D. (1996) 'The truth, the whole-class truth', *Times Educational Supplement*, 7 June, p. 21.
REYNOLDS, D. and FARRELL, S. (1996) *Worlds Apart? A Review of International Surveys of Educational Achievement Involving England*, London: OFSTED.
RICHARDS, C. (1988) 'Primary education in England: an analysis of some recent issues and developments', in CLARKSON, M. (Ed.) *Emerging Issues in Primary Education*, Lewes: Falmer Press.
RICHARDS, C. (1995) 'Utopia deferred, curriculum issues for primary and middle school education', in GALTON, M. and MOON, D. (Eds) *Changing Schools, Changing Curriculum*, London: Harper and Row.
RICHARDS, C. (1998) 'The primary school curriculum: changes, challenges, questions', in RICHARDS, C. and TAYLOR, P. H. (Eds) *How Shall We School Our Children? Primary Education and Its Future*, London: Falmer Press.
RICHARDS, M. and LIGHT, L. (1986) *Children of Social Worlds*, Oxford: Polity Press.
ROGERS, C. (1983) *Freedom to Learn for the '80s*, revised edn, Columbia, SC: Merrill.
ROGOFF, B. (1990) *Apprenticeship in Thinking*, Oxford: Oxford University Press.
ROGOFF, B. and WERTSCH, J. (Eds) (1984) *Children's Learning in the Zone of Proximal Development*, San Francisco, CA: Jossey-Bass.

References

ROHRS, H. (1995) 'Internationalism in progressive education and initial steps towards a world education movement', in ROHRS, H. and LENHART, V. (Eds) *Progressive Education Across the Continents*, Frankfurt am Main: Peter Lang.

ROHRS, H. and LENHART, V. (Eds) (1995) *Progressive Education Across the Continents*, Frankfurt am Main: Peter Lang.

ROSENTHAL, D. (1996) 'An effective blunt instrument', *Times Educational Supplement*, 7 June, p. 7.

ROUSSEAU, J.-J. (1911) *Émile*, New York: Everyman (first published 1762).

ROWLANDS, S. (1987) 'An interpretive model of teaching and learning', in POLLARD, A. (Ed.) *Children and Their Primary Schools*, London: Falmer Press.

RUDDUCK, J. and HOPKINS, J. (1985) *Research as a Basis for Teaching: Readings from the Work of Lawrence Stenhouse*, London: Heinemann Educational Books.

RUSSELL, P. (1996) 'Listening to children with disabilities and special educational needs', in DAVIE, R., UPTON, G. and VARMA, V. (Eds) *The Voice of the Child*, London: Falmer Press.

SAFSTROM, A. C. (1996) 'Education as a science within a scientific and rational discourse', *Journal of Curriculum Studies*, **28**, 1, pp. 57–71.

SALOMON, G. and GIBBERSON, T. (1987) 'Skill may not be enough: the role of mindfulness in learning transfer', *International Journal of Educational Research*, **11**, 6, pp. 623–37.

SAMMONS, P., HILLMAN, J. and MORTIMORE, P. (1995) *Key Characteristics of Effective Schools*, London: Institute of Education, for OFSTED.

SARTRE, J. P. (1948) *Existentialism and Humanism*, London: Eyre-Methuen.

SCHÔN, D. A. (1983) *The Reflective Practitioner*, New York: Basic Books.

SCRIMSHAW, P. (1983) *Educational Ideologies*, Unit 2 E204, Milton Keyes: Open University Press.

SCRUTON, R. (1987) 'Expressionist education', *Oxford Review of Education*, **13**, 1, pp. 39–44.

SHARP, A. and GREEN, R. (1975) *Education and Social Control*, London: Routledge and Kegan Paul.

SHARPE, K. (1997) 'Mr. Gradgrind and Miss Beale: old dichotomies, inexorable choices, and what shall we tell the students about primary teaching methods?', *Journal of Education for Teaching*, **23**, 1, pp. 69–83.

SHAYER, M. (1992) 'Problems and issues in intervention studies', in DEMITRIOU, A., SHAYER, M. and EFKLIDES, A. E. (Eds) *Neo-Piagetian Theories of Cognitive Development: Implications and Applications for Education*, London: Routledge.

SHERWIN, M. (1996) 'The law in relation to the wishes and feelings of the child', in DAVIE, R., UPTON, G. and VARMA, V. (Eds) *The Voice of the Child*, London: Falmer Press.

SHORT, G. (1991) 'Perceptions of inequality: primary school children's discourse on social class', *Educational Studies*, **17**, 1, pp. 89–106.

SIEGLER, R. S. (1991) *Children's Thinking*, 2nd edn, Englewood Cliffs, NJ: Prentice-Hall.

SILCOCK, P. J. (1990) 'Implementing the National Curriculum: some teachers' dilemmas', *Education 3–13*, **18**, 3, pp. 3–10.

SILCOCK, P. J. (1992) 'The "reflective practitioner" in the year of the SAT', *Education 3–13*, **20**, 1, pp. 3–9.

SILCOCK, P. J. (1993) 'Towards a new progressivism in primary school education', *Educational Studies*, **19**, 1, pp. 107–21.

SILCOCK, P. J. (1994a) 'Modern progressivism: a way forward from the 1993 ASPE Conference?', *Education 3–13*, **22**, pp. 3–7.

References

SILCOCK, P. J. (1994b) 'The process of reflective teaching', *British Journal of Educational Studies*, **XXXXII**, 3, pp. 273–85.
SILCOCK, P. J. (1995) 'Time against ideology: the changing primary school', *Oxford Review of Education*, **21**, 2, pp. 149–61.
SILCOCK, P. J. (1996) 'Three principles for a new progressivism', *Oxford Review of Education*, **22**, 2, pp. 199–215.
SILCOCK, P. J. and STACEY, H. (1997) 'Peer mediation and the cooperative school', *Education 3–13*, **25**, 2, pp. 3–8.
SILCOCK, P. J. and WYNESS, M. (1997) 'Dilemma and resolution: primary school teachers look beyond Dearing', *Curriculum Journal*, **8**, 1, pp. 125–48.
SILCOCK, P. J. and WYNESS, M. (1998) 'Strong in diversity: primary school inspectors beliefs', *Curriculum Journal*, **9**, 1, pp. 105–27.
SIMON, B. (1981a) 'The primary school revolution: myth or reality?', in SIMON, B. and WILLCOCKS, J. (Eds) *Research and Practice in the Primary Classroom*, London: Routledge and Kegan Paul.
SIMON, B. (1981b) 'Why no pedagogy in England?', in SIMON, B. and TAYLOR, W. (Eds) *Education in the '80s*, London: Batsford Educational.
SIXSMITH, C. and SIMCO, N. (1997) 'The role of formal and informal theory in the training of student teachers', *Mentoring and Tutoring, Partnership in Learning*, **5**, 1.
SKILBECK, M. (1976) *Ideology and Knowledge*, Milton Keynes: Open University Press.
SLEEGERS, P. and WESSELINGH, A. (1995) 'Dutch dilemmas: decentralisation, school autonomy and professionalisation of teachers', *Educational Review*, **47**, 2, pp. 199–207.
SMITH, L. (1996) 'With knowledge in mind: novel transformation of the learner or transformation of novel knowledge', *Human Development*, **30**, pp. 257–63.
SMITH, P. (1996) 'A social work perspective', in DAVIE, R., UPTON, G. and VARMA, V. (Eds) *The Voice of the Child*, London: Falmer Press.
SOUTHERN, R. W. (1970) *Medieval Humanism and other Studies*, Oxford: Blackwell.
STACEY, H. (forthcoming) 'An investigation into whether the "iceberg" system of peer mediation training and peer mediation, reduces levels of bullying, raises self-esteem, and increases pupil empowerment among upper primary age children', unpublished PhD thesis, University of Leicester, Nene College.
STENHOUSE, L. (1975) *An Introduction to Research and Curriculum Development*, London: Heinemann.
STENHOUSE, L. (1983) *Authority, Education and Emancipation*, London: Heinemann Educational.
STEVENS, E. JNR and WOOD, G. H. (1995) *Justice, Ideology and Education*, New York: McGraw-Hill.
SUGRUE, C. (1997) *Complexities of Teaching: Child-centred Perspectives*, London: Falmer Press.
SULLIVAN, K. (1996) 'Progressive education: where are you now that we need you?', *Oxford Review of Education*, **33**, 3, pp. 349–54.
SUMMERS, M. and KRUGER, L. (1994) 'A longitudinal study of a constructivist approach to improving primary school teachers' use of subject matter knowledge in science', *Teacher and Teacher Education*, **10**, 5, pp. 499–519.
SUTHERLAND, P. (1992) *Cognitive Development Today, Piaget and his Critics*, London: Paul Chapman.
SWANN, J. (1995) 'Realism, constructivism and the pursuit of truth', *Higher Education Review*, **27**, 3, pp. 37–55.
SWINGLEWOOD, A. (1991) *A Short History of Sociological Thought*, 2nd edn, London: Macmillan.

References

TABERRER, R. (1998) *Raising Standards, Improving Schools*, address to the Tenth Anniversary ASPE Conference (Association for the Study of Primary Education), Fitzwilliam College, Cambridge.
TARRANT, J. M. (1989) *Democracy and Education*, Aldershot: Gower.
TAYLOR, P. H. and RICHARDS, C. M. (1985) *An Introduction to Curriculum Studies*, 2nd edn, Windsor, Bucks: NFER Nelson.
THARP, R. and GALLIMORE, R. (1993) 'A theory of teaching as assisted performance', in DANIELS, H. (Ed.) *Charting the Agenda*, London: Routledge.
THELEN, E., CORBETTA, D., KAMM, K. and SPENCER, J. P. (1993) 'The transition to reaching. Mapping intentions and intrinsic dynamics', *Child Development*, **64**, pp. 1058–98.
THOMPSON, J. B. (1984) *Studies in the Theory of Ideology*, Cambridge: Polity Press.
TIZARD, B. and HUGHES, M. (1984) *Young Children Learning*, London: Fontana.
TOMLINSON, P. (1995) *Understanding Mentoring: Reflective Strategies for School-based Teacher Preparation*, Buckingham: Open University Press.
TOMLINSON, S. (1997) 'Edward Lee Thorndyke and John Dewey in the science of education', *Oxford Review of Education*, **23**, 3, pp. 365–83.
TRIGG, P. and POLLARD, A. (1998) 'Pupil experience and curriculum for life-long learning', in RICHARDS, C. and TAYLOR, P. H. (Eds) *How Shall We School our Children? Primary Education and its Future*, London: Falmer Press.
TUDGE, R. H. J. and WINTERHOFF, P. A. (1993) 'Vygotsky, Piaget and Bandura: perspectives on the relations between the social world and cognitive development', *Human Development*, **36**, pp. 61–81.
VALSINER, J. (1992) 'Social organization of cognitive development: internalization and externalization of constraint systems', in DEMITRIOU, A., SHAYER, M. and EFKLIDES, A. E. (Eds) *Neo-Piagetian Theories of Cognitive Development: Implications and Applications for Education*, London: Routledge.
VALSINER, J. (1996) 'Whose mind?', *Human Development*, **39**, pp. 295–300.
VAN BUEREN, C. (1996) 'The quiet revolution: Children's rights in international law', in JOHN, M. (Ed.) *Children in Charge: The Child's Right to a Fair Hearing*, London: Jessica-Kingsley.
VAN DER VEER, R. (1996) 'Vygotsky and Piaget: a collective monologue', *Human Development*, **39**, pp. 237–42.
VERBA, M. (1994) 'The beginnings of collaboration in peer interaction', *Human Development*, **37**, pp. 125–39.
VON GLASERFIELD, E. (1989) 'Cognition, construction of knowledge and teaching', *Synthesis*, **80**, pp. 121–40.
VON GLASERFIELD, E. (1995) *Radical Constructivism. A Way of Knowing and Learning*, London: Falmer Press.
VOSS, J. T. (1987) 'Learning transfer in subject-matter learning: a problem-solving model', *International Journal of Educational Research*, **11**, 6, chapter 1.
VULLIAMY, G. and WEBB, R. (1993) 'Progressive education and the National Curriculum: findings from a global education research project', *Educational Review*, **45**, 1, pp. 21–42.
VYGOTSKY, L. S. (1929) 'The problem of the cultural development of the child', *Journal of Genetic Psychology*, **6**, pp. 415–34.
VYGOTSKY, L. S. (1962) *Thought and Language*, Cambridge, MA: MIT Press.
VYGOTSKY, L. S. (1978) *Mind in Society: The Development of Higher Psychological Processes*, Cambridge, MA: Harvard University Press.
VYGOTSKY, L. S. (1979) 'Consciousness as a problem in the psychology of behaviour', *Soviet Psychology*, **17**, 4, pp. 3–35.

References

WAIN, K. (1985) 'Lifelong education and adult education — the state of the theory', *International Journal of Lifelong Education*, **12**, 2.

WALKERDINE, V. (1994) 'Developmental psychology and the child-centred pedagogy. The insertion of Piaget into early education', in HENRIQUES, J., HOLLOWAY, W., UNWIN, C. and WALKERDINE, V. (Eds) *Changing the Subject: Psychology, Social Regulation and Subjectivity*, London: Methuen.

WALLACE, G. (1996) 'Engaging with learning', in RUDDUCK, J., CHAPLAIN, R. and WALLACE, G. (Eds) *School Improvement: What Can Pupils Tell Us?*, Cambridge: David Fulton.

WARHAM, S. (1993) *Primary Teaching and the Negotiation of Power*, London: Paul Chapman.

WATERS, M. (1994) *Modern Sociological Theory*, London: Sage.

WEBB, R. (1993) *Eating the Elephant Bit by Bit*, London: Association of Teachers and Lecturers' Publications.

WEBB, R. and VULLIAMY, G. with HAKKINEN, K., HAMALAINEN, S., KIMONEN, E., NEVALAINEN, R. and NIKKI, M.-L. (1997) *A Comparative Analysis of the Management of Curriculum Change in England and Finland*, paper delivered to the BERA (British Educational Research Association) Annual Conference, University of York (obtainable from the Department of Educational Studies, University of York).

WEIR, S. (1989) 'The computer in schools: machine as humanizer', *Harvard Educational Review*, **59**, 1, pp. 61–73.

WELLS, G. (1986) *The Meaning Makers*, London: Heinemann Educational.

WERTSCH, J. V. (1979) 'From social interaction to higher psychological processes: a clarification and application of Vygotsky's theory', *Human Development*, **22**, pp. 11–22.

WERTSCH, J. V. (1991) *Voices of the Mind*, London: Harvester Wheatsheaf.

WERTSCH, J. V. (1994) 'Commentary', *Human Development*, **37**, pp. 343–5.

WERTSCH, J. V. and BUSTAMENTE SMOLKE, A. L. (1993) 'Continuing the dialogue: Vygotsky, Bakhtin, and Lotman', in DANIELS, H. (Ed.) *Charting the Agenda*, London: Routledge.

WESLER, H. N. (1990) 'Comparative perspectives in educational decentralization: an exercise in contradiction?', *Educational Evaluation and Policy Analysis*, **12**, 4, pp. 433–48.

WOODS, P. (1980) *Pupil Strategies*, London: Croom Helm.

WOODS, P. (1994) 'Critical students: breakthroughs in learning', *International Studies in the Sociology of Education*, **4**, 2, pp. 123–46.

WOODS, P. (1995) *Creative Teachers in Primary Schools*, Buckingham: Open University Press.

WORRALL, N. and INGRAM, J. (1993) *Partnership and the Negotiating Classroom*, London: David Fulton.

WYNESS, M. G. (1996) 'Policy, protectionism and the competent child', *Childhood*, **3**, 4, pp. 431–47.

WYNESS, M. G. and SILCOCK, P. J. (1997) *Market Values, Primary Schools and the Pupils' Perspective*, paper presented at the Values and Curriculum Conference, Institute of Education, London.

YEO, E. (1994) 'The rise and fall of primary education', in POLLARD, A. and BOURNE, J. (Eds) *Thinking and Learning in the Primary School*, London: Routledge/Open University Press.

ZEICHNER, K. and LISTON, D. (1987) 'Teaching student teachers to reflect', *Harvard Educational Review*, **57**, 1, pp. 23–48.

Index

Notes
1. Page numbers for chapters are shown in **bold**
2. Entries for *teachers* and *teaching* are omitted, as they are implied throughout

Abiko, T. 98
accelerated cognition 87
accountability of teachers 5, 29, 31, 135
Adey, P. 129
   curricular values 86, 87, 89, 90
   developmentalism 64, 65, 72
   informal teaching methods 107, 111, 113, 119, 120
   modern progressivism 137, 142, 143, 146, 147
Africa 41
Aitken, M. 23
Alexander, R. J.
   curricular values 85, 96, 98
   developmentalism 59, 75
   informal teaching methods 101, 103, 110
   major ideologies 23, 24, 32, 34, 35
   modern progressivism 141, 143
   National Curricula 39, 40, 42, 43, 44, 45
   value of ideologies 3, 12, 15, 18
Antony, W. S. 64, 143
Apple, M. W. 11, 17
applying ideologies 15–16, 26
Aristotle 127
Asia 2, 39, 40, 41, 98
assisted performance, teaching as 113
Association for Study of Primary Education (ASPE) 145
Astington, J. W. 62

Australia 92
authority *see* control
autonomy, pupil 124–33
   innate competence 61, 128–31
   teaching for 131–3
   see also involvement
Aviram, A. 25, 34

Back to Basics philosophy 5, 39
Badley, G. 35
Ball, S. J. 42
basic skills 49–50, 89, 92, 116
Batteson, C. 4, 39
beliefs arising from value-systems 13, 16, 19
   see also ideologies
Bell, B. 63, 86, 111, 146
Bennett, S. N. 4, 18, 23, 98
   developmentalism 59, 71, 74
   major ideologies 23
   modern progressivism 141–2, 143
Berlak, A. and H. 106
Berlin, I. 97
Biber, B. 43, 45
Bidell, T. R. 63
Biggs, J. B. 64, 72, 75, 88, 111, 143
Billig, M. 11, 14, 17, 18, 24, 26, 106
Black Paper 5, 77, 141
Blackham, H. J. 27, 96, 98
Blackie, J. 42
Blair, A. 5
Blatchford, I. S. and J. 85, 98, 146

163

Index

Blenkin, G. M. 30, 55
   curricular values 80, 81, 82, 89
   developmentalism 64, 72
   informal teaching methods 110, 112
Bliss, J. 118, 119
Blunkett, D. 5
Blyth, A.
   curricular values 82, 84, 86
   developmentalism 30, 55, 72
   informal teaching methods 110, 112
Bower, T. G. R. 128
Boyd, J. 93, 144
Brady, L. 91
Brandes, D. 66, 146
Brehony, K. J. 26, 93, 94, 110, 144
bridging perspective 63
Brimblecombe, N. 42
Bristol 43
Broadfoot, P. 51
Bruner, J. S. 6, 30, 128, 143
   developmentalism 60, 61-2
   informal teaching methods 111, 114, 119
bucket theory 79
Bueren, C. van 122
Burden, B. 130
Burtonwood, N. 80
Bustamente Smolke *see* Smolke

Caldwell, B. S. 104, 105
Callaghan, J. 4-5, 39, 101
Campbell, R. J. 36, 43, 47, 50, 51, 128, 144
capability *see* competencies
Cardelle-Elewar, M. 86, 89
Carr, D. 101
Carr, W. 104
CASE (Cognitive Acceleration through Science Education) 87
causal explanation of development 62
   see also Piaget
Central Advisory Council *see* Plowden
centralization of control 4-5, 41
   see also National Curricula
centrifugal and centripetal forces 41
Cerych, L. 41
Charles, HRH Prince of Wales 101
child-centred approach
   beliefs 1-2, 6
   and curricular values 67, 71-2, 77, 82-3, 86-90, 95-6

legislation controlling 14
and major ideologies 23, 30-1, 34
and National Curricula 43-9, 51
new 47-9
   see also modern/new progressivism
and new progressivism 55
and value of ideologies 18, 19, 21
see also choice; informal teaching methods; involvement; progressivism
children *see* learners
Children's Act (1994) 122
Chitty, C. 4, 101
choice 9, 68, **121-34**
   liberating learners 121-2
   rights 122-4
   see also autonomy, pupil
Clarke, C. 121
Clarke, K. 5, 121, 141
Clegg, Sir A. 18
co-construction 66, 73, 74, 75, 136
Code of Practice (1994) 122
coercion 80
cognitive/cognition
   accelerated 87
   change 117-18
   and culture 61, 66
   and curricular values 87-8
   development 30
      see also developmentalism
   metacognition 86, 87, 89, 113, 125
   outcomes of processes 91-3
   processes 30, 55
coherence of interpretation of ideologies 20-1
Cole, M. 33
   curricular values 92, 94
   developmentalism 59, 60-1, 66, 68, 69
commitment 17, 19, 132
competencies/competence 86, 88, 94, 103, 133
   innate 61, 128-31
complementarity of developmental views
   see reconciling traditions
computers 108
Connolly, P. 130
Conservatives 3, 5, 39
consistency of interpretation of ideologies 20-1

Index

constructivism and neo-Piagetians 36, 59
  and curricular values 85, 86–9
  and modern progressivism 137, 146
  see also Piaget
constructivism, social 59, 66–7
  see also Vygotsky
content of ideologies 14–15
contested nature of ideologies 16–17
context/contextual
  dimension of learning 88
  expression of innate competence 128–31
  and personal autonomy 129–30
continuing education 14–15
control and authority
  and curricular values 80, 88
  and major ideologies 28–9
  of schools and curricula 12, 13–14
    see also National Curricula
  see also centralization
Cooper, H. 102
Cousins, J. 128, 129
covert maintenance of ideologies 18
Cox, C. B. 5, 77, 141, 143–4
Cox, T. 34
creativity of teachers 116–17, 125
Cremin, L. A. 18, 26
critics
  of modern/new progressivism 140–4
  of National Curricula 144–5
Croll, P. 19
culture/cultural
  and cognition 61, 66
    see also Vygotsky
  and curricular values 78, 79–80
  and ideologies 15–16
  individual transformation of 112–17
  transcultural comparisons 2, 39, 40–2, 92, 98
  transformation of individuals 117–20
  values 40–2
  see also under individual
curricular values 9, 54, **77–99**
  learners' relationship with their knowledge 85–90
  progressivism and educational humanism 96–9
  traditional, problem with 77–81
  see also under processes

Darling, J. 6, 145
  curricular values 85–6, 96, 97
  major ideologies 26, 31
Dartington Hall 121
David, T. 146
Davie, R. 122, 125, 130, 147
Davies, T. 17, 23, 96
Dearden, R. F. 96, 127
Dearing Report 36
Deci, E. L. 99
deconstruction 25
defence of principles 56
defensive stance 46–7
defining ideologies 11–17, 25–8
  applying 15–16, 26
  content 14–15
  contested nature of 16–17
  function 12–14
  see also major ideologies
democracy/democratization 41, 54, 136
  and informal teaching methods 113, 118, 119
  and modern/new progressivism 137–8
  in primary school classroom 109–10
Désforges, C. 86, 90, 119, 147
developmentalism 8–9, 31, **59–75**, 144
  and autonomy 129–30
  complementarity of views *see* reconciling traditions
  and curricular values 77, 89, 92, 96
  developmental psychology 4, 6, 14, 55
  and modern/new progressivism 54–5, 136–7
Dewey, J. 6, 121
  curricular values 74, 83–4, 85, 96
  informal teaching methods 102, 109–12
  major ideologies 28, 30, 32
  modern progressivism 138, 139, 145
dichotomy, false 28
didacticism 25, 30, 80
  see also traditionalism
dilemmatic ideology 106–7
discipline, subject 85–6
distortion of ideologies, mental 17
diversity 41, 114
dogma and rhetoric 18
Driver, R. 63, 86, 111, 137, 146
dualisms 23, 33
Duffy, T. M. 63

165

Index

Durkheim, E. 17
Dykhuizen, G. 121
Dyson, A. E. 5, 77, 141, 143–4

Eccles, J. C. 98
Education Act (1988) ix
educational ideologies *see* ideologies
Edwards, D. 81, 82, 112
effectiveness research 104–5, 107
efficiency of formal teaching 35
Eliot, T. S. 27, 79
Elliott, J. 41
Ellis, T. 4, 15
Emery, H. 147
emotional dimension of learning 88
empiricism 55, 92, 107, 125, 140
empowerment 111
enabling 84
enactive thinking 30
Engeström, Y. 66
English primary schools and National Curricula 39, 42–9
   case study 44–6
   types of child-centredness 46–9
   see also primary schools
English/Welsh National Curricula *see* National Curricula
enjoyment of learning and teaching 47, 55, 85
Enlightenment 96
epistemological relations 82–3
Epstein, D. 93, 144
equilibrium 65
Eskeland, K. 130
Europe 41
examinations *see* tests
existentialism 97
external validity of progressivism 54

facilitation role 113
false dichotomy 28
Fang, Z. 19
Farrell, S. 1, 5, 39, 40, 142
Finland 41
first-hand experience, transforming 71–3
Fischer, K. W. 63
Fisher, J. 124–5, 146

fitness for purpose/goodness of fit 5–6, 32, 102–3
   see also pragmatism
Fitz, J. 1, 42
flexibility 102, 119–20
fluid contexts of culture 79–80
Fodor, J. A. 65
formal teaching methods 28, 29, 101
   and National Curricula 34–5, 42, 43
   nature of 102–3
Francis, L. J. 2, 4, 18
   major ideologies 23, 34
   National Curricula 39, 43, 49, 51
French, L. 63
function of ideologies 12–14

Gabella, M. S. 33
Gallimore, R. 63, 113, 143
Galton, M. 4, 19, 34, 40
   choice 125, 126
   curricular values 91, 98
   informal teaching methods 102, 107, 108
   modern progressivism 141–2, 143, 146
Gaskins, S. 64, 143
Gauld, A. 98
Geertz, C. 17
Genevan tradition *see* Piaget
Gibberson, T. 86, 90
Ginnes, P. 66, 146
Gipps, C. 41
Glaser, D. 122
Glaserfield, E. von 63, 81, 128
goals, long-term 82–3
goodness of fit *see* fitness
Green, R. 18, 141
Greenberg, D. E. 68
Griffiths, M. 105
Grimsley, R. 6, 26, 96
Grindle, Z. 2, 4, 18
   major ideologies 23, 34
   National Curricula 39, 43, 49, 51
group work 25
guidance and values 131

Hadow Committee and Report 26
   see also progressivism
Hakkinen, K. 41
Hall, E. and C. 96, 146

Halsey, A. H. 59, 143
Hand, B. 63, 86, 88
Harber, C. 41, 51, 111
Hargreaves, D. H. 129
Haroutunian, S. 65
Harré, R. 98
Haste, H. 60
Hendrick, H. 123
hermeneutic explanation of development 62–3
  see also Vygotsky
Hesketh, J. 23
Higgins, M. 107
high culture 27
Hill, D. 33, 93, 94
Hillman, M. 124
Hirst, P. H. 85–6
history, recent 3–7
HMCI (Her Majesty's Chief Inspector) 1, 5, 101
Hodge, M. 5, 6
holism *see* pragmatism
Holland 41
Holmes, B. 19, 51, 121
Holt, J. 99, 121, 122, 130
Hopkins, J. 30, 81, 82, 83, 84, 112
Hughes, M. 71, 143
humanism, educational 27
  and curricular values 96–9
  and developmentalism 65, 66
  and modern/new progressivism 54, 56, 137–8
  see also Piaget; progressivism
humanitarianism 16
humanities, study of 78, 84
humanization 41
Huxford, L. 63, 86, 87, 137, 142, 146

iconic thinking 30
identity, symbolic 69–70
ideologies
  defined 24
  major *see* developmentalism; major ideologies; pragmatism; progressivism; traditionalism
  and modern/new progressivism
    foundations 136–9
    roots 139–44
  value of *see* value of ideologies

individual/individualism 26, 48, 54
  and culture/society 96–8, 136–7
    social values 109–12
    transformations 112–20
    see also Dewey; humanism
  and developmentalism 60–1, 66
    see also Piaget
  see also child-centred approach; progressivism
infants 128–9
informal teaching methods 9, 23, 32, 56, **101–20**
  Dewey and democratic primary school classroom 109–10
  and National Curricula 43
  nature of 102–3
  pragmatic 103–9
  see also progressivism *and under* processes
information technology 108
Ingram, J. 147
Inhelder, B. 6, 60
innate capability/competence 61, 128–31
inspectors 1, 5, 101
  see also OFSTED
instrumental values 90
intentionality 66
interaction with others *see* society
interest, concept of 85
internal validity 26, 54
internalization 60, 63
international comparisons 2, 39, 40–2, 92, 98
interpretative explanation *see* hermeneutic
interventionism 64, 72–3, 87, 88
  and developmentalism *see* Vygotsky
involvement of learners in own education/ knowledge 30–1, 56
  and curricular values 85–90
  and developmentalism 64–7
  and informal teaching methods 112–13
  see also autonomy; child-centred approach; curricular values; Piaget

Japan 98
Jarvis, P. 15
Jeffrey, B. 125
John, M. 123, 147
Jonassen, D. H. 63
Jones, K. 93, 94, 110, 144

Index

Kainan, A. 11
Kant, I. 68, 96
Karmiloff-Smith, A. 69
Keiny, S. 63
Kellner, P. 5
Kelly, A. V. 13, 21, 145
  curricular values 80, 81, 82, 83, 84, 89
  developmentalism 64, 72
  informal teaching methods 102, 110, 112
  value of ideologies 27, 30, 55
Kemmis, S. 104
Kenny, J. 108
Kitchener, R. F. 59, 60, 143
knowledge
  creation 33
  learners' relationships with *see* involvement
  new and old 117–18
  particular *see* culture
  scaffolding 118–19, 120
  transfer 119–20
  transmission concept 26–7
Kruger, L. 63

Labour Party 4–5, 39, 101
  New Labour ix
Larrain, J. 11, 17
Lawlor, S. 27, 144
Lawrence, J. A. 62–3, 143
Lawton, D. 5, 144
  curricular values 93, 94
  major ideologies 23, 27
  value of ideologies 17, 18
learners
  comprehension 88
  enjoyment 47, 55, 85
  liberated by choice 121–2
  relationship with their knowledge 85–90
  relevance 90
  rights 122–4, 126–7, 133
  self-esteem 115–16
  see also autonomy; involvement
Lee, J. 1, 19, 42
Leeds 18
left-wing politics 11, 15–16, 94
  see also Labour Party; William Tyndale
Lenhart, V. 8, 41
Leont'ev, W. 66
life-long learning 14–15

Light, L. 59
listening to children 122, 125, 130
Liston, D. 105
Littledyke, M.
  curricular values 86, 87, 88
  developmentalism 63, 74
  major ideologies 24, 25, 27, 36
  modern progressivism 137, 142, 143, 146
Liu, M. 40
Liverta-Sempio, O. 61
LOGO (language) 108
London 18
  see also William Tyndale
Lowe, R. 93, 144
Luban, L. 108
Lubetsky, B. 93, 144
Lucariello, J. 61, 143
Lukes, S. 96

Macdonald, J. B. 28, 30
McIntyre, D. 105
Mackenzie, R. 101
  developmentalism 59, 74
  major ideologies 24, 25, 35–6
  modern progressivism 141, 143
MacLean, M. 41
Maclure, S. 5
major ideologies 8, **23–37**
  mixing 35–7
  numbers of 23–5
  see also defining; pragmatism; progressivism; traditionalism
Major, J. 5, 39
Mannheim, K. 17
Marchetti, A. 61
Marxism 11, 17
material content of ideologies 19
May, T. 127
Meadows, S. 65, 86, 128
Meighan, R. 23, 31, 121
mental distortion of ideologies 17
Menter, I. 43
metacognition 86, 87, 89, 113, 125
metatheories 33
methodologies, teaching 82
  hybridized 43
  and major ideologies 23, 28–9, 31
  and National Curricula 40, 43, 48

168

Index

and value of ideologies 12, 13
  see also formal; informal
mindfulness 86, 87
minds, transforming 71–3
mixing ideologies 35–7, 101
  see also pragmatism
modern/new progressivism 8, 9, **53–7**, 108, **135–47**
  ideological foundations 136–9
  ideological roots 139–44
  National Curricula criticised 144–5
Moll, I. 61, 143
Morris, P. 40
Morrison, K. 11, 23, 31
Mortimore, P. 104, 126
motivation 88
Mounce, H. O. 5, 32, 103, 110
Murphy, C. 40, 41
myth, progressivism as 19

National Curricula
  and choice 123, 124, 130, 132, 133
  and curricular values 80, 84, 91
  development stages 71, 72, 73
  and formal teaching methods 34–5, 42, 43
  and informal teaching methods 106, 112
  and major ideologies 26–7, 32, 35, 36–7
  and progressivism 1, 5, **39–51**
    alternative classroom ideologies 49–51
    international comparisons 40–2
    modern 144–5
    see also English primary schools
  and value of ideologies 12, 13, 20–1
National Curriculum of Finland 41
negotiation 124–5, 126
Neil, A. S. 43, 47, 51, 144
Neill, S. R. St. J. 121
Nelson, K. 62, 66, 69, 73, 74, 111, 143
neo-elementary 49–50
new progressivism *see* modern/new progressivism
Northam, J. 20

objectives, listing 81–2
OFSTED (Office for Standards in Education) 1, 5, 20, 145
  and informal teaching methods 104, 105, 107
  and major ideologies 29, 31, 42

O'Hear, A. 27, 77, 78, 79, 81, 110, 143
O'Keefe, D. J. 27, 144
Olson, D. R. 62, 128
Onore, C. 93
open-ended curriculum 114
ORACLE (Observational Research and Classroom Learning Evaluation) 82, 98, 107, 142, 146
origin of ideologies, validity of 26
Osborne, M. D. 95, 111, 118, 147
Osler, A. 122, 123, 147

PACE (Primary Assessment, Curriculum and Experience) project 43
Pacific Rim model 2, 39, 40
Panel, C. S. 40
Papert, S. 108
Patterson, C. H. 99
Peirce, C. S. 32
personal
  interests justifying practices 21
  outcomes of processes 95–6
  purpose of education 12
perspectivism 36
Peters, R. S. 4, 13, 85–6, 95, 140
phases of development 71–3
physical
  environment and development *see* Piaget
  transforming 67–71
Piaget, J. 6, 7, 90, 118, 143
  developmentalism 59–60
  value of ideologies 21, 33
  see also developmentalism; reconciling traditions
planning curricula 81–2, 84
Plowden Report 1, 2, 3–4, 6, 8–9, 26, 54, 59, 101, 141
  see also progressivism
pluralism 27, 138–9, 143
political/politics
  control 31
    see also National Curricula; OFSTED
  ideologies confused with educational 15–16
    see also left-wing; right-wing
Pollard, A. 2, 14, 23, 59, 105, 130
  modern progressivism 143, 144
  National Curricula 43, 51
Popper, K. R. 27, 80, 97, 98

169

Index

positivism 27
postmodernism 24, 25, 33–4, 36, 141
poststructuralism 24, 33
pragmatism 5–6, 24, 32–5, 85, 127
  defined 32–3
  informal teaching methods 103–9
  and modern progressivism 136, 139, 142
  and National Curricula 50–1
  see also Dewey
Prain, V. 25, 26, 33
prescription *see* regulation
Primary Assessment, Curriculum and Experience project 43
primary schools 13, 101, 126
  and curricular values 87–8, 92, 93
  democratic classroom 109–10
  specialist teaching in 3
  William Tyndale affair 4, 15–16, 94, 121, 141
  see also English primary schools; procedural principles
Pring, R. 24, 27, 98, 99, 109
priorities 13, 28
proactive role of learners *see* involvement
problems with ideologies 17–19
processes (procedural principles) 50
  cognitive 30, 55
  and curricular values 81–96
    cognitive outcomes 91–3
    personal outcomes 95–6
    social outcomes 93–5
  and informal teaching methods 112–20
    cultural transformation of individuals 117–20
    individual transformation of culture 112–17
  and progressivism 30, 31
professionalism and values 39
progressivism ix, 23–7 *passim*, 29–32, 35–6
  decline 43
  defined 25–6, 27
  and educational humanism 96–9
  mixed with traditionalism 35–6
  need to revise 2–3
  new ideology needed 1–3
  see also child-centred approach; modern/new progressivism *and under* National Curricula

psychology 82, 89
  see also developmentalism
public trust in progressivism, decline in 7
Punch, M. 121
pupils *see* learners
purposes of education 12–13

QCA (Qualifications and Curriculum Authority) 133–4
Quinn, V. 127

Ranaweera, A. M. 41
rationality and reason 97–8, 103–4, 105–6
reading, importance of 49–50, 92
reason *see* rationality
Reber, A. S. 69
reconciling traditions of Piaget and Vygotsky 61–75
  involvement of learners in own education 64–7
  socio-cultural developments 73
  transforming minds 71–3
  transforming physical 67–71
reconstructionism 94
Reed, E. S. 69
re-examination of beliefs 18
reflective practice 104–5, 106
regulation ix, 102, 122
  see also formal; National Curricula; OFSTED
religion 16
reports on education 26, 36
  see also Plowden
Resnick, L. B. 64
  curricular values 86, 87–8, 89
  informal teaching methods 107, 111, 117, 119
  modern progressivism 142, 146
responsibility *see* accountability
review process 56
revisionism 56
Reynolds, D. 1, 5, 39, 40, 142
Richards, C. x, 2, 23, 49, 59, 99, 103
  modern progressivism 135, 145
  value of ideologies 12, 14, 16, 17, 19
Ridley, K. 11, 23, 31
right-wing politics 3, 5, 27, 39, 77
rights 122–4, 126–7, 133
Rogers, C. 27, 66, 99, 115

170

Index

Rogoff, B. 60
Rohrs, H. 8, 18, 26, 41
Rosenthal, D. 5
Rousseau, J.-J. 6, 26, 29, 74, 96–7, 110, 145
Rowlands, S. 99, 124–5
Rudduck, J. 30, 81, 82, 83, 84, 112
rules *see* regulation
Ruskin College speech by Callaghan 4–5, 39, 141
Russell, P. 122
Russian tradition *see* Vygotsky
Ryan, J. M. 99

Safstrom, A. C. 32–3
Salomon, G. 86, 87, 90
Sammons, P. 104, 115
Sartre, J. P. 27, 97
scaffolding knowledge 118–19, 120
Schiller, C. 42
Schôn, D. A. 25, 27, 72, 104, 105, 106, 141
School Curriculum and Assessment Authority (SCAA) 80, 133–4
science 87, 91, 95, 96
Scrimshaw, P. 11, 17, 23
Scruton, R. 27
self
  -determination 89
  -esteem of learners 115–16
  -monitoring 86
  -sufficiency *see* autonomy
  see also individual
semiotics 67, 69–70
Sharp, A. 18, 141
Sharpe, K. 18, 24, 101
Shayer, M. 129
  curricular values 86, 87, 89, 90, 91
  developmentalism 64, 65, 72
  informal teaching methods 107, 111, 113, 119, 120
  modern progressivism 137, 142, 143, 146, 147
Sherwin, M. 122, 123
Shkolnik, D. 11
Short, G. 130
Shotter, J. 98
siege mentality 46
Siegler, R. S. 68, 128
signs *see* semiotics

Silcock, P. J. 2, 132
  curricular values 90, 98
  developmentalism 63, 64
  major ideologies 23, 27, 34, 35, 36
  modern progressivism 143, 144, 145, 147
  National Curricula 39, 42–51 *passim*
  value of ideologies 14, 20
Simco, N. 6, 147
Simon, B. 19, 108, 141
Sixsmith, C. 6, 147
Skilbeck, M. 23
skills acquisition 49–50, 82, 89, 92, 114–15, 116
Sleegers, P. 41
Smith, L. 122, 143
Smith, P. 59
Smolke, A. L. Bustamente 61, 68, 137
society/social 60–1
  constructivism 59, 66–7
  education as antidote to 29–30
  outcomes of processes 93–5
  purpose of education 12
  socio-cultural developments 73
  socio-political dimension of learning 88
  see also constructivism, social; Vygotsky
Song, M. J. 63
South America 41
Southern, R. W. 96
specialist teaching in primary school 3
Spinks, J. M. 104, 105
Stacey, H. 125
stages of development 71–3
standardization 20–1, 45
  tests (SATs) 46
  see also National Curricula
Stenhouse, L. 30, 81, 82–3, 84, 112, 114
Stevens, E. Jr 42
structural nature of ideologies 19
structural validity of ideologies 26
study skills 115–16
subject
  -based learning not emphasised in Plowden 4
  discipline 65–6
  see also knowledge
Sugrue, C. 4, 19, 42
  curricular values 96, 98
  major ideologies 24, 25, 34
  modern progressivism 141, 142, 146

171

Index

Sullivan, K. 19
Summerhill 121
Summers, M. 63
Sutherland, P. 6, 63, 72, 86, 137, 146
Swann, J. 79
Swinglewood, A. 11, 17
Sylva, K. 59, 143
symbolic identity 69–70
symbolic thinking 30

Taberrer, R. 142
Taiwan 40
Tann, S. 105
Tanner, R. 42
Tarrant, J. M. 96, 97
Tate, N. 80, 81
Taylor, P. H. 11–12, 14, 16, 17
technical rationality 103–4, 105–6
  see also OFSTED
technology, information 108
tests 46, 91–2, 95
Tharp, R. 63, 143
Thatcher, M. 5
Thelen, E. 128
thinking see cognitive
third way option 5
  see also pragmatism
Thompson, J. B. 11, 14, 15
Tizard, B. 71, 143
Tomlinson, P. 108
Tomlinson, S. 85, 102
tools 67, 68
traditionalism 1, 23, 24–5, 28–9, 49
  and curricular values 77–81
  defined 27
  mixed with progressivism 35–6
  and modern progressivism 135, 143–4
  renewed see National Curricula
transference of learning 86
transformation
  of culture, individual 112–17
  of individuals, cultural 117–20
  of minds 71–3
  physical 67–71
transmission concept 79–80
Treagust, D. F. 63, 86, 88
Trigg, P. 14, 130
Tudge, R. H. J. 60
Tunstall, P. 41

understanding, importance of 82
United Nations Convention on Rights of
  Child 122
United States 41, 42, 108
  see also Dewey
utilitarian purpose of education 12

validity of ideologies 26, 54
Valsiner, J. 60, 62–3, 64, 111, 143
value of ideologies 8, **11–22**
  coherence and consistency of
    interpretation 20–1
  justifying practices 21–2
  problems 17–19
  see also defining ideologies
values/value systems 40–2, 90, 95
  and developmentalism 65–6
  see also beliefs; culture; curricular
    values
Van Bueren, C. 122
Veer, R. van der 60
Verba, M. 66
verbal mediation 68–9
vocational purpose of education 12
Von Glaserfield, E. 63, 81, 128
Voss, J. T. 86, 90, 119
Vulliamy, G. 2, 135
Vygotsky, L. S. 6–7, 36, 136–7, 143, 146
  see also developmentalism; reconciling
    traditions

Wain, K. 15
Walkerdine, V. 24, 33, 93, 144
Wallace, G. 86
Warham, S. 126, 127
Waters, M. 15
Webb, R. 2, 34, 39, 41, 42, 43, 135, 144
Weir, S. 108
Wells, G. 59, 71, 143
Wertsch, J. V. 59, 60–1, 66, 67–8, 69, 109–10, 137
Wesler, H. N. 42
Wesselingh, A. 41
William Tyndale school 4, 15–16, 94, 121, 141
Williamson, J. 146
Winterhoff, P. A. 60
Wood, G. H. 42

Woodhead, C. 1, 5, 101
Woods, P. 43, 86, 89, 99, 116, 125, 143
Worrall, N. 147
Wyness, M. G. 2, 144
  choice 124, 132
  curricular values 90, 98
  major ideologies 23, 35, 36

National Curricula 39, 42, 43, 44, 45, 46, 49–50, 51
value of ideologies 14, 20

Yellow Book 4, 101
Yeo, E. 78, 85

Zeichner, K. 105